Woodstock

WOODSTOCK

AN ENCYCLOPEDIA OF THE MUSIC AND ART FAIR

JAMES PERONE

GREENWOOD PRESS
Westport, Connecticut • London

Library of Congress Cataloging-in-Publication Data

Perone, James E.
   Woodstock : an encyclopedia of the music and art fair / James Perone.
      p. cm.
   Includes set lists for the musicians appearing at the Festival.
   Includes bibliographical references (p.   ) and index.
   ISBN 0–313–33057–3 (alk. paper)
   1. Woodstock Festival (1969 : Bethel, N.Y.)—Encyclopedias. 2. Music
festivals—New York (State)—Bethel. I. Title.
   ML38.B48W669   2005
   781.66'079'74735—dc22   2004018006

British Library Cataloguing in Publication Data is available.

Library of Congress Catalog Card Number: 2004018006
ISBN: 0–313–33057–3

First published in 2005

Greenwood Press, 88 Post Road West, Westport, CT 06881
An imprint of Greenwood Publishing Group, Inc.
www.greenwood.com

Printed in the United States of America

∞™

The paper used in this book complies with the
Permanent Paper Standard issued by the National
Information Standards Organization (Z39.48–1984).

10 9 8 7 6 5 4 3 2 1

Contents

Illustrations

Preface

Woodstock. That one word conjures up images of long hair, hard rock music, protests against the Vietnam conflict, recreational drug use, free love, the hippie lifestyle, and a period of time in August 1969 in which nearly a half a million young people enjoyed a long weekend of peace, love, understanding, rain, traffic tie-ups, and music. Although the Woodstock Music and Art Fair started out as an attempt to use an open-air rock music festival as a means to finance construction of a commercial recording studio, Woodstock became a symbol of the ideals of the 1960s counterculture: for a little more than a weekend, these young people *lived* outside the confines of conventional American society. Woodstock was not the first rock music festival of the 1960s, nor was it even the first large rock festival of 1969. It was preceded by several major festivals in 1969, all of which included or featured rock music despite their names, including the following: the Atlantic City Pop Music Festival, the Newport Jazz Festival, and the Newport Folk Festival. These 1969 events were preceded by the 1968 Miami Pop Music Festival, an event produced by one of the eventual principals of Woodstock Ventures, and by the 1967 Monterey International Pop Music Festival, the first major rock music festival in the United States.

This book includes a chapter on the rock festivals that preceded and that immediately followed Woodstock, including the Monterey International Pop Music Festival, the Atlantic City Pop Music Festival, the two 1969 festivals that took place in Newport, Rhode Island (and bear that city's name), The Rolling Stones' disastrous one-day festival at California's Altamont Speedway, the 1970 Isle of Wight Festival, and the Concert for Bangla Desh. My goal is to put the Woodstock Music and Art Fair into context by describing the events that led up to it, at least one of which drew nearly as many audience members but which has became a footnote in the history of pop music festivals, and the music festivals that began the decade of the 1970s. We then take a look at the Woodstock festival itself, including information about the four principals who would form Woodstock

Ventures in order to build a recording studio. The chapter on the Woodstock Music and Art Fair presents the events that led up to the festival and information about the event itself. I also try to answer the question, Why was it Woodstock that captured the consciousness of the nation and not, say, the Atlantic City Pop Music Festival?

Chapters on the Woodstock '94 festival, which marked the twenty-fifth anniversary of the 1969 event, and on Woodstock 1999 follow. In each of these two chapters I describe the events, the music, and musicians who made each event what it was, and I compare and contrast the two anniversary festivals—neither of which, incidentally, was held at the site of the 1969 festival—with the original Woodstock Music and Art Fair. These chapters also include discussion of the competing, but much smaller, anniversary festivals that *were* held on the site of the famous 1969 festival.

Many interesting people, including musicians, concert promoters, artists' managers, technical staff, doctors, security personnel, New York state politicians, town governments, village governments, citizens committees, landowners, lawyers, food concessionaires, designers, visual artists, counterculture politicos, commune members, hotels, highways, and weather phenomena were part of the Woodstock story. The A-to-Z of Woodstock, which follows the chapters, presents snapshots of many of these interesting people, places, and corporate bodies. Some of the entries are included in the chapter on the 1969 Woodstock Music and Art Fair, but some are not. The purpose of the A-to-Z chapter is to present more detailed information on some of the people, locations, and corporate entities that are mentioned in the chapter, as well as to give recognition to some of the figures that played important roles but whose contributions did not necessarily fit into the chapter.

Appendix I includes set lists for the musicians who appeared at the Woodstock Music and Art Fair. Study of previous books on Woodstock and of the numerous Web sites that include set lists reveals a great deal of incomplete and contradictory information. Many of the lists that have appeared throughout the years have relied on audio and film recordings made during the festival. Some musicians were not recorded, and some of the film shot for the documentary film of the festival has not been issued commercially. As a result, some of the songs performed by various acts are not precisely known. Compilers of set lists have also collected correspondence from Woodstock attendees and musicians who recall that certain musicians performed particular songs. Interestingly, none of the Web sites on which I have found set lists include a list of songs performed by the Keef Hartley Band, an important band in the late 1960s British blues scene. While knowledge that Hartley had released an album shortly before Woodstock suggested to me some of the possible titles—rock musicians of the late 1960s tended to perform music that was available on their latest records for commercial reasons—all it took was an e-mail to Keef Hartley's current record company to confirm a partial list. If we do not have documentary evidence (recordings), for musicians, like the Keef Hartley Band, accurate set lists are difficult to compile. For one thing, some of these acts were traveling extensively during 1969 and 1970, all the while making adjustments to their sets without writing the running order down for posterity. I have tried to compile set lists that are as inclusive and accurate as possible from looking at evidence from both primary and secondary sources. Incidentally, the original Woodstock festival was a sociological phenomenon of such great importance and one that had so many unfortunate gaps in its documentation that Woodstock '94 and Woodstock 1999 were attended by graduate student researchers who documented the sociology of the events, real-time, at-the-time-of-the-event oral histories, and, yes, accurate set lists. Despite the real-time reporting, the cable television coverage, the extensive Web rings that have developed, and the scholarly study of Woodstock '94 and Woodstock 1999, however, neither of the official anniversary festivals managed to become a sociological phenomenon to match the 1969 festival.

Appendix II includes information pertaining to the various audio recordings and films of the Woodstock Music and Art Fair, Woodstock '94, and Woodstock 1999. I have included lists of the artists and songs that appear on the audio recordings with the hope that having this information in one location might make it easy for readers who want to hear these documentaries of the festivals to see what is commercially available.

My aim in this project has been to create a guide to the 1969 Woodstock Music and Art Fair and its legacy. It is my hope that it captures the history and significance of the event and its context in such a way that the book can be enjoyed on its own. I also hope, though, that the book will make a companion to the various audio and video releases that are currently available from all three Woodstock festivals.

Acknowledgments

This book could not have been written without the valuable assistance of a number of people. I wish first to thank Karen Perone for offering moral support
throughout this and all of my book projects for Greenwood Press and for offering much-needed input at every stage of every project.

Over the course of writing several books, the entire staff of the Greenwood Publishing Group has been most helpful and cooperative. I wish to extend special
thanks to Senior Editor Rob Kirkpatrick and to Carol Lucas and Andrew Hudak,
copy and production editors, respectively, for helping me in the fine-tuning of this
book.

I also wish to thank the folks at Photofest for making their fine collection of
Woodstock and other late 1960s photographs available to me and for being most
accommodating as I went through the selection process. Special thanks to Ian
Southworth of Kashmir Records for the information on the Keef Hartley Band's
Woodstock set list.

Popular Music Festivals of the Late 1960s and Early 1970s

Although the Woodstock Music and Art Fair of 1969 generated the most interest and affected the greatest number of Americans, including many who did not actually attend the event, it was preceded and followed by other significant pop music concert events, including the following: the Monterey International Pop Music Festival, the first rock music festival in the United States; the 1969 Newport Jazz Festival; the 1969 Newport Folk Festival; the 1969 Atlantic City Pop Music Festival; The Rolling Stones' Altamont Speedway concert; Britain's Isle of Wight Festivals; and the 1971 Concert for Bangla Desh. Each of these concert events helped to define the 1967 to 1971 era. In some cases these festivals exposed new forms of pop music to the nation and to the world, in other cases they exposed what can happen when a mob mentality overtakes a large public gathering, and in other cases they show the philanthropic good that pop music and pop musicians can do.

MONTEREY INTERNATIONAL POP MUSIC FESTIVAL

The summer of 1967 was known across the United States as the "Summer of Love." Nowhere was this more in evidence than in the San Francisco Bay Area. The experimentation with LSD that had been centered in San Francisco for several years had reached a high point in terms of the drug's influence on rock music and musicians, not to mention a free, counterculture lifestyle that was being enjoyed by thousands of young people.[1] San Francisco, particularly in the Haight-Ashbury district, was the scene of free food, free love, significant amounts of experimentation with marijuana and LSD, and a great deal of innovative psychedelic rock music. Area bands such as The Grateful Dead, Big Brother and the Holding Company, the Jefferson Airplane, Santana, and The Steve Miller Band were starting to garner national attention. In this atmosphere the first of the great

American rock music festivals, the Monterey International Pop Music Festival, took place.

Monterey Pop, as the event soon became widely known, was held June 16–18, 1967, at the Monterey County Fairgrounds and attracted approximately 60,000 fans.[2] In many respects, it was the right event at the right time. It hastened the national exposure for San Francisco Bay Area bands, including those listed above and several others. The festival also provided another reason for young people to travel to the San Francisco area to take part in the Summer of Love. The festival and the entire San Francisco hippie scene were glorified in song during the summer of 1967, which increased interest in the events in the Bay Area. Singer-songwriter John Phillips, of the folk-pop vocal group the Mamas and the Papas, composed the song "San Francisco (Be Sure to Wear Flowers in Your Hair)," a song that glorified the hippie scene in the city. The Phillips composition was a hit single for folksinger Scott McKenzie and received significant amounts of radio airplay.[3] It was no coincidence that Phillips was one of the producers of the Monterey International Pop Music Festival; his composition served as a call to a nation of freethinking young people to journey to a land in which this new hippie lifestyle was especially prominent. The British group Eric Burdon and the Animals highlighted the Bay Area hippie scene in their song "San Franciscan Nights," another hit single during summer 1967.[4] It was probably no coincidence that the aforementioned Mamas and the Papas, Scott McKenzie, and Eric Burdon and the Animals all performed at the Monterey International Pop Music Festival.

The organization of a festival like Monterey Pop, or Woodstock for that matter, is never the work of one person. Monterey Pop, like Woodstock, was a group effort; however, compared with the Woodstock festival of 1969, the organization of the Monterey International Pop Music Festival included several additional layers. The organizing committee, which was largely responsible for selecting the talent to be invited, included Derek Taylor (onetime publicist for both The Beatles and The Beach Boys), record producer Lou Adler, and record producer Terry Melcher. A separate Board of Governors—something Woodstock did not have—signed on to endorse the festival. This prestigious board included Brian Wilson (The Beach Boys), Paul McCartney (The Beatles), John Phillips (Mamas and the Papas), Mick Jagger (The Rolling Stones), and Paul Simon (Simon and Garfunkel). While the members of this board may not have had much to do with the actual organization and running of the Monterey festival, they were active in promoting the event and in inviting and encouraging prominent popular musicians to perform. This contrasted with many such boards, which often consisted of a group of people who simply lent their names to an event.

According to Board of Governors member Brian Wilson, The Beach Boys were among the first groups invited to perform at the Monterey International Pop Music Festival.[5] Due to the fact that the festival went from being a paid performance to a nonprofit, charity event (meaning that performers would not be paid) and due to the fact that The Beach Boys eventually became afraid of being considered old-fashioned compared with the likes of Jimi Hendrix, Janis Joplin, and other performers who had been signed or were likely to be signed, the band bowed out. The fact that The Beach Boys canceled their appearance did not go unnoticed by the younger acid rock musicians. Jimi Hendrix, for example, issued a famous proclamation during his performance at Monterey that the world had seen the end of surf music. The roster of musicians who actually did appear at the Monterey Pop Festival was quite impressive and included the following acts: The Byrds, Eric Burdon and the Animals, The Electric Flag, the Paul Butterfield Blues Band, Country Joe and the Fish, the Mamas and the Papas, The Steve Miller Band, Canned Heat, Scott McKenzie, Big Brother and the Holding Company (which featured vocalist Janis Joplin), African musician Hugh Masekela (who enjoyed a period of popularity in the United States in the late 1960s), The Buffalo Spring-field, Johnny Rivers, Quicksilver Messenger Service, The Grateful Dead, Laura Nyro, Lou Rawls, Moby Grape, The Association, The Blues Project, the Jefferson Airplane, The Jimi Hendrix Experience, Ravi Shankar, Simon and Garfunkel, The Who, and Otis Redding (who was backed by members of two of the best soul bands of the day, Booker T. and the MGs and The Markeys). Most of these performers appeared free, as the event was to raise funds for an area foundation. Ultimately, the money raised by the festival and the subsequent film seems to have vanished.[6] Unfortunately, this would establish something of a trend: some of the most culturally significant and even some of the best-planned rock festivals of the future would achieve less-than-stellar financial results.

As remarkable as the roster of Monterey Pop performers might seem to some people, at least one prominent rock music critic was not particularly impressed. Jann Wenner, one of the most well respected writers on rock music of the era and soon to be one of the mainstays of *Rolling Stone* magazine, lamented that "the most important artists were not at Monterey."[7] In particular, Wenner noted the absence of The Beatles and The Rolling Stones, arguably the most watched bands of the three years leading up to the Monterey festival. Interestingly, other critics would make the same point about the Woodstock Music and Art Fair: that The Beatles, The Rolling Stones, and Bob Dylan (who happened to live relatively close to the site of the Woodstock festival) were noticeably absent. Given Wenner's comment about The Beatles being missing from the lineup of Monterey Pop performers, it should be noted that the group's final live performance had taken place in the Bay Area at San Francisco's Candlestick Park on August 29, 1966,[8] less than a year before the Monterey Pop festival. Wenner made some interesting observations about the performers who did perform at Monterey, including his praise of Elvin Bishop's guitar playing with the Paul Butterfield Blues Band and his down-playing of the importance of Jimi Hendrix as a guitar player at the event. Wenner felt that Hendrix's showmanship, which included setting his guitar on fire at the conclusion of a performance of the song "Wild Thing," outshone his guitar playing.[9] Although Jann Wenner might not have been overly impressed, Hendrix's flamboyant performance helped to establish the guitarist-singer-songwriter with American audiences—although Hendrix was from Seattle, he had made his initial impact as a psychedelic musician in England—and the performance inspired Micky Dolenz, drummer of The Monkees, to request that Hendrix be hired as the opening act for The Monkees' upcoming tour.[10]

Since the festival highlighted San Francisco Bay Area bands, and since those bands and their fans tended to be part of the hippie scene in all of its ramifications—including an emphasis on a communal lifestyle and the use of psychedelic drugs—perhaps it was natural that drugs (and the communal lifestyle) would play a role at Monterey Pop. For example, Ellen Sander's report on the festival not only suggests what a "trippy" scene it was but also the points out some of the faulty business decisions that arose from the "trippiness" of the scene and details the sociological importance of the first of the great American rock festivals. For example, Sander describes Country Joe and the Fish being "so wiped out of their minds that they forgot to sign the release" to have their performance included in the film of the festival,[11] and she writes of the festival, "It touched an ancient lost connection with tribalism, it beckoned toward a vision of a future worth celebrating."[12]

The drug use that Ellen Sander described resulted in more than a few bad trips on LSD. Tom Law, a member of the Hog Farm commune, which was also to play a key role at the Woodstock Music and Art Fair in 1969, was on hand at Monterey to help concertgoers come down from these negative drug reactions. Law would sit people down in front of a fire near a tepee and talk them down from their bad trips. This system of dealing with bad trips ran counter to what was done by medical personnel, who would usually sedate the person experiencing the bad trip using the drug Thorazine. Law and other members of the Hog Farm found their drug-free method to be very successful. They would use the same kind of techniques at Woodstock.

The Monterey International Pop Music Festival not only was the first one of the great rock festivals of the 1960s and 1970s but was well documented through audio recording and through a fine documentary film. While the commercial audio recording was left unreleased for two decades due to contractual disputes between the various record companies involved, the film, directed by D. A. Pennebaker, was an immediate classic. Not only was Pennebaker's *Monterey Pop* the first filmed documentary of America's first rock music festival, but it set a high standard for subsequent concert films. *Monterey Pop* has been widely available on video and in DVD format. In 2002, Criterion Collection released *The Complete Monterey Pop Festival* on video and DVD, including many outtakes not used in the original Pennebaker film release of 1968.

THE BEATLES' ROOFTOP "CONCERT"

The last official concert by arguably the most important, and unquestionably the most commercially successful, rock band of the 1960s, The Beatles, took place at San Francisco's Candlestick Park on August 29, 1966. Years of touring and performing in front of screaming crowds who could not hear the music,[13] combined with something of a fiasco created by John Lennon's pretour statements about the state of Christianity and several protocol-related controversies that marred the Asian part of The Beatles' 1966 tour, *and* the fact that their new music was becoming too complicated for the band to perform live,[14] made it clear that The Beatles would be a studio group after their performance at Candlestick Park.

Although it was not technically a "concert," in the sense that no one save the sound and film crews and a few friends who were assembled knew in advance that they would be hearing a live performance by The Beatles on January 30, 1969, the group performed a set atop the roof of Apple Records in London's rather posh financial district. Since this was not even a concert in the traditional sense, it was also hardly a music festival to compare with the others described in this chapter. It was notable, however, as an example of the kind of unpredictability that marked, in some cases for good and in some cases for bad, live rock performances of 1969. Like Woodstock, Monterey Pop, and Altamont, The Beatles' rooftop concert has achieved a sort of iconic status within the world of rock music.

After recording the studio-oriented and heavily orchestrated music of *Sgt. Pepper's Lonely Hearts Club Band* (1967) and *Magical Mystery Tour* (1967), The Beatles had returned to a more basic form of rock and roll in 1968. Their 1968 double album, *The Beatles*,[15] featured a number of songs that could be performed live. Their next major project, tentatively titled *Get Back*, started out as an attempt to "get back" to musical roots/basics even further: the album was to include no studio overdubs or other effects that could not be reproduced onstage. Although the rehearsal and recording sessions started in mid-January 1969, and although the rooftop concert took place at the end of that same month, the project would not be commercially released until 1970, as the film and album *Let It Be*.[16]

The forty-two-minute performance by The Beatles and American keyboardist Billy Preston made a huge impact on Alan Parsons, who later gained fame as a leading British record producer and brains behind the studio "band" The Alan Parsons Project. Parsons was the young tape operator for the audio recording of the January 30, 1969, concert. According to Parsons, "That was one of the greatest and most exciting days of my life. To see The Beatles playing together and getting an instant feedback from the people around them, five cameras on the roof, cameras across the road, in the road. It was just unbelievable . . . a magic, magic day."[17]

The Beatles and Billy Preston performed in order the following songs: "Get Back" in two versions, "Don't Let Me Down," "I've Got a Feeling," "The One after 909," "Dig a Pony," a second version of "I've Got a Feeling," a second version of "Don't Let Me Down," and a third version of "Get Back."

Alerted to the performance by businesspeople complaining about the "noise" emanating from the rather conservative financial district, the London police half-heartedly tried to stop, or at least to quiet down, the proceedings. The *Let It Be* film captures the London bobbies' attempt. Paul McCartney alludes to it in the final version of "Get Back," when he sings about the song's character Loretta getting into trouble for playing on the roof again. Incidentally, the film also captures young people on the street rushing toward Apple Records as they hear the rock music emanating from the roof and, presumably, realize just who is performing there.

The events of January 30, 1969, could have turned out to be viewed as a callous publicity stunt or as a casual attempt to capture some interesting footage for the *Let It Be* film. The rooftop concert, however, has gained iconic status among Beatles fans as the last live appearance of the band. The surprise nature of the event and the fact that it took place in the generally conservative Savile Row part of London added to the notoriety surrounding the performance. The performance also helped to generate considerable speculation that The Beatles might be returning to live concert performances with their new, simplified rock and roll material: some fans believed that the band was trying out the material on the roof in preparation for a new tour. As the year 1969 became *the* year for famous rock concerts, rumors of possible surprise Beatles appearances abounded, especially because of the rooftop "concert" and the implications it held for rock music fans.

THE NEWPORT JAZZ FESTIVAL (1969)

Established by jazz impresario, club owner, and pianist George Wein, the Newport Jazz Festival had been an East Coast mainstay since the 1950s. The Newport Jazz Festival of 1969, however, had a distinctively rock sound to it and therefore stood in sharp contrast to previous festivals. Held July 4–6, 1969, the Newport Jazz Festival included such acts as jazz-rock group Blood, Sweat, and Tears, virtuoso rock guitarist Jeff Beck, Savage Rose, soul superstar James Brown, blues-rock guitar virtuoso Johnny Winter, soul and pop chart favorites Sly and the Family Stone, and the blues-based heavy metal superstars Led Zeppelin. Other rock acts that appeared at Newport included Jethro Tull, Frank Zappa and the Mothers of Invention, and Ten Years After. The 1969 edition of the Newport Jazz Festival was not entirely about rock music: jazz luminaries such as Buddy Rich, Sun Ra, Bill Evans, Anita O'Day, Gerry Mulligan, Miles Davis, Phil Woods, the amazing multi-instrumentalist Rahasaan Roland Kirk, and others also performed. It was the pop-rock-oriented nature of the festival, however, that made this edition of the festival unusual and made it function as a sort of kickoff to a summer of rock festivals of major significance.

Among the performers who would be at Woodstock approximately a month and a half after the Newport Jazz Festival was Blood, Sweat, and Tears. This group was taking America by storm after replacing their founder and original lead singer, Al Kooper, with the dynamic David Clayton-Thomas. Blood, Sweat, and Tears turned in a sensational, audience-pleasing performance at Newport, one of the main reasons that they were asked to play Woodstock.

With acts such as Sly and the Family Stone (who also would perform at Woodstock), Johnny Winter (who would be a last-minute addition to the Woodstock roster), and Led Zeppelin, the 1969 edition of the Newport Jazz Festival attracted a younger and somewhat "trippier" (and certainly less disciplined) audience than the totally jazz-oriented Newport events of the past. Although there was no scientific demographic study done of the 1969 Newport Jazz Festival audience, what documentary evidence there is supports the contention that a great many young people, probably rock fans, populated the event. Photographer Joseph J. Sia published his photographs of major pop music festivals of 1969 in the book *Woodstock '69, Summer Pop Festivals: A Photo Review.* Photographs from Woodstock, the Newport Jazz Festival, the Newport Folk Festival, and the Atlantic City Pop Music Festival suggest a very similar audience makeup: many young people who look very much like the hippies of the day.[18]

Because of the nature and the larger than usual size of the audience, the City of Newport, Rhode Island, experienced problems that it had never witnessed at earlier Newport Jazz Festivals. For one thing, the young people who attended the festival to hear the rock and rhythm and blues acts could not afford the hotels in the area and tried to sleep on the beach, something that would be entirely in line with the back-to-the-land, communal hippie lifestyle. The City of Newport, however, had laws against sleeping on the beaches within the city limits. In addition, there were some unruliness and gate-crashing. This seems to have been a result of both the nature of the crowd and the unusually large number of people who showed up for this installment of the Newport Jazz Festival. The performers, too, seemed to incite the crowd. As George Wein writes in his autobiography, "Sly [Stone] stood on the stage at Newport before a sea of faces. The sight intoxicated him. He went into a sort of crazed rapture. The audience went berserk right along with him. As the band's allotted time came to an end, and I signaled to them, they kept on playing. It was a mess; people had spilled over the box seats and into the photography pit. . . . Pandemonium was like a drug to Sly Stone, and instead of calming his fans he incited them. . . . It's a miracle that we avoided a riot."[19] Recapping the festival, Wein writes, "Total attendance for the 1969 Newport Jazz Festival—85,000 people—broke all previous records. By almost any standard, it had been a huge success. . . . But I never gave this scenario a second thought. The 1969 Newport Jazz Festival had been four of the worst days of my life."[20]

Given the diverse nature of the performers who appeared at the 1969 edition of the Newport Jazz Festival, it seems appropriate to deal with the question of to what extent rockers like Johnny Winter, Jeff Beck, and Led Zeppelin truly represented "jazz." Led Zeppelin, in particular, while they may have featured some improvisation (one of the essential components of jazz), certainly did not swing, in the conventional sense of the "swing" rhythmic interpretation of most jazz. The concert program booklet for the festival includes a quote from George Wein suggesting that the newer rock acts offered a rhythmic drive and excitement that jazz seemed to lack at the time. Wein asks, however, the rhetorical question, "Is it jazz?" in the concert booklet.[21] Although several musical ensembles were combining jazz and rock in 1969, most, like Chicago and Blood, Sweat, and Tears, were essentially pop groups with horn sections. The lines between jazz and rock would blur considerably within a few years of the 1969 Newport Jazz Festival when Miles Davis began combining the two disparate genres and younger musicians who routinely combined the two styles emerged; the group Weather Report and guitarist John McLaughlin with his Mahavishnu Orchestra were two notable examples. Frank Zappa, who appeared at the 1969 Newport Jazz Festival, would increasingly incorporate aspects of jazz into his groups in the 1970s. What Johnny Winter brought to the Newport Jazz Festival was a direct connection to electric rhythm and blues, a white perspective on the form but a direct connection nonetheless. Led Zeppelin, especially guitarist Jimmy Page, was connected to the British blues scene, which was based largely on the work of black American blues musicians like Sonny Boy Williamson, Muddy Waters, and Howlin' Wolf. Insofar as blues and instrumental jazz are connected, then, the rock musicians who appeared at the 1969 Newport Jazz Festival may not have "swung" in the traditional jazz rhythmic sense, but they were part of the tradition by means of their connection to the blues. Ultimately, though, with a few exceptions like John McLaughlin, Miles Davis, and some of Jeff Beck's work, the years following the 1969 Newport Jazz Festival did not see the great merger of the two styles that some thought might take place.

Concert organizer George Wein and several prominent music critics considered the rock experiment to be a failure, despite the unusually large number of tickets that were sold, and the Newport City Council voted to forbid future rock performances in the city in reaction to the 1969 Newport Jazz Festival. What the festival did accomplish was to suggest the extent to which rock was becoming part of the American cultural mainstream—here the genre found itself in a most unusual setting: one formerly reserved for strictly jazz and folk music related to jazz. This was an indication of the level of importance the rock genre had achieved by 1969. It is notable that rock's coming-of-age as part of the popular music festival mainstream at Newport—and for that matter at the other festivals that took place in summer 1969—happened at almost exactly the same time as public opinion turned against the U.S. involvement in the Vietnam conflict. The connection? What had been a counterculture political and social movement tipped the balance of public opinion at nearly the same moment as rock, a counterculture musical genre, found its way into the venerable institution of the Newport Jazz Festival.

THE NEWPORT FOLK FESTIVAL (1969)

Like the Newport Jazz Festival, impresario George Wein had for many years produced the Newport Folk Festival. In fact, Wein and folk musician Pete Seeger essentially founded the festival back in the late 1950s during the ascendancy of popularity of folk revival music. The Newport Folk Festival was originally a purely acoustic folk-styled musical counterpart to the jazz festival. Things had changed somewhat, however, in 1965, when Bob Dylan plugged in an electric guitar and performed "Maggie's Farm" backed by a rock band. Dylan's move infuriated many folk purists (including the aforementioned Seeger, who reportedly tried to cut the electrical cables in order to silence the rock music) and seemed not to have a great deal of effect on the subsequent Newport Folk Festivals.

Like the Wein-produced jazz event, however, the Newport Folk Festival of 1969 stressed greater diversity and a leaning toward the roots of rock music, in this case, blues and country music. The festival took place July 16–20, 1969, and featured folk and folk revival musicians such as Arlo Guthrie and Pete Seeger; country-folk and country-pop musicians such as Johnny Cash, Ramblin' Jack Elliott, the Everly

Brothers, and John Hartford; and a large number of blues musicians, including Willie Mae "Big Mama" Thornton (the original performer of the Jerry Leiber and Mike Stoller song "Hound Dog," which would become one of Elvis Presley's most important early hits), Muddy Waters, Sonny Terry, Brownie McGhee, Sleepy John Estes, Yank Rachel, Son House, and Jesse Fuller. James Taylor, Van Morrison, and Joni Mitchell represented the pop-folk-rock side of the musical spectrum. The diversity of the festival was also enhanced by the Georgia Sea Island Singers, a group that preserved the unique African American Gullah language songs of the nineteenth-century islands just off the coast of the U.S. mainland.

Although the Newport Folk Festival did not feature the kind of high-intensity rock music that the city's Jazz Festival had just a couple of weeks before, Joseph J. Sia's photographic book *Woodstock '69, Summer Pop Festivals: A Photo Review* suggests that many who attended the festival were young and dressed in the trappings of hippies of the era.[22] The festival is also interesting because of some of the younger performers who were on the bill. Joni Mitchell and James Taylor, in particular, were just at the start of their careers and, within two years, would be major stars representing the new, introspective singer-songwriter style of the early 1970s. Van Morrison, too, had solid rock credentials, particularly on the strength of his garage-band anthem "Gloria," which although it had barely dented the *Billboard* top 100 in the United States in 1965 for Morrison's group Them, was widely covered by rock bands throughout the 1960s and in subsequent decades. Morrison might best be remembered, however, for his 1967 hit "Brown Eyed Girl."

Although the event might not have been as noteworthy as the 1969 Newport Jazz Festival experiment or the Woodstock Music and Art Fair, with its heavy emphasis on the blues, the pop-country sounds of performers like the Everly Brothers and Johnny Cash, and younger singer-songwriters like Van Morrison, Joni Mitchell, and James Taylor, the 1969 Newport Folk Festival represented well the kinds of chances that promoters and festival organizers were taking in mixing pop music styles at the end of the 1960s.

THE ATLANTIC CITY POP MUSIC FESTIVAL

Held August 1–3, 1969, at the Atlantic City Race Track, outside Atlantic City, New Jersey, the Atlantic City Pop Music Festival featured many acts that had either earlier appeared at the Newport Jazz Festival or Newport Folk Festival or would appear a couple of weeks later at the Woodstock Music and Art Fair. These included the following: Johnny Winter; Crosby, Stills, Nash, and Young; Joni Mitchell; Frank Zappa and the Mothers of Invention; Santana; the Jefferson Airplane; Creedence Clearwater Revival; the Paul Butterfield Blues Band; Janis Joplin; Canned Heat; Joe Cocker; and the Buddy Rich Big Band. The festival included sets by many other performers as well, including Chicago, Procol Harem, Booker T. and the MGs, The Sir Douglas Quintet, Little Richard, Dr. John, The Crazy World of Arthur Brown, Tim Buckley, Mother Earth, The Moody Blues, The Doors, the Buddy Miles Express, Hugh Masekela, and others. The event drew

110,000 people. Although the entire grounds of the racetrack provided plenty of space for the concertgoers, the size of the crowd proved to be something of a problem with regard to bathing facilities. As photographer Joseph J. Sia wrote, "Water was in short supply for bathing but the promoters managed to bring in water trucks which would hose down anyone willing to undertake such makeshift and public showers."[23]

The tribute to the past, to the roots of rock and roll, in the inclusion of Little Richard speaks well for the range of Atlantic City Pop Music Festival. The Miami Pop Festival of 1968 had also found new acts and pioneering musicians of 1950s rock and roll appearing at the same festival. Although one could argue that featuring one Little Richard and dozens of more modern acts hardly constitutes a balance of current trends with tradition, it was more than the Woodstock festival had. The sole "oldies" act to appear at Woodstock, Sha-Na-Na, performed second-generation 1950s-style rock and roll—they were a cover band[24] in place of the real article. The inclusion of such diverse musicians as Buddy Rich's jazz band and African musician Hugh Masekela further broadened the Atlantic City festival.

Given the breadth of musical styles at Atlantic City—the absence of Jimi Hendrix notwithstanding, its roster was arguably stronger in many ways than that of Woodstock—the fact that several of the acts later performed at Woodstock, *and* the relative closeness of the two venues, why did Woodstock become a 1960s icon and Atlantic City become something of a footnote in some accounts of the era? As far as can be determined, there has not been a scientific study of this question. The anecdotal evidence[25] suggests that, as those in the real estate business say, it was "location, location, location." The racetrack just did not seem to have the same kind of aesthetic appeal to the younger generation that a rural setting did. Part of the answer might also lie in the way in which Woodstock would be advertised, as an Aquarian festival of peace, love, and music—the Atlantic City festival received more mundane publicity that by all appearances did not try to paint the event as a sort of counterculture happening.

ALTAMONT

If the Woodstock Music and Art Fair represented what was positive about the hippie, counterculture era and lifestyle, then Altamont represented the antithesis. This one-day event took place December 6, 1969, and represented The Rolling Stones' "answer" to Woodstock. The Stones were near the end of a long American tour and decided to conclude the tour with a free concert at California's Altamont Speedway.[26] It was to be one of the great disasters of the 1960s.

Although The Rolling Stones were touring North America at the time of the Woodstock festival, Woodstock Ventures bypassed the group. The band was one of the leading rock groups of the 1960s and had reached a peak of popularity as a concert act by the end of the decade. Although Woodstock was to include performances by many of the luminaries of late-1960s rock, a few groups, like The Rolling Stones, were in a league of their own. The principals of Woodstock Ven-

The Rolling Stones perform at their Gimme Shelter rock concert at the Altamont Speedway in California on December 6, 1969. A fan was stabbed to death by a member of the Hells Angels motorcycle club, who were hired as bouncers to control the crowd. Hells Angels are on stage with the Rolling Stones' Mick Jagger and guitarist Mick Taylor, with back to camera. (AP/Wide World Photos)

tures realized that an appearance by the Stones would necessitate increased security, both for the band members and for the audience. The Stones had recently released several songs that dealt with violent themes, perhaps the best example of which is "Street Fighting Man," which happened to be the group's single at the time Woodstock Ventures was beginning to book acts. Woodstock Ventures feared that a song like "Street Fighting Man" could easily incite a riot, thus ruining what was being touted as an Aquarian Exposition of peace and love. This decision by the Woodstock promoters is especially interesting in light of the outbreaks of violence at Woodstock 1999, a festival in which several name bands actively incited the crowd, both with their onstage banter with the crowd and with lyrics that dealt frankly and sometimes quite sympathetically with violence.

Bypassed as they were for what turned out to be an event of immense cultural significance, The Rolling Stones decided to stage their own version of Woodstock, a free, one-day festival originally scheduled to take place in San Francisco's Golden Gate Park. Only days before the event was to take place, however, the San Francisco City Council refused to release the necessary permits. At the very last possible moment, the owner of the nearby Altamont Speedway offered his demolition derby racetrack as a venue for the self-proclaimed "Greatest Rock and Roll Band in the World" to conclude their U.S. tour. As The Rolling Stones and their associates planned what would now come to be known as the Altamont festival, they sought the advice of musicians who were better acquainted than they were with the personnel resources available in California. Members of The Grateful Dead made the fateful suggestions that the Hell's Angels motorcycle gang work security at the festival. The exact nature of the employment of members of the Hell's Angels has been a source of much contention, with widely circulated and reproduced reports suggesting that the motorcyclists were hired for $500 worth of beer. Other reports, from people close to The Grateful Dead, suggest that "everyone involved knew that the Angels would be there anyway, so it seemed sensible to let them hang out around the stage and make themselves useful."[27] The Rolling Stones hired some 300 members of the motorcycle club for that purpose.

In his 1967 book, *Hell's Angels*, counterculture writer-sociologist Hunter S. Thompson documented the tendency toward violence of the motorcycle gang. The author, in fact, was beaten up on more than one occasion while he spent time with the bikers. Perhaps the planners of the Altamont concert saw the Angels' image as enforcers as a positive. Perhaps The Rolling Stones and their associates thought that the American version of the Hell's Angels was more like the basically harmless members of the Hell's Angels branch in London.[28] Whatever the reason for the decision, the 300 bikers could not be adequately controlled. Members of the bike gang working the security detail near the stage stabbed and killed one concertgoer.[29] Interestingly, members of the Hell's Angels and other motorcycle clubs had been at the Woodstock festival, the difference between Woodstock and Altamont being that, at Woodstock, members of motorcycle gangs were not used as the security force.

The Altamont festival began with performances by Santana, The Grateful Dead, the Jefferson Airplane, Crosby, Stills, Nash, and Young, and The Flying Burrito Brothers. During Santana's set the violence began, with members of the Hell's Angels battling audience members with pool cues and also throwing cans of beer at the concertgoers. The Rolling Stones' road manager moved the Angels' beer close to the stage in order to keep the bikers in one location and in order to keep them close to the stage, in case any security issues would evolve that might prove threatening to the musicians. During the Jefferson Airplane's set, however, a member of the motorcycle gang knocked out the Airplane's Marty Balin. Paul Kantner of the Airplane announced from the stage that the Hell's Angels were responsible for initiating the fights that were taking place near the stage, a move that incited the bikers even more.

During The Rolling Stones' set, eighteen-year-old Meredith Hunter was near the stage with a knife and a gun. He was beaten and killed by the security force while The Rolling Stones performed the aptly named song "Sympathy for the Devil." Countless people have cited this as an example of white on black violence and have noted the irony that Hunter was black and that The Rolling Stones were perhaps the best-known white band to be very heavily influenced by African American music. Despite a brief interruption when the stabbing took place, the band continued their set, realizing that if they were to cancel the rest of their performance at this point, a full-scale riot might break out. There were also three accidental deaths at Altamont and numerous injuries from the fights. Although it was a one-day festival, the casualty count far exceeded that of the three-plus-day Woodstock Music and Art Fair.

Bad drug trips also marred the Altamont event. Although Monterey and Woodstock both had freak-out tents where concertgoers experiencing bad LSD trips and overdoses of other drugs could be given the psychological or physical care they required, Altamont produced more numerous bad trips than previous festivals. Adding to the drug-related problems was the fact that The Rolling Stones had not provided the kind of mechanism to help concertgoers through their bad trips that smoothed out the Monterey and Woodstock festivals.

So what was it that caused the atmosphere of American rock festivals to shift so radically from the cooperation and communal spirit of Woodstock to the hysteria, violence, and drug problems of Altamont? The violence of Altamont suggests that Woodstock Ventures' assessment of the possible problems that some of The Rolling Stones' material might cause may have been valid. Certainly, Altamont did not have the mix of rock, soul, and gentle folk music that had balanced Woodstock: the music and performance style of the Stones was high-energy and theatrical and included the references to violence in "Street Fighting Man" and "Sympathy for the Devil" that had caused Woodstock Ventures to pass over the band in the first place. Certainly, the dark side of the Hell's Angels that Hunter S. Thompson chronicled so well played a role. The demeanor and crowd-control tactics of the bikers who worked security at Altamont were worlds away from the gentle persuasion of members of the Hog Farm commune who assisted at Woodstock. They were also worlds away from the studied techniques of the off-duty New York Police Department officers who worked security at Woodstock. Even the types of "uniforms" that identified members of the Hell's Angels contrasted with the peaceful uniforms of Woodstock's security detail. The careful attention to detail with regard to the presentation and behavior of security at Woodstock gave way to carelessness and anarchy at Altamont. The demographics of the Woodstock audience have been documented, but no similar study is available for Altamont. Anecdotal evidence would suggest that the demographics were somewhat different. For one thing, the Woodstock audience was certainly more diverse, given the eclectic nature of the music acts that appeared at the festival. The Altamont audience was there to hear The Rolling Stones. No doubt Altamont attracted fewer of the gentle hippies of the late 1960s and more hard-core, hard rock fans.

Interestingly, at least one of the principals involved in the Altamont concert refused to place the blame for the fiasco at the California speedway anywhere but on what he perceived as the differences in the nature of Americans and the British. In early 1970, Rolling Stones guitarist Keith Richards was quoted as saying, "Really, the difference between the open air show we held here [in England] in Hyde Park and the one there is amazing. I think it illustrates the difference between the two countries. In Hyde Park everybody had a good time, and there was no trouble. You can put half a million young English people together and they won't start killing each other. That's the difference."[30] Of course, in making this statement,

Richards completely ignores all of the positive communal spirit that drove the Woodstock festival. Although the concertgoers were not necessarily "killing each other," England's Isle of Wight Festival later in 1970 found the audience members strangely at odds and even openly hostile with the musicians who were entertaining them. These actions at the Isle of Wight greatly diminished the validity of Richards' assessment of why The Rolling Stones' Altamont and Hyde Park concerts—both in 1969—differed so greatly.

THE ISLE OF WIGHT FESTIVAL (1970)

Although many discussions of the rise and fall of rock music festivals of the 1960s start with the Monterey International Pop Music Festival and end with The Rolling Stones' disastrous Altamont concert, the 1970 Isle of Wight Festival in England also deserves mention as it represents, like Altamont, a kind of antithesis to Woodstock. The festival saw young people turn on their rock idols en masse for the first time. This seems to have been caused by several factors, including the physical setup of the concert area and the growing financial and lifestyle gulf between audience members and rock stars.

In sharp contrast to Monterey Pop, Altamont, and the summer 1969 festivals, the Isle of Wight Festival had a tremendous physical gulf between the stage and the audience areas. Even in the larger stadium concerts of the 1960s at least some of the audience was close to the stage. The physical gulf between performers and audience worked in total opposition to the communal nature of the rock experience. Typically, rock audiences felt close (in many senses of the word) to their favorite rock musicians. Music critic Jon Landau alludes to this sense of connection and the way in which it was coming undone by the early 1970s in his 1972 book *It's Too Late to Stop Now*, in which he writes:

> Rock, the music of the Sixties, was a music of spontaneity. It was a folk music—it was listened to and made by the same group of people. It did not come out of a New York office building where people sit and write what they think other people want to hear. It came from the life experiences of the artists and their interaction with an audience that was roughly the same age. As that spontaneity and creativity have become more stylized and analyzed and structured, it has become easier for businessmen and behind-the scenes manipulators to structure their approach to merchandising music. The process of creating stars has become a routine and a formula as dry as an equation.[31]

Landau's statement also suggests the reason behind the other gulf that seems to have caused some of the problems at the Isle of Wight: the fact that young people were viewing rock stars as rich, corporate types or at least as rich people who were being manipulated by corporations. Certainly, the rock star as a businessperson was on the minds of British rock fans at the time of the concert. The Beatles had garnered headlines around the world when they announced the formation of their corporation, Apple Corps, in 1968. In their idealism members of The Beatles had described the corporation as a sort of communal support mechanism for deserving, but as yet undiscovered, artists. By the time of the Isle of Wight concert, The Beatles were finished as a band and Apple was an unmitigated business disaster. In the minds of many at the Isle of Wight festival, it was *them* (the rich rock stars) and *us* (the poor kids who could barely afford to attend the concerts). The physical gulf at the concert site only helped to emphasize that lack of emotional and social connection.

Unlike Woodstock and Altamont, the Isle Wight festivals were an annual event, dating back to 1968. The 1968 festival had been a rather small affair, with mostly British bands performing in front of approximately 10,000 fans.[32] The 1969 edition of the Isle of Wight festival found approximately 150,000 fans showing up. The 1969 festival took place August 30–31. This was just after the Woodstock Music and Art Fair, and several Woodstock performers (The Band, The Who, Richie Havens, and Joe Cocker) appeared at the English festival. The biggest stir, however, was caused by Bob Dylan's performance at the 1969 Isle of Wight festival. His set, backed by The Band, included "She Belongs to Me," "I Threw It All Away," "The Mighty Quinn," "Maggie's Farm," "Wild Mountain Thyme," "It Ain't Me, Babe," "To Ramona," "Lay Lady Lay," "Highway 61 Revisited," "One Too Many Mornings," "I Pity the Poor Immigrant," "Like a Rolling Stone," "I'll Be Your Baby Tonight," "Minstrel Boy," "Rainy Day Women #12 and 35," "Mr. Tambourine Man," and "I Dreamed I Saw St. Augustine."

Other performers who appeared at the 1969 edition of the Isle of Wight festival included Blodwyn Pig, Blonde on Blonde, Fat Mattress, Marsha Hunt, and other, primarily British musicians. The festival also included an Environmental Playground, "with jousting between beautifully painted, bizarre-shaped cars," giant phallic-shaped balloons, and an area filled with soapsuds in which concert attendees could cavort.[33] Despite, or perhaps because of, some of these oddities, however, the 1969 Isle of Wight festival generally went off well.

Taking place over the course of five days—August 26–30, 1970—the 1970 the Isle of Wight festival attracted approximately 500,000 fans.[34] The 1970 edition of the festival featured a wide range of British, American, and international acts, including Judas Jump, Kathy Smith, Rosalie Sorrels, David Bromberg, Redbone, Kris Kristofferson, Mighty Baby, Gary Farr, Supertramp, Andy Roberts Everyone, Howl, Black Widow, The Groundhogs, Terry Reid, Gilberto Gil, Fairfield Parlour, Arrival, Lighthouse, Taste, Tony Joe White, Chicago, Family, Procol Harum, the Voices of East Harlem, Cactus, John Sebastian, Shawn Phillips, Joni Mitchell, Tiny Tim, Miles Davis, Ten Years After, Emerson, Lake and Palmer, the Doors, The Who, Sly and the Family Stone, Melanie, Good News, Ralph McTell, Heaven, Free, Donovan with the Open Road, Pentangle, The Moody Blues, Jethro Tull, Jimi Hendrix, Joan Baez, Leonard Cohen, and Richie Havens. Despite, or per-

haps because of, the inclusion of numerous big-name performers, the festival's promoters encountered challenges with the programming. The biggest challenge was
that the venue did not lend itself well to the folk-oriented acoustic music performed by musicians like Melanie and Joan Baez. Another problem was that at
least some of the lesser-known acts were probably deservedly lesser known. Another major problem was created by the way in which the festival was paced: the
audience seemed to want to hear rock music at precisely the time folk performers took the stage.

There were other problems as well. The festival site itself was inadequate for
the crowds[35] and included a hilly area where nonpaying onlookers had nearly as
good a view of the festival as those who bought tickets. As one might imagine,
this caused a great deal of resentment among those who had purchased tickets.
There were also various politically radical factions in attendance that felt strongly
that the musicians who could have been helping their political and social causes
were in the music industry only for money, sex, and drugs. The high fees com-
manded by some of the acts, in fact, caused considerable resentment. In the film
footage shot at the Isle of Wight concert there is a very poignant scene of Joan
Baez trying to calm down the audience and bring them to the realization that the
musicians who are performing at the event share many of the same values. Baez,
in fact, seems to have been one of the musicians who were booed most vehemently.
Seen as having been very much aligned with the radical Left of the early 1960s,
she was seen by members of the Isle of Wight audience as a performer who had
abandoned radical politics in order to make money.

Some acts, notably Joni Mitchell, were booed because the half a million audience members wanted to hear rock music and not acoustic folk music by the time
of her appearance on Saturday, August 29. Ironically, some audience accounts suggest that Mitchell performed one of the better sets of the festival. The less-than-
perfect programming of acts by the festival's promoters, however, caused Mitchell's
fine set not to be well received.[36] Other acts did not perform up to their high standards of the past, including Jimi Hendrix, who would be dead of drug-related
causes in less than three weeks. Similarly, The Doors disappointed many in the
audience with their erratic performance. The Doors' difficulties seem to have been
caused by singer Jim Morrison, who was suffering at the time from the effects of
serious drug and alcohol abuse.

Doors keyboardist Ray Manzarek, however, has other memories of the 1970
Isle of Wight Festival. According to Manzarek,

> It was an incredible lineup. Jimi Hendrix, who would be dead
> two weeks later; the Who, with the debut of *Tommy*[37]; Miles
> Davis, with his new electronic funk aggregation; Joni Mitchell;
> Sly and the Family Stone; Jethro Tull . . . and the Doors. And half
> a million English hippies. A sea of soft garments and colors and
> nubile bodies. An ocean of humanity. An amazing two days.
> There was some absolutely brilliant music. Brilliant playing.
>   Our set was subdued but very intense. We played with a con-

trolled fury and Jim was in fine vocal form. His voice was rich and powerful and throaty. He sang for all he was worth but moved nary a muscle. He remained rigid and fixed to the microphone for the entire concert. Dionysus had been shackled. They [the authorities who had charged the singer with exposure at a Miami, Florida concert, and with unruly behavior onboard an aircraft, both serious crimes] had killed his spirit. He would never be the same in concert again. They had won.[38]

By the last day of the festival, the fences were ripped down by some of the radical politicos, stage announcements had become frantic and even condescending to the audience, and organizationally, the festival basically fell apart. As festival promoter Ron Foulk was widely quoted as saying on Monday, September 1, 1970, the day after the festival ended, "This is the last festival. Enough is enough. It began as a beautiful dream, but it has got out of control and become a monster." Indeed, the 1970 Isle of Wight Festival seems to have been so distasteful that not only was there not another Isle of Wight Festival, but some of the production and promotional figures never again worked on rock music festivals at all.

Filmmaker Murray Lerner captured the 1970 Isle of Wight Festival on film. Castle Music Pictures and the British Broadcasting Corporation, in association with Initial Film and Television released the videorecording *Message to Love* in 1997. Lerner's documentary includes performances by Joan Baez, Leonard Cohen, Miles Davis, Donovan, The Doors, Bob Dylan, Emerson, Lake and Palmer, Family, Free, The Great Awakening, Jimi Hendrix, Jethro Tull, Kris Kristofferson, Joni Mitchell, The Moody Blues, John Sebastian, Taste, Ten Years After, Tiny Tim, and The Who. The film captures some of the unfortunate backstage intrigue and the rift that developed between concertgoers and the musicians, both of which cast the festival as one of the low points (along with Altamont) of the hippie lifestyle.

THE CONCERT FOR BANGLA DESH

After having been told about the plight of refugees in Bangla Desh by his friend and mentor Ravi Shankar, former-Beatle George Harrison decided to undertake a massive benefit concert at New York's Madison Square Garden.[39] Harrison contacted musician friends and assembled an all-star group for the August 1, 1971, event (the concert was repeated the next day). Eric Clapton, Bob Dylan, Ringo Starr, Billy Preston, Leon Russell, Badfinger, Allan Beutler, Jesse Ed Davis, Ravi Shankar's ensemble, and other singers and instrumentalists performed in the first major rock benefit megaconcert. The Concert for Bangla Desh set the stage for later philanthropic popular events such as Live Aid, Farm Aid, and other such events.

Harrison biographer Geoffrey Giuliano writes of Harrison's quick work in lining up performers for the concert, "To say that George fully drew on his extensive web of show-business connections with almost unparalleled efficiency is an understatement. The truth is that from the first day he committed himself to the cause he acted like a man obsessed."[40] In fact, by all accounts, the Concert for Bangla Desh was almost single-handedly put together by Harrison.

Sitarist Ravi Shankar, tabla player Alla Rakah, sarod player Ali Akbar Khan, and tamboura player Kamala Chakravarty led off the concert with music from the Indian subcontinent. George Harrison led the rock ensemble in his Beatles and post-Beatles songs "Wah-Wah," "My Sweet Lord," "Awaiting on You All," "While My Guitar Gently Weeps," "Something," "Here Comes the Sun," and several others. Ringo Starr sang his recent post-Beatles hit "It Don't Come Easy." Leon Russell was the lead singer for a cover of The Rolling Stones' "Jumpin' Jack Flash" and the early rock and roll hit "Youngblood."

Although Bob Dylan had participated in the rehearsal the day before the first of the Bangla Desh concerts, he had reserved the right not to perform if he did not feel like making an appearance. During the first part of the August 1, 1971 concert, as he was waiting backstage, Dylan reportedly expressed concern that the audience might not want to hear him perform. When convinced that he had to perform in order to support his friend Harrison, Dylan took the stage to thunderous applause. Although Dylan was reclusive at this point in his career and did not often perform, he sang his compositions "A Hard Rain's Gonna Fall," "It Takes a Lot to Laugh/It Takes a Train to Cry," "Blowin' in the Wind," "Mr. Tambourine Man," and "Just Like a Woman."

The Concert for Bangla Desh nearly was of even greater musical importance. Former Beatle John Lennon was prepared until the last minute to perform; he backed out when it became clear that his wife, conceptual artist/musician Yoko Ono, would not be permitted to perform. There was also the slim chance, or at least a hope among fans, that Paul McCartney would appear. McCartney's business differences with his former bandmates, however, probably never would have found him on the same stage as Lennon, Starr, and Harrison in 1971. Despite the lack of a full Beatles reunion, Harrison, Starr, Russell, Shankar, Dylan, Clapton, and the backing musicians put together a critical and philanthropic success. This was especially important in light of the disasters of Altamont and the 1970 Isle of Wight Festival. Harrison and his compatriots showed that a rock festival (in this case, a single, indoor, very long concert) could be nonviolent, musically satisfying, and socially responsible.

The Concert for Bangla Desh was filmed and audio-recorded. Royalties generated by the subsequent movie and three-record set, as well as from ticket sales from the concerts themselves, ultimately raised approximately $15 million for relief efforts in the ravaged nation. The money, however, was slow in coming, and tax-related complications managed to keep the final tally of dollars much lower than it might have been. As an unprecedented event, organized primarily by one musician and in a very narrow time frame, and as a model of sorts for the philanthropic music festivals of the later 1970s through the present, the Concert for Bangla Desh was a great success and certainly an event that was intimately tied to the Woodstock spirit of peace, love, and music. The concert's philanthropic legacy continued into the 1990s: all proceeds from the 1991 compact disc reissue on the

Capitol Records label were donated to the United Nations Children's Fund (UNICEF), which continues to support relief efforts for refugees and others.

NOTES

1. San Francisco Bay Area author Ken Kesey had been using the royalties from his successful book *One Flew over the Cuckoo's Nest* to finance LSD parties (which are well documented in Tom Wolfe's book *The Electric Kool-Aid Acid Test*). His followers, known as the Merry Pranksters, were among the first hippies. Former Harvard psychological researcher Dr. Timothy Leary was the acid guru of the East Coast. Unlike Kesey and the Merry Pranksters, who encouraged everyone to use LSD (and in a partylike atmosphere), Leary placed strict guidelines on who should try the drug and under what circumstances. Leary's rules were designed to ensure against bad trips.

2. Some estimates suggest that as many as 200,000 young people were gathered in the general vicinity of the Monterey County Fairgrounds. *Monterey International Pop Music Festival—1967*, http://members.tripod.com/Yelnats_Yarkled/Monterey/. Accessed March 2004.

3. McKenzie's recording of "San Francisco (Be Sure to Wear Flowers in Your Hair)" peaked at number 4 on the *Billboard* pop singles charts and still receives radio airplay on oldies stations over thirty-five years after the "Summer of Love."

4. Eric Burden and the Animals' "San Franciscan Nights" spent ten weeks on the *Billboard* pop charts, peaking at number 9. The band followed up this single with the single "Monterey," which chronicled the Monterey International Pop Music Festival. "Monterey" peaked at number 15 on the *Billboard* pop singles charts.

5. Wilson, Brian, with Todd Gold, *Wouldn't It Be Nice* (New York: HarperCollins, 1991), p. 167.

6. Ward, Ed, "The Monterey Pop Festival," Britannica.com, http://www.Britannica.com/psychedelic/testonly/monterey.html.

7. Wenner, Jann, "British Groups 'Smash' at Monterey," *Melody Maker* 42 (June 24, 1967), pp. 8–9.

8. The Beatles actually did another live "concert" in January 1969 atop the roof of the building that housed Apple Records in London. Since the rooftop performance was not advertised and was primarily heard by passers-by on the street, it could scarcely be called a "concert" in the traditional sense. (See discussion that follows.)

9. Wenner, "British Groups 'Smash' at Monterey," pp. 8–9.

10. Jimi Hendrix opened for The Monkees at the start of the tour, but after being booed by Monkees fans who wanted only to see their idols and who were not expecting Hendrix's brand of loud, driving, psychedelic music, Hendrix withdrew from the tour.

11. Country Joe and the Fish were quite well known and popular among members of the counterculture during the mid- to late-1960s but achieved little commercial success on the record charts. The exposure that the group might have gained from being included in the documentary could have affected their nationwide popularity. This would not be the last example of poor business decisions being made with regard to rock festivals in the 1960s. Some of these decisions might have been made because of a lack of sobriety, as Sander suggests, but others were made because some performers and managers, at the time, did not grasp the commercial and sociological significance of the rock festivals of the 1960s. For example, although there is some evidence to the contrary, it has long been con-

tended that the Keef Hartley Band's performance at the Woodstock festival was not recorded or filmed because the group's manager failed to recognize the importance of the exposure that the concert recording and documentary film would eventually have.

12. Sander, Ellen, "Monterey," *Trips: Rock Life in the Sixties* (New York: Charles Scribner's Sons, 1973), pp. 91–95. Reprinted in Budds, Michael J., and Marian M. Ohman, eds., *Rock Recall* (Needham Heights, Massachusetts: Ginn Press, 1993), p. 291.

13. Nor could members of The Beatles adequately hear themselves with the concert amplification technology of the day.

14. The Beatles album *Revolver* was released on August 5, 1966. The album featured studio overdubs, backwards tape material, electronically manipulated voices and instruments, and additional orchestral instruments. Many of these recordings were so complicated that the four musicians playing alone onstage simply could not adequately re-create the sound of the recordings. Material like the song "Strawberry Fields Forever" (the recording of which began in November 1966) and most of the songs of the mid-1967 album *Sgt. Pepper's Lonely Hearts Club Band* would be impossible to re-create onstage. When The Beatles did live television performances in 1967 and 1968, the better part of a full symphony orchestra was assembled in order to make the performances of songs like "All You Need Is Love" and "Hey Jude" sound like the records.

15. *The Beatles*, which was released with a stark, white album cover, is generally and unofficially known as "The White Album."

16. The legendary record producer Phil Spector worked on the *Let It Be* tapes, adding brass, string, and choral parts to some of the songs. A compact disc, *Let It Be: Naked* was released in late 2003 and went to the top of the *Billboard* album charts. This new release is purported to represent the "bare-bones" sound that members of The Beatles had actually intended for the original album. The astute listener who is familiar with the original version of *Let It Be* will note that not only does *Let It Be: Naked* present the non-Spectorized tracks, but it also includes several complete takes that differ from those that Spector used as the basis of his version of the *Let It Be* album.

17. Quoted in Lewisohn, Mark, *The Beatles Recording Sessions: The Official Abbey Road Studio Session Notes, 1962–1970* (New York: Harmony Books, 1988), p. 169.

18. Sia, Joseph J., *Woodstock 69, Summer Pop Festivals: A Photo Review* (New York: Scholastic Book Services, 1970).

19. Wein, George, with Nate Chinen, *Myself among Others* (Cambridge, Massachusetts: Da Capo Press, 2003), p. 284.

20. Wein with Chinen, *Myself among Others*, p. 286.

21. Wein with Chinen, *Myself among Others*, p. 283.

22. Sia, Joseph J., *Woodstock 69, Summer Pop Festivals: A Photo Review* (New York: Scholastic Book Services, 1970). It should be noted that part of the photographer's art is in picking his or her subjects. Sia's audience photographs may not necessarily have been fully representative of the Newport Folk Festival's audience demographics.

23. Sia, *Woodstock 69, Summer Pop Festivals: A Photo Review*.

24. Cover bands perform music made popular by other performers, often trying overtly to imitate the famous version of a song.

25. This anecdotal evidence includes the recollections of Woodstock attendees, some of which are published in Makower, Joel, *Woodstock: The Oral History* (New York: Doubleday Press, 1989), and several of which are part of the Youngstown State University Department of History's Oral History Project. I have included citations for the transcripts of the Youngstown State University interviews. These include, but are not limited to, the fol-

lowing: Mallory, Kenneth, *Woodstock, 1969* (Youngstown, Ohio: Youngstown State University, 1995); Nelson, Tribby, *Woodstock, 1969* (Youngstown, Ohio: Youngstown State University, 1994); Turk, John R., *Woodstock Concert of 1969* (Youngstown, Ohio: Youngstown State University, 1989); and Vansuch, Alexandra, *Woodstock, 1969* (Youngstown, Ohio: Youngstown State University, 1995).

26. The event originally was to have taken place in San Francisco. As the organizers realized that too many people would show up, and as the San Francisco City Council failed to approve the necessary permits, a new venue needed to be found. The Altamont Speedway site was secured less than twenty-four hours before the festival began. This probably accounts for some of the lack of planning for sanitation facilities and for a hastily constructed stage that, by many accounts, was far too low and close to the audience.

27. *Grateful Dead: The Illustrated Trip* (New York: DK, 2003), p. 105.

28. The Rolling Stones had, in fact, utilized the London-based Hell's Angels as a security force for their free concerts in London's Hyde Park earlier in the summer of 1969.

29. As many commentators have pointed out, it was highly ironic that a black man was the victim, as he was surrounded by whites listening to a white band that specialized in playing black-influenced music.

30. Burks, John, "In the Aftermath of Altamont," *Rolling Stone* n51 (February 7, 1970), pp. 7–8.

31. Landau, Jon *It's Too Late to Stop Now* (San Francisco: Straight Arrow Books, 1972), p. 40.

32. The Jefferson Airplane was the only big-name American band to appear at the 1968 Isle of Wight Festival.

33. *The Isle of Wight Festival* 1969, http://tinpan.fortunecity.com/ebony/546/iow1969-press.html, accessed December 23, 2003.

34. Some unconfirmed accounts place the number closer to 600,000.

35. One festival attendee described it as "a prison camp atmosphere." *The Isle of Wight Festival 1970*, http://tinpan.fortunecity.com/ebony/546/iow1970menu.html, accessed December 23, 2003.

36. Interestingly, the programming skills of concert organizers would later be blamed in part for the violence of the Woodstock 1999 festival.

37. Contrary to Manzarek's recollections, the bulk of *Tommy* was performed by The Who at Woodstock months before the group's appearance at the Isle of Wight festival.

38. Manzarek, Ray, *Light My Fire: My Life with the Doors* (New York: G. P. Putnam's Sons, 1998), p. 340.

39. The troubles arose when the West Pakastani government attempted to reduce the population of East Pakistan (Bangla Desh). Over 1 million Bengals were murdered, and approximately 10 million Bengali refugees fled to India. Lipski, Alexander, and Suzenna Martin, "Bangla Desh," Liner notes to *The Concert for Bangla Desh*, Apple Records STGX 3385, 1971, p. 3.

40. Giuliano, Geoffrey, *Dark Horse: The Private Life of George Harrison* (New York: Dutton, 1990), pp. 131–32.

The Woodstock
Music and Art Fair

The story of the Woodstock Music and Art Fair is the saga of a venture that really never started out to be what it ultimately became. The original idea was to build a recording studio in Woodstock, New York, a small town into which several prominent rock musicians had moved by the late 1960s. Then, a concert to promote the studio was proposed. And then, a rock music festival that would fund the recording studio by means of ticket sales to the 50,000 to 100,000 fans who might be expected to attend over a couple of days was planned. Then, the festival idea took hold—leaving any plans for a recording studio on the back burner—and the proposed venue moved from Woodstock to Saugerties (located in Ulster County, New York), albeit very briefly, and then to the Town of Wallkill (located in Orange County, New York) and eventually to the Village of White Lake in the Town of Bethel, Sullivan County, New York. The festival was plagued by bad weather, a crowd far exceeding anything any of the principals in the venture ever anticipated, a lack of food, a lack of adequate sanitation, and a lack of medical staff but became the greatest, most significant three days of many young people's lives and the high point of the hippie philosophy of peace, love, and understanding put into action. Due to the ever-evolving nature of the enterprise, the quickness with which plans were made and changed, and the fact that no one tried adequately to document the entire enterprise at the time,[1] it has been difficult to sort out an exact chronology of the events that led up to the festival itself as well as exactly what transpired once the festival began. The four principals involved with planning and implementing the festival have disagreed with each other and have contradicted themselves in interviews and in print—it seems that even they had difficulty making sense of the whole thing. Let us take a look at the whirlwind of activity that led up to one of the most significant musical and sociological happenings of the 1960s.

THE FOUR ORGANIZERS

We begin our look at the events leading up to the festival itself by looking at the four principals involved in actually conceptualizing the Woodstock Music and Art Fair and then getting it off the ground: Michael Lang, Artie Kornfeld, John Roberts, and Joel Rosenman.

Michael Lang was the visionary of the group. Originally from Brooklyn, New York, he had run a head shop[2] in Florida in 1966 before branching out into rock concert production. Lang and Mel Lawrence, who would later serve as director of operations for the Woodstock Music and Art Fair, produced the Miami Pop Festival in 1968, organizing the event together in an amazingly short three weeks—remarkable considering the lack of previous experience the two had with concert production. The festival attracted approximately 40,000 fans but, foreshadowing Woodstock, lost a considerable sum of money. What Lang and Lawrence did achieve was an artistic success, primarily built upon an impressive breadth of talent and styles among the artists who appeared at the festival. In addition to well-established masters such as blues master John Lee Hooker and the early rock and roll pioneer Chuck Berry, Lang and Lawrence's festival featured modern acts such as The Jimi Hendrix Experience, The Crazy World of Arthur Brown, Blue Cheer, and many others.

Lang returned to New York and began managing the rock band Train in 1968.[3] Attempting to secure a recording contract for his charges, Lang made the rounds of the New York City record companies. In the course of these meetings, he encountered Artie Kornfeld, only slightly older than Lang but already a highly successful pop songwriter, record producer, and executive at Capitol Records. Kornfeld's credentials included his co-authorship of the highly successful song "Dead Man's Curve," which hit number 8 on the *Billboard* pop charts for Jan and Dean in 1964. Like Lang, Kornfeld was a self-acknowledged "head," known for smoking marijuana and hashish in his office.[4] Lang had gotten into Kornfeld's office by telling the Capitol Records director of East Coast Contemporary Product's secretary that he was from Kornfeld's old neighborhood. Although the rock band Train went nowhere in the recording industry, they played an important role in bringing together two of the principals of Woodstock Ventures, for after their initial meeting, Michael Lang and Artie Kornfeld and their wives became close friends. By early 1969, Lang and Kornfeld had taken notice of the number of prominent folk and rock acts that had relocated to the little town of Woodstock, New York. Lang and Kornfeld believed that the fact that musicians like Jimi Hendrix, Tim Hardin, Janis Joplin, The Band, Van Morrison, and Bob Dylan now lived in the rural community, not all that far away from New York City, made Woodstock a ripe target for starting a state-of-the-art recording studio.

Artie Kornfeld, born in 1942 in Coney Island, New York, received his first main exposure to the music industry and to music outside of the middle-of-the-road pop mainstream when his family moved to Charleston, North Carolina, in the mid-1950s.[5] His family later moved back to New York City, and Kornfeld gradually became a part of the city's music scene. In 1963, the budding songwriter met Don Kirschner, the head of Aldon Music. Aldon Music was an important company in the Brill Building era of popular music in the late 1950s and early 1960s. Brill Building songwriters penned many of the top pop and rock and roll hits of the time and included such figures as Carole King, Gerry Goffin, Ellie Greenwich, John Barry, Barry Mann, Cynthia Weil, and Neil Sedaka. Other future singing stars, notably Neil Diamond and Paul Simon, also honed their crafts at various Brill Building publishers before they became nationally known as performers.

In this world of almost factory-like pop song production Kornfeld found his songwriting success. He co-wrote songs that hit the *Billboard* singles charts for the Shirelles and the Angels. As mentioned previously, however, Kornfeld's biggest success came in the form of "Dead Man's Curve," a song recorded by Jan and Dean. Kornfeld co-authored the number 8 pop hit with Jan Berry and the legendary Beach Boys singer-songwriter-keyboardist-bass guitarist-producer Brian Wilson.

In 1967 the New York City music publishing and recording industry was taking notice of the San Francisco "Summer of Love" hippie lifestyle. At the time, Artie Kornfeld was the director of artists and repertoire for Mercury Records. Through his work in matching songs with performers, he became aware of a new multigenerational family group known as The Cowsills. Incidentally, this group was the real-life inspiration for the popular 1970s television program *The Partridge Family*.[6] Kornfeld co-wrote the "Summer of Love"-influenced song "The Rain, the Park and Other Things" for The Cowsills, whose recording of the song reached number 2 on the *Billboard* pop singles charts in late 1967. Based on his success with the Cowsills' first hit, Kornfeld left his position with Mercury Records and took up management of The Cowsills, writing for, producing, and managing them into 1968.

Under Kornfeld's management and record production leadership, The Cowsills were tremendously successful. Kornfeld then left his independent production work to take a position at Capitol Records. Kornfeld's position, director of East Coast contemporary product, assured that he would be in contact with yet-to-be-discovered acts and in contact with their managers. It was in this context that Michael Lang, manager of the rock band Train, met Kornfeld in November 1968.

Joel Rosenman grew up in Cold Spring Harbor on Long Island, New York. He entered Princeton University in 1959, graduating with a degree in English literature in 1962. During his university days, Rosenman worked for a time as a nightclub singer. Until the time of his later work with John Roberts, this very much part-time nightclub singing was the extent of Joel Rosenman's experience in the music industry. Rosenman, who needed to find a profession and who was something of an academic overachiever, then entered Yale Law School in 1962. Upon his graduation from Yale, Rosenman began practicing law but soon discovered that the traditional practice of law was not as exciting as what he had hoped it would be. He was looking for a new direction and new opportunities. A fortuitous weekend of golf would provide that new direction.

John Roberts had been born into a wealthy family in New York City in 1945. Upon the death of his mother in the early 1950s, Roberts inherited a sizable sum of money.[7] In 1961, Roberts enrolled at the University of Pennsylvania, although according to most accounts, his main concern in college was in having fun. When Roberts reached age twenty-one, he received the first $400,000 of his inheritance. Although the bulk of the inheritance remained tied up in a trust, Roberts already had the means to invest in attractive projects. After college, he entered the investment world, making highly speculative investments on Wall Street. At the same time he was taking graduate courses in Philadelphia at the Annenberg School of Communications.

One of Roberts' friends in college had been Douglas Rosenman. In 1966, Rosenman invited Roberts to spend a weekend out of the city playing golf. Also golfing on that day was Douglas Rosenman's brother Joel. Joel had just graduated from law school and was trying to make his start in the legal profession.

Rosenman and Roberts quickly became friends and decided to share an apartment in New York City. The two young men, one with business training and the financial means to invest in new projects and the other with a legal background, decided to become venture capitalists, and John Roberts dropped out of Annenberg in March 1967. The two would-be entrepreneurs placed an advertisement in the *Wall Street Journal* that read, "Young Men with Unlimited Capital looking for interesting and legitimate business ideas." According to Rosenman, Roberts, and their co-author Robert Pilpel, the idea behind the ad was to provide Rosenman and Roberts with possibilities for working in venture capital.[8] According to their later recollections, recorded by Joel Makower in his book *Woodstock: The Oral History*, however, the ad was meant to generate plot ideas for a television situation comedy Roberts and Rosenman were planning to write.[9] Incidentally, Robert Stephen Spitz, in his book *Barefoot in Babylon*, agrees that the *Wall Street Journal* advertisement was placed in order to generate story ideas for a television program.[10] Whatever the initial reason for the advertisement, Rosenman and Roberts received thousands of responses, some of which were quite silly, really the type of material that could provide fodder for a television sitcom. Some of the ideas, however, actually seemed to be workable business ideas.

In 1967, Roberts and Rosenman were involved with the construction of a new recording studio in New York City, called Media Sound. As one might guess, this was one of the workable business ventures that Roberts and Rosenman had uncovered. It also would eventually become one of the key ingredients in bringing the four Woodstock principals together.

Miles Lourie, a lawyer, knew Roberts and Rosenman and also happened to represent Michael Lang. Knowing of Roberts and Rosenman's work in developing the Media Sound recording studio and of Lang and Artie Kornfeld's plans to construct a studio in Woodstock, New York, Lourie introduced Lang, Roberts, and Rosenman in February 1969. After Rosenman, Lang, Roberts, and Kornfeld cemented their business association as Woodstock Ventures, Lourie continued to act as one of the new enterprise's attorneys. Eventually, Miles Lourie's father, Felix, who had important political connections in New York state government, would also assist Woodstock Ventures in their work.

As the four Woodstock principals made their plans for the studio in early 1969, they simultaneously developed plans for a music festival to be held in Woodstock, New York. Originally, the festival was to be a means of financing the studio. For a time, too, the idea to hold a yearly rock festival, modeled to some extent on what George Wein had been doing for years in other musical genres in Newport, Rhode Island, was bounced around.

Somehow when the four principals eventually got together, they complemented each other nearly perfectly. Together they had important contacts in the music industry, had knowledge of the youth and counterculture market, had the financial means to put some of their plans into action, and had some legal background. Interestingly, though, Kornfeld was the only one with substantial experience in the music business. The real music business experience of the others was considerably more modest. Lang had managed a rock band that had gone nowhere, and he had produced one rock festival, which was basically rained out. Rosenman and Roberts had worked to get one recording studio established. In some respects, the entire story of Woodstock being planned and put together was a case of "let's put on a rock festival, we'll call all our friends." In fact, many commentators have remarked about the "Andy Hardy" nature of the entire enterprise.

FINDING A CONCERT SITE AND PLANNING THE FESTIVAL

Part of the Andy Hardy meets Rube Goldberg nature of what was now called Woodstock Ventures can be seen in the story of the organization's office, which was set up at 47 West 57th Street in Manhattan in spring 1969. In their book, *Young Men with Unlimited Capital*, Joel Rosenman, John Roberts, and Robert Pilpel tell, in hilarious detail, the story of the redecorating of the 57th Street offices by a group known as Curtain Call Publications, Inc.[11] Like many of the schemes promoted by Michael Lang, the work done by Curtain Call sounds as if it must have resembled something from a film by Frederico Fellini, a bizarre, surreal experience that could have taken place only in the psychedelic drug-influenced late 1960s.

Despite the unlikely nature of the Woodstock Ventures enterprise, plans continued for the music festival, as well as for the recording studio.[12] The originally proposed site was owned by Alexander Tapooz and was located in Woodstock. Due to objections from local residents and several other factors, the Woodstock, New York, site quickly fell out of contention. Michael Lang and Artie Kornfeld thought that they had found a new site for the Woodstock festival in March 1969, when they found a landowner in Saugerties, New York, who agreed to lease his property for the event. When the businessmen of the Woodstock Ventures team, John Roberts and Joel Rosenman, met with the landowner's attorney on March

26, 1969, however, there seemed to have been a change of heart on the part of
the landowner. The attorney raised serious concerns about the financial stability
of Woodstock Ventures. In the course of the discussions it became clear to Rosenman and Roberts that the landowner probably had had second thoughts about
the financial stability of the organization perhaps based on the youth of the four
principals and on Michael Lang and Artie Kornfeld's hippie-like demeanors and
reputations.

With time elapsing and with the questions that had arisen in discussions in
Saugerties, Rosenman and Roberts sensed that a new site would have to be found,
and fairly quickly at that. As Roberts put it, "As was our custom, we decided to
act boldly, i.e., without proper thought."[13] The pair came upon a realtor who specialized in industrial parks. The realtor contacted Howard Mills, owner of the yet-
to-be-developed, 600-acre Mills Industrial Park in the Town of Wallkill, New
York.[14] On March 30, 1969, the two promoters, who still had not been in touch
with Lang and Kornfeld about their find, met with Mills, who indeed was interested in leasing the property to Woodstock Ventures for $10,000.[15] Howard and
Pat Mills, working with their attorney Herbert Fabricant, formed an agreement
with the would-be concert promoters. The one sticking point, however, was that
the use of this Walkill property for a music and art festival would still have to be
approved by the town's Zoning Board.

Although Woodstock Ventures had several attorneys, the principals realized that
they would need local representation at the meeting with the Town of Wallkill
Zoning Board. The company retained the services of Samuel W. Eager Jr. of Mid-
dleton, New York.[16] Roberts and Rosenman met with the Wallkill Zoning Board
of Appeals on April 18, 1969, and secured preliminary approval for the festival.
Through May 1969, the Mills property still looked to be the site for the concert.
Some Wallkill residents, however, began to fear what might happen when their
little town witnessed an invasion of hippies. Their suspicions were heightened
when they learned of a no-marijuana-smoking memo that had been circulated
among Woodstock Ventures employees. It was clear to Wallkill residents that, if
Woodstock Ventures had to order its employees not to smoke the illegal drug in
order to maintain good public relations, those same employees must already be
using marijuana on a regular basis. This proved to be the proverbial straw that
broke the camel's back. Despite all the efforts of Samuel Eager, the Concerned
Citizens Committee of Wallkill, which included vocal local residents such as
Richard Dow and Cliff Reynolds and which was represented by attorney Jules
Minker, succeeded in applying pressure on the town's politicians to rethink the
preliminary approval that had been given to Woodstock Ventures. New zoning
legislation was proposed and passed by the town government, which was represented by attorney Joseph Owen, that effectively made it impossible for a gathering of more than 5,000 people to take place. Woodstock Ventures was hoping to
attract between ten and twenty times that number.[17] Once again, it became apparent that a new venue for the Woodstock Music and Art Fair would have to be
secured.

Although Michael Lang, Artie Kornfeld, John Roberts, and Joel Rosenman each provided his own expertise and his own flavor to Woodstock Ventures, Lang and Kornfeld felt that their image would connect best with potential audience members than the more straitlaced, big-business, big-money corporate image of their partners. In May 1969, Rosenman and Roberts noticed that Lang and Kornfeld were mentioned in several wire reports as being the organizers of the festival, while no mention was made of Rosenman and Robert. Upon confrontation, Lang and Kornfeld claimed that they had asked the reporter who interviewed them only to keep Rosenman and Roberts low-profile in the story, so as not to offend members of the counterculture, who would be the probable audience members. This would not be the last time a wedge would be placed between the four partners. In fact, as the spring progressed, it became clear to Kornfeld, Rosenman, and Roberts that Lang had been trying to control the entire Woodstock operation so as to produce the festival the way *he* wanted to produce it by playing his three partners off against each other. Rosenman and Roberts tell in their book of a June 4, 1969, meeting at which they and Kornfeld intended to confront Lang with their discovery of Lang's behind-the-scenes manipulations. Apparently not much came of the confrontation, as the partnership continued, and Lang continued to act as something of a lone wolf.

The festival's slogan, "Three Days of Peace and Music . . . An Aquarian Exposition" and the famous dove and guitar logo[18] were finally all in place by early summer 1969. The posters and other advertisements for the festival were calculated to draw attention to the event as a sort of all-encompassing hippie happening. Unlike previous rock festivals, Woodstock's advertising did not focus on the names of performers. Although youth who might expect to intend the festival had some idea of who would be performing, the effect of the advertising campaign made the names or even the fame of the acts almost superfluous. In retrospect, it was probably this type of advertising that helped the festival draw the huge crowds that it did and to draw not just audience members for a day but people who arrived early and stayed for much of the festival, camping outside.

Also in June 1969, counterculture political activist Abbie Hoffman was in Michigan at a rally of the White Panther Party, where he learned of the Woodstock festival. Upon his return to New York City, Hoffman heard talk on the street of the festival, suggesting to him that the event was going to be of major importance. Hoffman had a reputation for being extremely suspicious of corporate rip-offs. Convinced that the Woodstock Music and Art Fair was another example of such a rip-off, Hoffman demanded a meeting with the Woodstock Ventures team. Joel Rosenman, Michael Lang, Hoffman, and members of his Young People's International Party (Yippies) met at the Yippies' East Village headquarters. According to reports from Rosenman in various sources, Lang was very nervous about the prospects, thinking that Hoffman possessed tremendous political power among members of the youth counterculture. According to Rosenman's recollections, Hoffman demanded $10,000 to ensure that the festival would not be disrupted by members of his organization, a move that Rosenman described as "a shakedown."[19] Hoffman remembered the meeting as a negotiation, not as an attempt at extortion.[20] Regardless of the true motivation behind the negotiations with Hoffman, the political activist and members of the Yippies helped to publicize the festival among the counterculture and helped to ensure that young people did not see the festival as a corporate rip-off. In the end, apparently only a couple thousand dollars was exchanged, and Woodstock Ventures provided concessions space for the political Left to distribute literature.

Despite the minor concessions of cash and booth space for the distribution of left-wing literature that had been made to Abbie Hoffman and his Young People's International Party, the goal of Woodstock Ventures was to make Woodstock's sole focus on the art of the counterculture and not on its politics. The organizers knew that politics would be part of the proceedings but wanted to ensure that the focus was on rock music and contemporary visual arts. The view of Rosenman, Lang, Roberts, and (to lesser extent) Kornfeld (who seemed to grow increasingly less involved with the festival as time went on), reflects a growing realization within the counterculture that neither violent protest nor politics would bring about the truly revolutionary change the counterculture sought. A complete change of lifestyle was what was needed.

Talk about Woodstock was heard not only in Michigan and on the streets of New York City. Woodstock co-producer Joel Rosenman recalled talking just before the start of the festival to one parking lot attendant who had hitchhiked to Woodstock from his home in Minnesota. The young man told Rosenman, "Everybody in Minnesota had been talking about Woodstock for months."[21] Just what was it that created the Woodstock mystique? Why this particular festival of 1969 instead of the Newport Jazz Festival, the Newport Folk Festival, the Atlantic City Pop Music Festival, or one of several other such music festivals?

The answer to that question probably had something to do with the idyllic, bucolic location at which the Woodstock festival took place. Max Yasgur's dairy farm and the surrounding community stood in sharp contrast to, say, the racetrack at which the Atlantic City Pop Music Festival had taken place. Even before Yasgur's farm became the site of the festival, the other proposed sites were similarly removed from the trappings of organized and urbanized gathering venues. Part of the answer probably lies in Michael Lang and Artie Kornfeld's decision to highlight their roles in the planning of the festival, de-emphasizing the roles of the "straighter" acting and dressing financiers John Roberts and Joel Rosenman. Given the iconic status that the festival's guitar and dove logo and self-billing as "An Aquarian Exposition" quickly acquired, the carefully calculated advertising campaign that Woodstock Ventures mounted also played a role.

Throughout the late spring and nearly up to the opening of the festival, Woodstock Ventures was booking performers. Lang, Kornfeld, Rosenman, and Roberts established a kind of "most-favored nation"-type fee policy for the musicians, offering to pay acts more or less equally. While this policy worked out particularly well for the lesser-known acts, it made it necessary for at least one long-established, well-known band to reject an offer to perform at Woodstock. Specifically, The Moody Blues had been touring the United States during summer 1969—the band appeared at the Atlantic City Pop Music Festival—but had to return to England before the Woodstock festival, due to commitments back home. The group's management determined that The Moody Blues would lose a great deal of money by making the return trip to the United States to play at Woodstock. Other bands had other reasons for turning down offers to perform at Woodstock. The Doors, arguably one of the most important American rock bands of the late 1960s, also appeared at the Atlantic City Pop Music Festival and were invited to perform at Woodstock. The band turned down the offer, due to singer Jim Morrison's paranoia that he might be assassinated at the concert, according to Bill Belmont, who was working with The Doors doing tour bookings at the time.[22]

As the musical acts were signed, Woodstock Ventures worked with and through several notable booking agents, but probably no one as well known as Bill Graham. Graham had established himself as a major player in the rock music world, particularly through his Fillmore East in New York City and the Fillmore Auditorium in San Francisco. These two venues were the scenes of many important rock shows in the mid- and late 1960s. Graham happened to be a man of complex temperament. As Doors keyboardist Ray Manzarek recalled, "Bill Graham was always a gracious host to us [when The Doors played the Fillmore in San Francisco], although he could be—when he flipped his rage switch on—the meanest man in San Francisco. I saw him freeze a gaggle of hippies at fifty paces with a mere shout."[23] Legendary concert promoter and producer that he was, Bill Graham was said to harbor some resentment that Lang, Kornfeld, Rosenman, and Roberts were producing what was looking to be a major rock festival practically in Graham's own backyard. Although there were some tension and fears among those working for Woodstock Ventures that Graham might try to buy them out or make it impossible for some musicians to appear at Woodstock, Graham eventually was persuaded by Michael Lang to work with the Woodstock producers rather than against them.

The acts booked for Woodstock varied considerably in terms of their popularity and even just how generally well known they were. For example, Jimi Hendrix, Sly and the Family Stone, The Who, and Janis Joplin were very widely known, and the jazz-rock group Blood, Sweat, and Tears and the roots-rock band Creedence Clearwater Revival were topping the pops charts in 1969. Melanie, however, made her debut at Woodstock. Several of the acts that Woodstock Ventures booked were undoubtedly signed for what could be labeled self-serving purposes. Bert Sommer, for example, was managed by Artie Kornfeld, and the group Quill, which was unknown outside Boston, was managed by Michael Lang. Some acts were booked due to pressure from some of the established rock managers of the day. Bill Graham, for example, made the appearance of Santana contingent upon Woodstock Ventures also booking It's a Beautiful Day. Ironically, although they were booked, It's a Beautiful Day never performed at the festival. Jeff Beck and the heavy metal band Iron Butterfly were also booked but did not perform.

Although the principals of Woodstock Ventures would experience a great deal of difficulty in securing a site for their festival, they were at least working through the process in June 1969. They were also developing and implementing their advertising campaign and signing performers. It was in June, however, that Woodstock Ventures realized that they had completely overlooked making arrangements for food concessions for the festival. Peter Goodrich had been a friend of Michael Lang since the latter's days in Florida, and Lang knew that Goodrich had contacts in the food industry. Goodrich contacted the trio of Charles Baxter, Lee Howard, and Jeff Joerger, who had some experience in food service and who had in fact done the concessions work for Lang's Miami Pop Music Festival in 1968. The trio, however, had no working capital. After their recruitment by Goodrich, the trio, known as Food for Love, Inc., received up-front financing from Woodstock Ventures.

Woodstock Ventures sensed that they might need to have some sort of official endorsement of their planned music and art festival in order to make the event more palatable to the government and citizens of Wallkill, New York. Miles Lourie, who had introduced Joel Rosenman and John Roberts to Michael Lang and Artie Kornfeld initially, happened to have a father who was very well connected in Albany. Felix Lourie helped to set up a meeting between himself, Rosenman, Roberts, and New York state's lieutenant governor Malcolm Wilson. Rosenman and Roberts hoped that this meeting would result in some sort of official endorsement of the festival from the New York state political establishment. An endorsement of this sort, it was thought, would quiet some of the opposition to the Woodstock festival that seemed to be growing in Wallkill. When the meeting with the lieutenant governor failed to produce an endorsement, Felix Lourie arranged for Rosenman and Roberts to meet with one of Governor Nelson Rockefeller's executive secretaries to see if an endorsement could be secured directly from the governor's office. This time the outcome was a letter welcoming Woodstock Ventures and their music and art festival to New York state. Unfortunately for Woodstock Ventures, the letter stopped far short of endorsing the festival and arrived too late for a crucial meeting of the Wallkill, New York, Town Board that took place on June 12, 1969. This meeting found opposition to the Woodstock festival solidifying. At this meeting the Wallkill Town Board was convinced by the Concerned Citizens Committee to consider legislation that would limit the size of any future gatherings in the town. By July 1969 the village had enacted the new local law mentioned earlier that regulated gatherings of over 5,000 people. Since Woodstock Ventures was counting on a crowd of between 50,000 and 100,000, Wallkill's new law effectively put an end to Woodstock Ventures' plans for the locale.

By mid-July 1969 it was clear that the festival would not be taking place in Woodstock, Saugerties, or Wallkill, New York. The question of ticket refunds came up, as the Concerned Citizens Committee of Wallkill announced in a press conference that people who had bought tickets should seek refunds, implying that if the advertised festival did not take place in Wallkill, it was unlikely that it would take place at all. At the time, over $500,000 in tickets had been sold.[24] The principals of Woodstock Ventures feared that they might actually have to process the refunds, as time was running out to find a location for the mid-August festival. Woodstock Ventures placed advertisements in local newspapers all around the Woodstock-Wallkill-Bethel, and so on region north of New York City. Dairy farmer Max Yasgur and his wife, Miriam, saw one of these ads. As several associates of Woodstock Ventures scouted the region for suitable sites for the music festival, Yasgur contacted the festival organizers through a middleman, real estate salesman Morris Abraham. Abraham introduced Yasgur to Michael Lang and Mel Lawrence. Yasgur's property turned out to be perfect for the festival, with a natural amphitheater in what would turn out to be the performance area. The negotiations moved along smoothly and quickly.

The Yasgurs were well respected in the conservative, predominantly Jewish community of Bethel, New York. This respect was the result not only of the high-quality dairy products the Yasgurs supplied to the leading resorts of the region but also of the couple's personal integrity. When Max and Miriam Yasgur spoke out in support of the plans of Woodstock Ventures, area residents took the endorsement with much more than a grain of salt. Although there was resistance from some Bethel and White Lake residents, it was tempered by the outspoken trust in the outsiders that the Yasgurs expressed.

Having been through the disastrous attempts to stage the music and art festival in Woodstock proper and in Wallkill, Woodstock Ventures decided to hit the Bethel/White Lake area with a sort of public relations blitz. Reverend Don Ganoung, who had been a Roman Catholic priest, served as the head of community relations for the Woodstock Ventures organization. Ganoung preached sermons in area churches and youth centers in order to provide a service to the community and also to show that Woodstock Ventures was not all about sex, drugs, and rock and roll. Reverend Ganoung also organized concerts in the area by the Boston-based band Quill, a group that was not particularly well known but that generated goodwill among the young people of the area. Some of the public relations efforts undertaken by festival promoters, however, failed. The baseball games involving area youth and members of the Woodstock "team" were seen by White Lake area residents as being transparent attempts to win them over. The games were widely perceived as political maneuvering and, therefore, backfired. Ganoung organized a mini-Woodstock just in advance of the actual Woodstock Music and Art Fair in another attempt to show that contemporary arts (rock music and modern theater) could be at least something approaching wholesome entertainment. Unfortunately, the Earthlight Theatre, a politically and social-protest-based theater company, appeared and managed to offend many of the townspeople in attendance. Despite the unevenness of the public relations attempts by Woodstock Ventures, any opposition to the festival that existed in the Bethel/White Lake area was considerably more muted than that which had been in place in Wallkill. The festival seemed finally to have found a home.

Although progress was clearly being made, securing the necessary permissions for the festival to take place on the Yasgur farm did not proceed entirely smoothly. The last two weeks of July and the start of August found the principals of Woodstock Ventures appearing in public forums and in court trying to assure Bethel–White Lake residents that the festival would not adversely affect the area. The Bethel Businessman's Association voted to support the festival at its proposed site at Max Yasgur's dairy farm. Association member and spokesperson Ken Van

Loan's assessment of the coming festival was, "This is the greatest thing that ever happened to Sullivan County, and it just fell into our lap. Besides, the festival will be a cloudburst and a great thing for the area's young people since they're always complaining that they have nothing to do."[25] On July 29, 1969, the day after the Bethel Businessman's Association voted to support the festival, however, a hearing was held before Judge George L. Cobb in the Village of Catskill, New York, in which the owners of four summer camps in the area attempted to stop the festival. The camp owners feared that an invasion of hippies would adversely affect their camps. Paul Marshall, one of Woodstock Ventures' New York–based attorneys, negotiated an out-of-court settlement. Co-owners of a summer home adjacent to Max Yasgur's farm, however, had also filed papers in the same court trying to stop the festival. Marshall was unable to negotiate a settlement with the owners of the vacation home, and Judge Cobb heard arguments on the case. Weighing the possible impact on the owners of the summer home against the financial commitment Woodstock Ventures had already made to the festival, Judge Cobb decided that the festival could not be stopped on the basis of the homeowners' lawsuit.

Security can be a most important concern at large gatherings of people; failure to recruit a proper security force had deadly consequences at the Rolling Stones' Altamont rock festival, for example. Woodstock Ventures engaged the services of Ralph Cohen, a member of the New York City Police Department (NYPD), and Deputy Inspector Joe Fink of the NYPD to recruit off-duty police officers to work security at the Woodstock Music and Art Fair. Fink took the lead in these recruitment efforts but had his job complicated by the fact that Police Commissioner Howard Leary overturned an earlier approval for the off-duty officers to work at Woodstock just days before the festival was scheduled to open. Fink was sympathetic to the festival promoters' decision to use the security force as unarmed peace officers. This was to be done so as to avoid possible conflicts between members of the activist, counterculture audience and the police. Fink's sympathies came from his work on New York City's Lower East Side, a hotbed of counterculture activity in the late 1960s and into the 1970s. Interviews with prospective security officers were constructed in such a way as to try to detect any prejudices against hippies among the policemen. Because of Commissioner Leary's ban on a mass movement of off-duty NYPD officers to Bethel for the music festival, many officers joined the ranks of Woodstock peace officers, using assumed names on their applications for the job. When it eventually became evident that hundreds of thousands more young people would be attending the festival than had ever been anticipated, members of the Hog Farm commune also assisted with security.

As the Yasgur farm site was finalized and the various legal challenges to the festival appeared to be wrapping up, all reports indicate that Michael Lang continued to act as a visionary and lone wolf, largely trying to run the festival his own way. Although this caused him to run into conflicts with the other principals of Woodstock Ventures, he seems to have represented the free, hippie spirit of the festival better than Rosenman, Roberts, Kornfeld, or Mel Lawrence. In fact, Lang continued to act as the media representative for the Woodstock festival, as his

The pond, located at the edge of Max Yasgur's farm, provided drinking water and served as a source of relaxation for swimmers. (Courtesy of Photofest)

image made a favorable connection with the potential concert attendees more readily than the images projected by his partners.

Less than a week before the start of the festival, however, some important details still had not all been entirely worked out. On August 11, 1969, Chris Langhart, Woodstock's technical director and designer, notified Joel Rosenman that the large pond on the edge of the Yasgur property, a pond that Woodstock Ventures had assumed was owned by the dairy farmer, was instead owned by a group of other area residents. Clearly, the festival organizers would have to secure permission from the owners to use water from this pond, the nearest usable source of freshwater to the site. William Filippini, one of the pond's co-owners and a local chicken farmer, negotiated a ten-day lease on water from the pond for $5,000.

The various accounts of the actual construction of the stage, lighting towers, and other structures found in several books, including Joel Makower's *Woodstock: The Oral History*, Robert Stephen Spitz's *Barefoot in Babylon: The Creation of the Woodstock Music Festival, 1969*, and Joel Rosenman, John Roberts, and Robert Pilpel's *Young Men with Unlimited Capital*, suggest that it was something of a wonder these structures held up as well as they did. Mel Lawrence worked on the construction with a crew who ended up calling themselves the Bastard Sons. The main problems were that construction started later than it should have and took longer than anticipated, and once the festival started, structures were repeatedly compromised by overly eager concertgoers. Climbing the sound towers, in particular, seemed to present an attractive challenge to some of the more adventurous audience members; however, the towers were not designed to be subjected to this type of activity. Significantly, the stage itself was sufficiently elevated in the Yasgur farm's natural amphitheater that performers could easily be seen and the audience could be close to the stage, but audience members could not easily climb onto the

Built by members of the Woodstock construction crew, which called themselves the Bastard Sons, and by members of the Hog Farm Commune, the sound and lighting towers proved to be desirable, although precarious, vantage points for some audience members. (Courtesy of Photofest)

stage. Stage height seems to have played a significant role in the tragedy that would take place several months after the Woodstock Music and Art Fair at The Rolling Stones' Altamont festival.

As the Woodstock festival's opening day approached, young people began traveling into the Bethel area from New York City and elsewhere. Hints that Woodstock would become a happening of major and unprecedented proportions were observed as concertgoers got closer and closer to the festival site. Joel Makower quotes Woodstock attendee Alan Green, who described a very obvious change that he observed as he drove his newly purchased Volkswagen Beetle from Teaneck, New Jersey, to the festival. Green observed no one hitchhiking in the immediate New York City area, but as he got closer and closer to the festival, more and more hitchers appeared. As Green said, "it was really obvious that something was happening and there was this—it was sort of weird."[26] Other attendees described the funneling of traffic from the New York State Thruway onto two-lane roads, with backups and the use of the entire road surface, plus the shoulders being used to move one way: to Woodstock. The traffic congestion caused many concertgoers to abandon their vehicles, which in turn created more congestion. The New York State Police and New York state transportation director Harrison Dunbrook would be forced to close such major, well-traveled routes as the New York State Thruway and New York Route 17.

Despite the ironic road sign for Happy Avenue, the 1969 Woodstock festival created one of the worst traffic jams in U.S. history. Not only were small access roads like this completely blocked with cars, but so were major thoroughfares like New York 17 and the New York State Thruway. (Courtesy of Photofest)

One of the things that plagued the Woodstock festival was the unevenness of the pace of preparations, especially in light of the crowd that would began assembling for several days in advance of the festival's official starting date. For example, while rented pastures had been turned into well-marked parking lots in advance of the arrival of crowds, the ticket gates and fencing of the performance area never quite were finished. This is partially to blame for the tens of thousands of concertgoers who arrived in advance and camped out in the performance area.

John Roberts' recollections of the last-minute preparations suggest that the early arrival of tens of thousands of concertgoers by August 13 in turn hindered the efforts to install the fencing and ticket booths and, in effect, rendered them useless.[27] Even so, at one point, Michael Lang approached Ken Babbs, Wavy Gravy, and Tom Law of the Hog Farm commune to ask that the Hog Farmers clear the site of the by-then-50,000 early arrivals. Lang's goal was to make sure that the early arrivals reentered through the ticket gates so that ticket revenues could be prop-

Fences, designed to keep early arrivals out of the performance area at the 1969 Woodstock festival, were late to be put up and ultimately proved to be ineffective. (Courtesy of Photofest)

erly generated—remember that the festival at this point was still viewed by Woodstock Ventures as a way to generate profits for the construction of a recording studio. According to Wavy Gravy, Tom Law asked Lang, "Do you want a good movie or a bad movie?,"[28] referring to the deal Lang and his associates had worked out for the distribution of the documentary film Michael Wadleigh was to shoot. Lang and his associates, realizing that 50,000 angry hippies could easily ruin the festival and the film, allowed the early attendees to stay, even though they had not necessarily purchased tickets. The influx of young people became something akin to a snowball rolling down a mountain. By the first day of the actual festival, it would be clear that there would be no way to collect tickets, due to the lack of preparation and the crowd, which by then numbered an estimated 400,000 people.

As concessions booths were being constructed and it was becoming increasingly evident that more people would be attending Woodstock than anyone had anticipated and taxing the resources of Food for Love, Inc., Woodstock Ventures and the concessionaires ran into business disagreements. For a time, Food for Love threatened to pull out of the festival. Had such a move taken place, it would have created a disaster for the concert promoters. Woodstock Ventures was forced to renegotiate their contract with the concessionaires.

Not only did the size of the crowd cause enormous traffic problems and necessitate the principals of Woodstock Ventures making the decision to make the festival a free event, but it also created serious problems in the areas of food and water supply, sanitation, and medical care. It must be remembered that no one in the Woodstock organization had an inkling that more than perhaps 150,000 people would attend, and then over the course of three days. All of the advance plans had been done with this as a possible maximum head count in mind.

A system of scrips was set up instead of using money for concessions. In large part this was supposed to expedite service by eliminating the need to make change. The system, however, soon broke down. Some audience members didn't purchase the scrips and found that they could not buy the food or beverages they wanted when they got to the concessions booths. An even bigger problem developed early on in the festival: Food for Love, Inc., ran out of food.

An emergency appeal for food went out from the organizers, but members of the Hog Farm have always contended that there really was no shortage of food at Woodstock. Attendees simply did not bother to go to the wooded area where the Hog Farmers had set up their kitchen.[29] The macrobiotic, vegetarian fare prepared by Lisa Law and other members of the Hog Farm apparently did not appeal to many of the young people. As the size of the audience became apparent and as the need for food became known, community members came together to support the young people, gathering food to be taken out to the festival site. Various community centers and churches in the towns and villages close to the festival site served as collection and serving points. The festival's relative proximity to New York state's Catskills region also worked to the advantage of Woodstock Ventures: some of the large resorts so popular with vacationers from New York City offered to help out with food.

Stanley Goldstein, a member of the Woodstock Ventures staff who had worked at Criteria Sound in Miami and had worked with Michael Lang and Mel Lawrence providing sound for the Miami Pop Music Festival, had acted as a sort of head-hunter as planning for the Woodstock festival progressed. Goldstein enjoys at least part of the credit for enlisting the services of the Hog Farm commune. Study of the various roles played by members of the Hog Farm, including intervention in bad LSD and other drug trips, helping young people from the city learn to live off the land, cooking macrobiotic food for festival attendees, assisting in security, leading the concertgoers in morning yoga exercises (these were led by Tom Law), making stage announcements (frequently handled by Wavy Gravy), and other sundry tasks, makes it clear that the commune was an essential ingredient to the mix that made the Woodstock Music and Art Fair function as well as it did. If anyone at the time had been looking for a model group of "hippies," a group that truly lived out the ideals of the hippie lifestyle, the Hog Farmers would certainly have scored many points at Woodstock.

It was not the good done by members of the Hog Farm, however, that the general public saw in the media when groups of hippies were portrayed. Just before the festival, the gruesome Sharon Tate murders were committed by members of Charles Manson's hippie "family." Although the general public would not necessarily definitively link the Tate and LaBianca mass murders to a particular hippie communal cult for some time, these tragic events cast a pall over the entire nation. It almost seemed as though the news media was looking for the next major counterculture-related disaster to take place. So, the traffic problems, the rain, the bad drug trips, the destruction of the fences, and the injuries some festival attendees sustained all made headlines. Interestingly, in virtually every subsequent publication (book, magazine article, interview) in which a Woodstock performer or festival attendee speaks of the festival, Woodstock is held up as one of the important, if not *the* most important, positive events in the person's life.

THE DEMOGRAPHICS OF THE AUDIENCE

One of the more interesting features of the Woodstock festival and one that distinguished it from the other music festivals of 1969 was that it seemed to capture the attention of the entire nation. Starting in the counterculture underground, it seemed as though thousands of people just spontaneously decided that this was an event that they wanted and needed to attend. This was seen as having the potential to be the ultimate happening of the 1960s, even before the music actually started. Perhaps this was due in part to the advertising campaign dreamed up by Michael Lang and his associates—a campaign aimed squarely at the counterculture.

Attempts to establish just who attended the Woodstock Music and Art Fair have had to be done in retrospect, using surveys of a large enough sample of concert attendees so as to achieve statistically meaningful results. One such study suggested that 55 percent of the crowd was male and 45 percent was female; 95 percent was

Although the overwhelming majority of the audience members at the 1969 Woodstock Music and Art Fair were born between 1940 and 1952, some young children were also present. (Courtesy of Photofest)

white, 1.5 percent black, 1 percent Hispanic, 1 percent other, with 2 percent not identifying themselves by race; 3 percent identified themselves as being upper-class, 30 percent thought of themselves as upper-middle-class, 43 percent were middle-class, 18 percent were lower-middle-class, and 5 percent identified themselves as lower-class economically; 30 percent were from the northeastern United States, 21 percent were from the South, 24 percent were from the central/midwestern United States, and 25 percent were westerners; 43 percent were born between 1950 and 1952, 40 percent were born between 1946 and 1949, and 17 percent were born between 1940 and 1945; 43 percent were single, 30 percent were married, 14 percent were cohabitating, and 13 percent were divorced; 1 percent had some high school education, 5 percent were high school graduates, 31 percent had done some college study, 27 percent were college graduates, and 35 percent had done some postgraduate work.[30] In general, then, Woodstock attendees tended to be white, predominantly male, generally well educated, middle- to upper-middle-class, and between the ages of seventeen and twenty-three.

Mere statistics, however, do not tell the entire story of who attended Woodstock and why. It has been suggested by some that the festival primarily appealed to loners, kids who were misfits in the U.S. society of 1969. Writer Joseph Sobran wrote a twentieth-anniversary reflection on the Woodstock festival for the conservative magazine *National Review*. According to Sobran, the festival had attracted disenfranchised loners—societal misfits. As evidence he cites interviews with various Woodstock attendees and Janis Joplin's stage announcement in which she said, "We used to think of ourselves as little clumps of weirdos. But now we're a whole new minority group." According to Sobran, "The hippies weren't rebels. They were positively hungry for authority. They settled for the only form they could get, which was peer pressure."[31]

What brought these people together? Lawrence J. Dessner in his essay " 'Woodstock,' A Nation at War," suggests that consciously or unconsciously the journey of so many young people to Woodstock and the high level of cooperation and community that was exhibited for three days was tied to the antiwar movement. Dessner and others suggest that the young people, who generally shared a commitment to the antiwar movement, felt that the futility of traditional politics had been shown in the 1968 presidential campaign and that the futility of protests had been borne out in the riots of 1968, particularly in the violence that broke out at the 1968 Democratic National Convention in Chicago. Many activists, in fact, point to the 1968 convention as a crucial turning point for the entire 1960s and

It has proven to be impossible to accurately determine exactly how many people attended the Woodstock festival. Rough estimates of over 400,000 people seem to be supported by the massive crowd pictured at the site in this photograph. (Courtesy of Photofest)

early 1970s counterculture. The Back to the Land movement and the growth of interest in establishing self-sufficient communes were tied to this feeling of futility. In some respects, then, Woodstock simply happened at the right place (in natural, rural surroundings) at the right time (when the only alternative to trying to change "straight" American society's values through traditional politics and protest rallies was a complete change of lifestyle). The Woodstock audience did not engage in massive protests; they simply lived for three days in a manner that showed a complete rejection of suburban, military-industrial-complex-based concepts of what America should be. Some who attended the festival have since commented on the feelings that they had seeing hundreds of thousands of like-minded individuals, all of whom seemed to be committed to the same causes, gathered together in one place. For example, Glenn Weiser writes, "Every town has it's [sic] hippies, but now enormous numbers of us had massed in one area. Friday afternoon brought home to everyone there how broad-based the movement really had become."[32]

THE MUSIC BEGINS[33]

As thousands of young people gathered at Max and Miriam Yasgur's farm, in spite of all the highway closures and traffic congestion, some of the musicians were having difficulty getting to the concert site even on the first day of the festival, Friday, August 15, 1969. Among their numbers were some musicians who were scheduled to perform near the beginning of the event. Although his bass player had not yet arrived, guitarist-singer-songwriter Richie Havens and most of his backing group were ready to take the stage to kick off what would become the most famous rock festival in history. Havens, an African American folk musician who co-wrote (with the later-famous actor Louis Gossett Jr.) the antiwar anthem "Handsome Johnny," had toured and recorded but was not counted among the most widely known of the musicians who would perform at Woodstock. The fact that Havens opened the Woodstock festival and was featured in a fine performance in the subsequent Woodstock documentary film exposed his name and music[34] to a much wider audience. Havens and his band performed three songs by Beatles songwriters John Lennon and Paul McCartney: "With a Little Help from My Friends," "Strawberry Fields Forever," and "Hey Jude." He also performed his own compositions, reworkings of traditional folk songs, and folk-styled songs by other songwriters to complete his set. These songs included "Minstrel Came Down from Gault," High Flyin' Bird," "I Had a Woman," "I Can't Make It Anymore," "Handsome Johnny," and "Freedom." The performance of "Freedom" was improvised on the spot and received an especially passionate treatment by Havens.

Festival organizers Rosenman and Roberts described Havens' "Freedom" as being a highly symbolic statement that in many respects set the stage for the entire festival. They later wrote, " 'FREEDOM! . . . ' he exalted. 'FREEDOM! . . . FREEDOM! . . . FREEDOM! . . . ' he bellowed into the microphone. And the sound system piled wattage onto his voice and blew it out into the ears of the generation on the hillside, the unprecedented hundreds of thousands who at that instant grasped the wonder of their emancipation. They had arrived. They were legion. . . . Nothing could control them—except themselves."[35]

Not only had Richie Havens' bass player been unable to get to the concert site, but other musicians were also continuing to have difficulty. In order to provide music to the hundreds of thousands of people who were now gathered, Woodstock organizers prevailed upon Country Joe McDonald to perform an impromptu solo set. McDonald and his group, the Fish, were scheduled to perform later in the festival, but McDonald, a singer-guitarist-songwriter best known for his antiwar song "I-Feel-Like-I'm-Fixin'-to-Die Rag," agreed to go it alone on the festival's opening day. McDonald performed "Janis," "Rockin' All around the World," "Flyin' High All over the World," "I Seen a Rocket," and "I-Feel-Like-I'm-Fixin'-to-Die Rag."

Perhaps the best-remembered part of Joe McDonald's set, however, was his leading of "The 'FISH' Cheer." As Robert Stephen Spitz recounts:

> "Gimme an F!" he screamed. A quarter-million voices responded obediently. "Gimme a U! Gimme a C! Gimme a K!" The bowl had erupted in jubilation. "What's that spell?"
> "Fuck!" the audience shouted.
> "What's that spell?"
> "Fuck!"
> "What's that spell?"
> "Fuck!"
> "What's that spell?"
> "Fuck!"[36]

Although use of that particular pro-
fanity may seem commonplace in the
twenty-first-century world of R-rated
movies and rap music, to utter it publicly in the late 1960s was seen as an act
of great counterculture significance: it
was a tangible, yet nondestructive, way
to break one of "official" society's
taboos.

Even after Joe McDonald's set,
many acts were *still* having difficulty
negotiating the highway closure situation in order to make their scheduled
appearance times. John B. Sebastian,
who had been the principal songwriter,
lead singer, and rhythm guitarist of
the highly popular band The Lovin'
Spoonful, also agreed to make an unscheduled appearance to fill time. Sebastian sang "How Have You Been?,"
"Rainbows All over Your Blues," "I
Had a Dream," "Darlin' Be Home
Soon," and "The Younger Generation." Unfortunately, Sebastian was
not expecting to perform and had difficulty remembering the words to his
own compositions, as evidenced in the
documentary film of the concert. It has been widely
speculated that the singer-guitarist had been enjoying some of the intoxicants that were making the
rounds of the festival site and was not really up to
performing when he agreed to take the stage. Although he was not scheduled to perform, wanted just
to hang out backstage with some of his friends, was
singing some of his newer, underrehearsed material,
and had no backing band, John Sebastian's appearance was of major importance in establishing Woodstock as something more than just a rock concert: a
real event. As Robert Spitz writes, "Something magical transformed the stage when John Sebastian ambled out, waving at his fans, and it was at that
moment, [John] Morris thought, that the Woodstock
Music and Art Fair truly became a festival."[37]

The transportation difficulties that made it necessary for Havens to perform before his entire band had

Although he was only booked to appear with his band Country Joe
and the Fish later in the festival, Joe McDonald performed a solo set
on Woodstock's opening day to help promoters fill a gap between
acts. (Courtesy of Photofest)

John Sebastian, here seen in profile, performed an
impromptu set to help Woodstock promoters fill in
a gap on the opening day of the festival. (Courtesy
of Photofest)

been assembled and that made it necessary for Joe McDonald and John Sebastian to perform impromptu sets caused some scheduled performers not to appear at all. The most infamous of these cancellations was of hard rock/heavy metal band the Iron Butterfly. The Iron Butterfly was best known at the time of the Woodstock festival for their 1968 recording of the song "In-A-Gadda-Da-Vida," an album track that ran approximately seventeen minutes and that featured one of the longer, and some would suggest self-indulgent, rock drum solos ever committed to vinyl. The band was also known for powerful live performances and for being somewhat difficult to deal with for concert promoters. When it became clear that the group would not be able to make it to Yasgur's farm in a timely manner by highway, their manager demanded that the Iron Butterfly be flown in from New York City by helicopter. The demands were too much for the Woodstock Ventures principals, who simply canceled the band.

Not only did the travel difficulties mean that some impromptu performances took place and that some would-be performers never took to the Woodstock stage, but the order of performers who played Woodstock tended to be in flux, due in large part to transportation problems. Despite this unpredictability, the first day of the festival had a very definite acoustic, folk, eclectic style to it. The group Sweetwater, one of the lesser-known acts to perform at the festival, combined the sounds of female voice and "traditional" rock band instruments with the more unusual flute, cello, and conga drums. Stylistically, Sweetwater has been described as "California psychedelia with jazzy keyboards and a classical bent."[38] The group consisted of Nansi Nevins, August Burns, Elpidio Cobain, Alex Del Zoppo, Fred Herrera, Albert Moore, and Harvey Gerst. Sweetwater performed "Motherless Child," "Look Out," "For Pete's Sake," "Day Song," "What's Wrong," "Crystal Spider," "Two Worlds," and "Why, Oh Why?" Unfortunately, the group's lead singer, Nansi Nevins, was seriously injured in an automobile accident just a few months after the Woodstock festival. Although the group continued on for a time after Nevins' accident, Sweetwater disbanded in 1971 and has reunited only from time to time in more recent years.

Singer Bert Sommer followed Sweetwater. Sommer was another of the less-than-prominent artists on the Woodstock bill, although in 1967 he had recorded with keyboardist-songwriter Michael Brown of The Left Banke.[39] Sommer performed "Jennifer" and Paul Simon's well-known composition "America" as his contribution to the Woodstock festival. The singer released two albums within two years of Woodstock, both of which were produced by Artie Kornfeld. Interestingly, Sommer was the first, but not the last, act managed by either Michael Lang or Kornfeld that would take the stage on Max Yasgur's farm who would remain in relative obscurity despite having a built-in audience of nearly half a million people.

Born in 1941, Tim Hardin was a singer-songwriter who combined elements of jazz and blues in his folk music style. He was an established act on the folk circuit but was probably best known at the time and certainly is best remembered today for his composition "If I Were a Carpenter," which was a top-10 hit for pop singer Bobby Darin in 1966 and which has been recorded by numerous other mu-

Rain and mud marred the 1969 Woodstock Music and Art Fair. Here, the crowd just about manages to avoid a muddy puddle. (Courtesy of Photofest)

sicians. At Woodstock, Hardin performed this song, as well as "Misty Roses." A heroin addict from the mid-1960s on, Hardin's career faded in the early 1970s. He died of a drug overdose in 1980.

Beginning around 1965, the music of the Indian subcontinent began making a significant impact on British and American rock and pop music. The Beatles, for example, featured the Indian sitar (played by lead guitarist George Harrison) on the song "Norwegian Wood (This Bird Has Flown)" in 1965 and on several other recordings the band made between 1965 and 1968. The acknowledged master of the sitar in India was Ravi Shankar, who taught the instrument to several British rockers, including the aforementioned Harrison. Shankar and his ensemble, which featured such other Indian instruments as tabla (a type of Indian drums) and tamboura (a droning stringed instrument), performed at several U.S. pop festivals between 1967 and 1969, including Woodstock. Shankar and his ensemble performed *Raga Puriya-Dhanashri/Gat In Sawarital*, *Tabla Solo In Jhaptal*, and the multimovement improvisation *Raga Manj Kmahaj*. During Shankar's set a major rainstorm hit the area. Rain and the resulting mud would cause problems throughout the rest of the Woodstock festival.

Arlo Guthrie is best remembered for his composition "Alice's Restaurant Massacree," an epic antiwar talking song classic that clocked in at over eighteen minutes and later was the basis of a movie starring Guthrie. Guthrie, the son of folk music legend Woody Guthrie, performed three selections at Woodstock. The first of these, "Coming into Los Angeles," was one of the great songs of the 1960s related to the paranoia that psychedelic drug users felt with being arrested by "the man." Guthrie also performed "Walking Down the Line," and the traditional folk hymn "Amazing Grace."

The American folk revival "set" begun by Arlo Guthrie continued with the performance of one of the most significant figures of the folk/protest song movement, Joan Baez. Baez sang "Joe Hill," "Sweet Sir Galahad," The Byrds' "Drug Store

Truck Driving Man," the traditional folk song of the Civil Rights and antiwar movements, "We Shall Overcome," and the black spiritual "Swing Low, Sweet Chariot." Baez's Ensemble featured the talents of Jeffrey Shurtleff.

Interestingly, Baez had earlier in the day performed for a relatively small group of young people who were gathered at the free stage that had been set up, primarily for amateur performers. Although many of the musicians who performed at Woodstock were deeply entrenched in the counterculture and spoke, wrote, and sang of anticommercialism and the social idealism of the movement, Baez was the only major star to share her talents at the free stage.

The Incredible String Band was scheduled to perform after Joan Baez; however, the group was rescheduled to Saturday because of the rain. The twenty-two-year-old folksinger Melanie Safka (she used only her first name professionally) had not yet made the charts at the time of her Woodstock appearance. The singer-songwriter would later make the pop top 10 with her spring 1970 antiwar hit "Lay Down (Candles in the Rain)"[40] and with her late 1971 hit "Brand New Key." Melanie also wrote The New Seekers' 1970 hit "Look What They've Done to My Song, Ma." At Woodstock, this new talent sang "Beautiful People" and "Birthday of the Sun." Melanie's later nationwide success was largely attributed to the exposure that she gained from her "walk-on" appearance at Woodstock.

As it became evident early in the festival that medical supplies and staff were not adequate for the number of concertgoers, Woodstock Ventures' chief of security, Wes Pomeroy, contacted the New York State Police to try to get the site declared a disaster area. A declaration to that effect from New York governor Nelson Rockefeller would better enable the festival producers to secure additional medical staff and supplies in a very short amount of time. Some politicians in Albany wanted to send in the National Guard to shut down the festival and remove the hundreds of thousands of people who had assembled. John Roberts and Joel Rosenman dissuaded the use of the National Guard, fearing that it would cause a confrontation between the Guard and potentially thousands of angry young people. The cooler heads prevailed, Governor Rockefeller made his declaration, and Woodstock Ventures secured the needed supplies and personnel.

At approximately 2:00 A.M. on Saturday, the music stopped. A peaceful night followed for what, at that particular time, was the third most populous (after New York and Buffalo) "city" in New York state. By the early morning hours of Saturday, press coverage of the festival had made it clear that traffic had come to a standstill, that a crowd many times what had been anticipated was taxing the resources of the Yasgur farm, and that the state of New York was declaring the concert site a disaster area. Frantic parents began calling festival organizers, fearful of what was happening to their children. Although it would become increasingly clear that, despite the odds against it, Woodstock was working, press coverage would continue to be decidedly mixed.

The first order of business Saturday morning when stage announcements reconvened was for Mel Lawrence, director of operations for Woodstock Ventures, to ask the hundreds of thousands of young people to clean up the area in order to help the crew get set for the new day. Although Lawrence feared that his re-

A Woodstock concertgoer flashes the peace sign. (Courtesy of Photofest)

quest might be met with a negative response, audience members complied with the request. Those who saw this transpire took it as another sign that Woodstock as a utopian, Aquarian Exposition was indeed working. It also served as another very visible sign of the connection of the Woodstock Music and Art Fair and the Back to the Land movement, which emphasized protection of the environment.

The performances of Saturday, August 16, began with the Boston-based band Quill's performance of "Waiting for You." Quill was a Michael Lang-managed project that he had hoped to break into the big time at Woodstock. The group had worked for Woodstock Ventures doing concerts in the White Lake-Bethel area to help with prefestival public relations. Quill's appearance at Woodstock, like the Artie Kornfeld-managed Bert Sommer's Friday, August 15, performance before, failed to push the band into the national spotlight.

The festival continued with a set by British blues drumming legend Keef Hartley's band. Interestingly, a definitive set list for the Keef Hartley Band has never been established. Due to the fact that no one thought to document Woodstock performances except through audio recording and film, performances by musicians who were not recorded or filmed due to contractual restrictions have proved too difficult to reconstruct. Reportedly, Hartley's manager refused the request to have the band's performance filmed,[41] obviously not being aware that the Woodstock documentary film would be a massive hit and would push several performers squarely into the limelight. According to other reports, however, the Keef Hartley Band's set was filmed, but the film simply has never been released.[42] In either case, published documentation of the group's performance has been very sparse. According to a representative of Hartley's current (2004) record company,

Mike Shrieve, drummer with Santana, performing at Woodstock. (Courtesy of Photofest)

the band definitely performed "Sinning for You," "Born to Die," and "Leaving Trunk" and probably performed "Just to Cry."[43] These songs had all been included on the band's most recent pre-Woodstock album.

The Keef Hartley Band might not have enjoyed the benefits associated with exposure in the Woodstock film and the multialbum audio recording of the festival highlights, but the group that followed them, Santana, certainly did. Fronted by the Mexican-born electric guitar virtuoso Carlos Santana, the band had been part of the vital San Francisco rock scene for several years before Woodstock. Santana performed the heavily Latin-influenced songs "Persuasion," "Savor," "Soul Sacrifice," and "Fried Neckbones and Some Homefries" in their high-energy set at Woodstock. Due probably in part from their successful appearance at Woodstock (and in the subsequent film and album), Santana broke nationally just after the festival. The band's first chart single, "Jingo," made the charts in October 1969, and "Evil Ways" and "Black Magic Woman" both made the *Billboard* pop top 10 in 1970. The experience of performing at Woodstock left a long-lasting imprint on Carlos Santana. As the twenty-fifth anniversary of Woodstock approached, he was quoted as saying, "Woodstock gave me the feeling of what oneness is all about, and that's something that I've sought to maintain. If I play Fresno, I carry Woodstock in my heart."[44]

Although Carlos Santana expressed totally positive memories from Woodstock, not everything was completely rosy for Woodstock Ventures on Friday and Saturday in the area of dealing with the crowd and their effects on the surrounding community. Hippies were overrunning the nearby Monticello Raceway. The trespassing hippies and the blocked roads and traffic shutdowns had caused the raceway to have a poor night Friday. By Saturday, Leon Greenberg, president of the raceway, had lodged a formal complaint and lawsuit against Woodstock Ventures for failure to adequately control the audience members. Although a summons was served to the festival organizers, Monticello Raceway quickly withdrew the complaint. Apparently, Greenberg and the raceway realized that the attendant publicity would ultimately help them more than the invasion of hundreds of young people would hurt the corporation.

In the mid-1960s a musical subgenre known as raga rock emerged. This style featured extensive improvisations on scalar patterns that were commonly found in the music of India. Most of the bands that found themselves classified as raga rock bands relied on albums and live performances to bring their sounds to the public: typically, the usually long raga-based pieces were not 45-rpm singles material. The Incredible String Band was part of this raga rock movement, but the group's style went even beyond the influence of the Indian subcontinent and included Celtic, American folk, rock, and Middle Eastern music as well. The Incredible String Band, which consisted of Robin Williamson and Mike Heron, sometimes incorporated other musicians, as was the case at Woodstock when their girlfriends, Licorice McKenzie and Rose Simpson, joined them onstage. At Woodstock, the group performed "Catty Come," "This Moment Is Different," and "When You Find Out Who You Are." As *All Music Guide* critic Jim Powers suggests, the acoustic style of The Incredible String Band did not fare particularly well on the Saturday program at Woodstock when they were sandwiched between loud, high-energy rock bands.[45] Interestingly, though, *Yahoo* music reviewer Jim Derogatis described The Incredible String Band as "one of the few good groups that played at Woodstock."[46]

Several late-1960s white rock bands found some of their inspiration in earlier African American rhythm and blues and even acoustic blues music. The so-called boogie band,[47] Canned Heat, was one such unit. The band's lead singer and harmonica player, Bob "Bear" Hite, appeared to be a performer of contradictions: Hite was a rather imposing physical presence but sang with an almost delicate falsetto style. Hite's vocal style was actually inspired by some of the early black rural blues musicians. Canned Heat performed "A Change Is Gonna Come," "Leaving This Town," "Woodstock Boogie," "Going up the Country,"[48] "Let's Work Together," and "Too Many Drivers at the Wheel" during their Woodstock set.

Those who appeared onstage at Woodstock did not include solely performers and announcers. Although the principals of Woodstock Ventures were not expecting him, the Indian guru Swami Satchadinanda arrived at the performance area with his entourage. The guru and his associates and followers convinced the concert production crew that they should allow the swami to speak to the crowd in order to give the proceedings something of an official Hindu blessing—an invocation. While some of the concertgoers undoubtedly believed in the swami's message about Woodstock representing the expression of peace and love, others initially thought that Woodstock represented something else. Woodstock attendee Glenn Weiser recalls that the swami "was extolling the concert as a holy gathering in his melodious Indian accent. I listened to him and thought that it was all bullshit. This was going to be a huge drug party, pure and simple, and to masquerade it as a spiritual gathering seemed phony to me."[49] Soon enough, however, Weiser realized that "although Woodstock certainly was the psychedelic spree of all time, it turned out to be much more than just that."[50] Weiser found that a spirit of brotherhood and sisterhood he had never anticipated quickly developed at the festival—the very thing about which and for which Swami Satchadinanda had preached and prayed.

Record producer and musician Felix Pappalardi and guitarist Leslie West founded the group Mountain, largely as a showcase for West's virtuoso guitar work. This power-rock band had one substantial pop hit, "Mississippi Queen," but not until after their appearance at Woodstock. Mountain's set at the Woodstock festival included "Blood of the Sun," "Stormy Monday," "Long Red," an at the time untitled song that would eventually be known as "For Yasgur's Farm," "Theme from an Imaginary Western," "Waiting to Take You Away," "Dreams of Milk and Honey," "Blind Man," the legendary Carl Perkins composition "Blue Suede Shoes," "South Bound Train," and "Mississippi Queen." Leslie West would reemerge at the 1999 A Day in the Garden festival, which was held on the site of the 1969 Woodstock festival. West reprised several of the songs he had originally performed at the site thirty years before.

If there was one rock band at Woodstock that was definitely "hot" on the charts at the time of the festival, it was the John Fogerty-led Creedence Clearwater Revival. The band had reached number 2 on the *Billboard* pop singles charts three times in 1969 prior to the festival. Creedence Clearwater Revival would reach the top 10 six more times within two years of their Woodstock appearance. At Woodstock, CCR, as they are sometimes known, performed several covers of songs initially made popular by other performers, including "Ninety-Nine-and-a-Half (Won't Do)," "I Put a Spell on You," "Night Time Is the Right Time," and "Susie Q." The rest of the band's rather lengthy set included the following songs written by John Fogerty: "Born on the Bayou," "Green River," "Commotion," "Bootleg," "Proud Mary," and "Keep on Chooglin.' "

Despite rain, which plagued the festival and would plague later reunions, despite inadequate sanitation facilities and food supplies, and despite the fact that the audience count reached multiples of what had been anticipated, all in all Woodstock was proceeding remarkably well through its first two days. This fact was not lost on the site's owner, Max Yasgur, who addressed the crowd Saturday night, saying, "I'm a farmer. I don't know how to speak to twenty people at one time, let alone a crowd like this, but I think that you people have proven something to the world: that half-a-million kids can get together and have three days of fun and music. And have nothing but fun and music. And I 'God Bless You' for it."[51]

Woodstock audience members enjoying the music and the atmosphere. (Courtesy of Photofest)

Early on in the Woodstock festival it became painfully evident to the producers that they needed to have the musicians play longer sets than what had been stipulated in the original contracts. This was due in part to the fact that performers continued to run into challenges reaching the festival site and due in part to the size of the crowd. The producers feared that such a large crowd might grow restless and possibly violent if there were too many dead spaces in the festival. Although not all the musicians were willing to perform extralong sets, many did. This, combined with the unscheduled solo appearances by musicians like John Sebastian, Country Joe McDonald, and Melanie, had helped the festival's organizers make music available for the crowd for most of the days and nights.

The requests for extra music did play a role, however, in one of the near-disasters of the festival. By the time Woodstock Ventures representatives met with The Grateful Dead, a rumor was circulating among performers that the festival producers were asking for longer sets because they might not have adequate funds to pay the musicians. Given the fact that everyone knew that Woodstock had become a free festival due to the enormous crowd and the early problems getting fences and ticket booths ready, it probably would have been surprising had such rumors *not* arisen. In any case, management for The Who and The Grateful Dead demanded that their fee be paid in cash. The producers did not have sufficient cash on hand, and cashier's checks were locked away in the Bethel, New York, branch of the Sullivan County National Bank at the time the demand was made. Charlie Prince, the bank's branch manager, was called at home, awakened from his sleep, and asked to go to the bank to retrieve cashier's checks. As soon as Prince got the checks, the festival organizers dispatched a helicopter to pick them up.

Due to a variety of circumstances, problems arose from time to time involving the sound system throughout the Woodstock festival. Concertgoers attempted to climb the sound towers several times and had to be dissuaded from doing so by means of stage announcements. The Grateful Dead's set on the Saturday of the festival suffered more than most from amplification problems. The band jammed onstage while Woodstock personnel fixed problems with the sound system, which included such things as the amplifiers picking up radio signals and ungrounded equipment that caused minor shocks to performers, and ended up playing a very long and not necessarily very coherent set. At least one concertgoer who was not familiar with the band thought that the impromptu improvisations, with only some of the group's personnel audible, represented a typical Grateful Dead performance. They were not at all impressed. As attendee Glenn Weiser recounted, "All we in the crowd heard was aimless riffing from the stage as the crew tied [*sic*] to fix things, but no one bothered to explain to us what the difficulty was. As a result, I mistakenly assumed this was

Jerry Garcia, guitarist with The Grateful Dead, poses backstage at Woodstock. (Courtesy of Photofest)

the Dead's actual style of music. I thought they were so bad that I didn't see them again until 1983."[52] In assessing Weiser's comments, it must be remembered that Woodstock was far and away the biggest rock festival up to that point in history and that for part of the time it was one of the rainiest and therefore one of the most electronically challenged ever. Interestingly, there also is some evidence that The Grateful Dead's Woodstock performance was not necessarily that unusual for the band—that it might not have been entirely due to the need to buy time while the sound crew attempted to work their magic. Ray Manzarek of The Doors wrote the following of a 1967 concert at which The Doors and The Grateful Dead were on the same bill:

> They have a sound check in the afternoon and it takes forever. They noodle, they fool around, they play out of tune, they try to tune up . . . but fail . . . and finally play a song. Vocals are out of harmony, guitars are tuned to some arcane, eccentric mode that each musician has kept as his own private secret, not telling the fellow next to him what the mode is, and the rhythm section is at cross purposes with each other, laying down what seems to be two separate and distinct rock beats that have no relation to each other. In other words, it's a typical Grateful Dead song/jam.[53]

Incidentally, insiders among The Grateful Dead's camp have acknowledged for years that the Woodstock performance was among the band's worst.[54] The famed psychedelic band from San Francisco eventually performed "St. Stephen," "Mama Tried," "Dark Star," "High Time," and "Turn on Your Lovelight."

According to many published accounts of recollections from the Woodstock festival, Janis Joplin gave one of the most disappointing performances of the three-plus-day event. The blues-rock singer performed "Raise Your Hand," "As Good As You've Been to This World," "To Love Somebody," "Summertime," "Try (Just a Little Bit Harder)," "Kozmic Blues," "Can't Turn You Loose," "Work Me Lord," "Piece of My Heart," and "Ball and Chain." There was much speculation that drug and alcohol abuse seriously marred Joplin's performance. In fact, she would die in October 1970 of a heroin overdose.

The Who made a much more favorable impression at Woodstock than Janis Joplin had. The British band played a set of formidable length that included several of their earlier hits, nearly the entire rock opera *Tommy*, as well as covers of songs made popular by other artists. Not only was the amount of material impressive, but The Who turned in an exciting, musically exhilarating performance, according to many accounts. Woodstock's official photographer, Henry Diltz, had been a folk musician and as a photographer had worked with numerous famous rock acts. According to Diltz and festival organizer Michael Lang, The Who's performance more than made up for the audience's disappointment with Janis Joplin's set.[55] The Who's Woodstock set included "Heaven and Hell," "I Can't Explain," "It's a Boy," "1921," "Amazing Journey," "Sparks," "Eyesight to the Blind,"

"Christmas," "Tommy, Can You Hear Me," "Acid Queen," "Pinball Wizard," "Do You Think It's Alright?," "Fiddle About," "There's a Doctor I've Found," "Go to the Mirror, Boy," "Smash the Mirror," "I'm Free," "Tommy's Holiday Camp," "We're Not Gonna Take It," "See Me, Feel Me," "Summertime Blues," "Shakin' All Over," "My Generation," and "The Naked Eye." The Who's performance at the festival was also notable for the onstage appearance of radical political activist Abbie Hoffman. The story of Hoffman's appearance and the controversy it produced requires some background information.

Early Saturday morning, Abbie Hoffman had been working with the festival medical personnel, helping to organize them and having informational leaflets printed up and distributed to concertgoers to alert them as to what to do in various medical emergency situations. According to Hoffman's recollections, he was at least partially responsible for getting medical supplies sent into the festival site by helicopter.[56] In the years preceding the Woodstock festival, Abbie Hoffman had earned a reputation as a sort of radical punk-clown. He and fellow left-wing activist Jerry Rubin had, for example, staged a massive antiwar demonstration at the Pentagon at which they and the assembled crowd attempted to levitate the massive building. They also attempted an exorcism at the Pentagon. Hoffman's techniques typically were, to use a more recent colloquial phrase, "in your face." John Morris, production coordinator for the Woodstock festival, thanked Hoffman from the stage over the festival's public address system for his work at the medical tents. Hoffman was upset by this public expression, since he guarded his well-deserved reputation as a political radical closely. Hoffman was afraid that the announcement would make him appear to be "soft." Shortly after Morris' announcement, in the middle of the set by The Who, Hoffman took to the stage to make an announcement in support of John Sinclair, the leader of the radical White Panther Party who was in prison over what many in the counterculture considered a trumped-up drug charge.

Accounts vary as to exactly what happened when Hoffman began his speech about John Sinclair. According to some Woodstock attendees, Pete Townshend, guitarist of The Who, deliberately hit Hoffman on the back of the head with his guitar. Others, including Hoffman himself, contend that Townshend may have accidentally bumped the left-wing politico but meant and caused no harm to Hoffman. Ultimately, however, the most important part of The Who's appearance was not the infamous incident with Hoffman, but the music.

Woodstock's production coordinator John Morris also gained fame for another of his late Saturday–early Sunday announcements. Just prior to Sly and the Family Stone's performance in the early A.M. hours of Sunday, Morris announced, "This is the largest crowd of people ever assembled for a concert in the history, but it's so dark out there we can't see and you can't see each other. So when I say 'three,' I want every one of you to light a match." Many of the hundreds of thousands of young people in attendance followed Morris' directive. This tradition of raising a flame in the air at rock concerts was not entirely new at Woodstock,[57] but the spectacle of so many people doing so in unison firmly cemented the practice. The awesome sight of these thousands of tiny flames raised in unison in the rain inspired Melanie to write possibly her best-known song "Lay Down (Candles in the Rain)."

As had occurred at their 1969 performance at the Newport Jazz Festival, Sly and the Family Stone's set at Woodstock found musicians and audience members feeding off each other to create a performance of great intensity and exuberance. Although George Wein, producer of the 1969 Newport Jazz Festival, expressed concern that the near-fever pitch to which Sylvester Stewart (aka Sly Stone) and his ensemble took the audience might result in a riot,[58] Woodstock co-producers Joel Rosenman and John Roberts praised the group's efforts in Bethel. Rosenman, Roberts, and Robert Pilpel wrote in their book *Young Men with Unlimited Capital*, "Sly chanted, and the crowd answered him, 'HIGHER!!!' again and again, each time from a more rarefied eminence, until height and depth lost meaning and there was only the moment, the eternally transient Now of existence."[59] Based on Rosenman, Roberts, and Pilpel's description, this was a performance similar to the intensity of Sly's appearance at Newport; however, one might surmise from the description that, unlike Newport, this intensity was welcomed at Woodstock. Sly and the Family Stone performed the following songs at Woodstock: "M'Lady," "Sing a Simple Song," "You Can Make It If You Try," "Stand!," "Love City," and a medley of "Dance to the Music," "Music Lover," and "I Want to Take You Higher." At the time of their Woodstock performance, Sly and the Family Stone were near the height of their popularity. The group had hit the *Billboard* top 10 before the festival with the songs "Dance to the Music" and "Everyday People" (their biggest hit). The song "Hot Fun in the Summertime" would reach number 2 shortly after the Woodstock festival, and the curiously titled topical song about racism, "Thank You (Falettinme Be Mice Elf Agin)," would reach number 1 in early 1970.

By the time Sly and the Family Stone had ended their set in the early hours of Sunday, August 17, the crowd was beginning to thin. One must remember, however, that in this case "thin" was a relative term. Hundreds of thousands of young people remained at the Yasgur farm through the Sunday morning sleeping hours and into the resumption of music after daybreak.

The Jefferson Airplane had made its initial impact as one of several San Francisco bands that came out of the early hippie movement in the mid-1960s and its ties to the use of psychedelic drugs like LSD. Probably best known for their song "White Rabbit," which combines imagery drawn from author Lewis Carroll and from the LSD experience, the band had appeared at the 1967 Monterey International Pop Music Festival. At Woodstock, the Jefferson Airplane performed "The Other Side of This Life," "Plastic Fantastic Lover," "Volunteers," "Saturday Afternoon," "Won't You Try," "Eskimo Blue Day," "Uncle Sam's Blues," "Somebody to Love," and the aforementioned "White Rabbit."

The British singer Joe Cocker was not particularly well known in the United States at the time of his Woodstock appearance. In fact, festival organizers were at first reluctant to book the singer because they had never heard of him. Cocker would find fame primarily because of Woodstock and his massive "Mad Dogs and

The Jefferson Airplane pose for a portrait in San Francisco, August 3, 1968. From left: Spencer Dryden, drummer, Marty Balin, rear, vocalist; Jorma Kaukonen, lead guitar; Grace Slick, vocalist; Paul Kantner, electric guitar; and Jack Casady, bass guitar. (AP/Wide World Photos)

Englishmen" tour of 1970. Cocker was something of a rarity in the rock music world of the late 1960s and early 1970s: a singer who specialized in singing songs written by others. Cocker was a rarity in this regard because after the "British Invasion" of groups like The Beatles, The Rolling Stones, The Kinks, and The Who in 1964 and 1965, it became fashionable, if not nearly compulsory, for rock musicians to write their own material. At Woodstock, Cocker performed "Delta Lady" (composed by Leon Russell), "Something's Goin' On," "Just Like a Woman" (composed by Bob Dylan), "Dear Landlord" (another Dylan composition), "Let's Go Get Stoned" (a Jo Armstead, Nickolas Ashford, and Valerie Simpson composition that had been popularized by Ray Charles), "I Shall Be Released," and Lennon and McCartney's "With a Little Help from My Friends." Readers unfamiliar with Joe Cocker are likely to be surprised if they see his Woodstock performance in the documentary film (or any other performance by the singer). Cocker would appear almost spastic in performance—an affectation he reportedly developed in imitation of Ray Charles' motions at the keyboard.[60]

Country Joe and the Fish followed Joe Cocker onstage at Woodstock. Joe McDonald's band was well known among the counterculture, largely on the strength of the sarcastically humorous antiwar song "I-Feel-Like-I'm-Fixin'-to-Die Rag." Country Joe and the Fish performed "Barry's Song,"[61] "Not So Sweet Martha Larraine," "Rock and Soul Music" (included on the audio recording release of Woodstock highlights), "Thing Called Love," "Love Machine," and the aforementioned

Alvin Lee, guitarist and singer with Ten Years After, performing at Woodstock. (Courtesy of Photofest)

"I-Feel-Like-I'm-Fixin'-to-Die Rag." As was customary for the band, the "Rag" was preceded by the profane version of "The 'FISH' Cheer."[62]

The group Ten Years After created a sensation on the British blues-rock scene in 1968 and 1969. The band had seen some success in the United States, but their appearance at Woodstock brought Ten Years After a significantly larger audience in the United States. Consisting of virtuoso guitarist Alvin Lee, keyboard player Chick Churchill, bass guitarist Leo Lyons, and drummer Ric Lee, Ten Years After's biggest claim to fame at the Woodstock festival was their nine-minute rendition of the Alvin Lee composition "I'm Going Home." This song was included on the multidisc recording of highlights from the festival. The group also performed "Good Morning Little Schoolgirl," "I Can't Keep from Crying Sometimes," and "I May Be Wrong, but I Won't Be Wrong Always."

The Band, a group that featured guitarist Robbie Robertson, drummer Levon Helm, bassist Rick Danko, and keyboardists Richard Manuel and Garth Hudson, had been formed in Woodstock, New York, in 1967. The mostly Canadian group backed Bob Dylan, who had also relocated to Woodstock in the late 1960s. Although they were not a "name" group at the time of their Woodstock appearance, The Band would produce hit singles and albums from 1969 through 1976 and was inducted into the Rock and Roll Hall of Fame in 1994. They were particularly effective as a live band and combined rock and roll, folk, and country styles in a way that had a broad appeal. At Woodstock, The Band performed "Chest Fever," "Baby Don't You Do It," "Tears of Rage," "We Can Talk," "Long Black Veil," "Don't You Tell Henry," "Ain't No More Cane," "Wheels on Fire," "Loving You Is Sweeter than Ever," "The Weight," and "I Shall Be Released."[63] Incidentally, Robbie Robertson's composition "The Weight" gained fame through its inclusion in the 1969 film *Easy Rider*, a favorite of the counterculture.

When acts were being booked in summer 1969, one of the major signings for Woodstock Ventures was Blood, Sweat, and Tears. Although Chicago would later be the best known and the most commercially successful jazz-rock group of the 1970s, Blood, Sweat, and Tears was the group that initially popularized this fusion of styles. Prior to their appearances at the Newport Jazz Festival and Woodstock, the group had scored two number 2 pop hits in "You've Made Me So Very Happy" and "Spinning Wheel." Blood, Sweat, and Tears' performance at Newport was highly successful, and the Woodstock organizers broadened *their* festival's stylistic range considerably by signing the popular band. The group, which featured singer David Clayton-Thomas,[64] performed the following songs at Woodstock: "All in a Day,"[65] "More and More," group founder Al Kooper's composition "I Love You Baby More than You'll Ever Know," David Clayton-Thomas' composition "Spinning Wheel," the rhythm and blues standard "I Stand Accused," and "Something Coming On."

The albino blues guitarist Johnny Winter had been a last-minute addition to the Woodstock lineup. Winter had performed at the Newport Jazz Festival earlier in 1969 and was just starting to garner national exposure in 1969. Although he was a virtual unknown, Columbia Records offered him a lucrative recording contract and gave him considerable publicity. Columbia, in fact, promoted Winter as the next great superstar of the electric guitar. Although ultimately Winter did not achieve the standing of a Jimi Hendrix or an Eric Clapton, he was in the midst of Columbia's promotional campaign at the time of his Woodstock performance. Winter's set at Woodstock was one of the underdocumented performances. Although early set lists include only his performance of "Mean Town Blues," there is evidence that Winter's set also included "Talk to Your Daughter," "Six Feet in the Ground," "Tell the Truth," "Johnny B. Goode," "Rock Me Baby," "Mean Mistreater," "I Can't Stand It," and "Tobacco Road."[66] Winter's brother, singer and keyboardist Edgar, who would later record the number 1 hit single "Frankenstein," reportedly made a guest appearance during his brother's performance of "Tobacco Road."[67]

Although the new supergroup (every member of the band had achieved success as part of other groups) Crosby, Stills, and Nash had already made their debut shortly before they traveled to Bethel, New York, their appearance at Woodstock thrust them into the international spotlight. Neil Young, who would join the three full-time shortly after Woodstock, joined them onstage for part of their set. David Crosby, Stephen Stills, Graham Nash, and Neil Young were all primarily singers and guitarists. Their performance was filled out by drummer Dallas Taylor, who years later would sue his former bandmates for back royalties he claimed he had been promised but never paid. At Woodstock Crosby, Stills, Nash, and Young performed "Suite: Judy Blue Eyes," "Blackbird," "Guinnevere," "Marrakesh Express," "4 + 20," "Mr. Soul," "Sea of Madness," "Wooden Ships," and "Find the Cost of Freedom." Crosby, Stills, Nash, and Young's performance was prominently featured in the Michael Wadleigh film *Woodstock: Three Days of Peace and Music*. The group was also connected to the Woodstock story through their hit recording of Joni Mitchell's song "Woodstock." The Crosby, Stills, Nash, and Young recording of Mitchell's tribute to the festival and the spirit of peace and love that it generated went to number 11 on the *Billboard* pop singles charts in 1970.

As Sunday moved into Monday, three performing groups remained on the Woodstock docket. The first of these was the Paul Butterfield Blues Band. Although this group's name might not be as instantly recognizable as that of many

Graham Nash, of Crosby, Stills, Nash, and Young, sings with gusto at Woodstock. (Courtesy of Photofest)

of the other Woodstock performers today, Butterfield's ensemble was quite well respected by blues-rock fans in the late 1960s. In fact, Paul Butterfield's group and John Mayall's Bluesbreakers were two of the premier groups that welded blues and rock in the 1960s. Butterfield was a blues harmonica player from Chicago who is credited with being the first white performer on his instrument to establish an authentic Chicago-style electric blues voice. His was also one of the premier racially integrated blues bands in the mid-1960s. At the time of their appearance at Woodstock, Butterfield's band featured lead guitarist Elvin Bishop, who had favorably impressed critics with his playing at the 1967 Monterey International Pop Music Festival.[68] The Paul Butterfield Blues Band performed the following songs at Woodstock: "Everything's Gonna Be Alright," "Driftin'," "Born under a Bad Sign," "All My Love Comin' Through to You," and "Love March."

One of the very noticeable features of the Woodstock festival, especially when compared with the earlier pop music festivals of 1969, was a lack of representation from the pioneers of rock and roll. In fact, the only group on hand to represent the rock styles of the 1950s and early 1960s was Sha-Na-Na, a group that had been formed by Columbia University students earlier in 1969. Many members of the audience, who by this time had experienced a lot of hard rock music and some folkish music, were shocked by these second-generation "greasers." In fact, many members of the audience initially thought that Sha-Na-Na was a joke. The group certainly played up the humor of the music of the 1950s and early 1960s in their performances over the years, as well as in their late-1970s comedy-variety television program. Despite

In this, one of the most famous movie stills from the documentary *Woodstock: Three Days of Peace and Music*, a couple hugs as the festival winds down. (Courtesy of Photofest)

this, Sha-Na-Na really did want to pay tribute to the music and lifestyle of the early rock era. At Woodstock they performed songs that had initially been hits for the likes of Elvis Presley, Danny and the Juniors, the Coasters, and others. Sha-Na-Na's Woodstock set included the following: "Na Na Theme," "Yakety Yak," "Teen Angel," "Jailhouse Rock," "Wipe Out," "The Book of Love," "Duke of Earl," and "At the Hop."

Rock guitar legend Jimi Hendrix performed the final set at Woodstock. He made his appearance at approximately 9:00 A.M. and was joined onstage by drummer Mitch Mitchell, bass guitarist Billy Cox, guitarist-vocalist Larry Lee, and percussionists Juma Sultan and Jerry Velez.[69] Hendrix and his augmented band—Hendrix had earned most of his fame through his work with the trios The Jimi Hendrix Experience (Noel Redding, bass, and Mitch Mitchell, drums) and (after the Woodstock festival) Band of Gypsys (Billy Cox, bass, and Buddy Miles, drums)—performed a lengthy set, which included the following songs: "Message to Love," "Getting My Heart Back Together Again," "Spanish Castle Magic," "Red House," "Master Mind," "Here Comes Your Lover Man," "Foxey Lady," "Beginnings," "Izabella," "Gypsy Woman," "Fire," "Voodoo Chile (Slight Return)," "Stepping Stone," "The Star-Spangled Banner," "Purple Haze," which was preceded by an improvised seque, "Woodstock Improvisation," "Villanova Junction," and "Hey Joe."

Hendrix's unaccompanied performance of "The Star-Spangled Banner" has been cited as one of the most potent antiwar messages of the entire counterculture era. Writers Joan and Robert Morrison edited a series of reminiscences by members of the 1960s and early 1970s counterculture. The Morrisons quote Woodstock attendee Jason Zapator as saying that Hendrix's performance of the American national anthem "was probably the truest rendition of that song I've ever heard, because Hendrix was using sound effects through the guitar to complement the lyrics." According to Zapator, members of the audience caught a sense of heavy irony in the performance, because Hendrix's "playing was reminding everybody that 'the rockets' red glare' and 'the bombs bursting in air' was really the napalming of the villages [of Vietnam].[70] The performance, then, seemed to be at once a strong patriotic statement, supporting the ideals of the Constitution of the United States of America, and an equally strong statement against the activities of the U.S. military in Southeast Asia. According to Hendrix biographer David Henderson, famed jazz composer-saxophonist Ornette Coleman called Hendrix's performance of "The Star-Spangled Banner" "a work of true genius."[71]

DRUGS AT WOODSTOCK

Although it is difficult, if not impossible, to verify, reports from Woodstock attendees suggest that the police helped to maintain peace but ignored the drugs that were being used in enormous quantities around them. Some minor drug arrests may have been made, but by and large, the police helped to maintain order and to get young people who were experiencing bad trips to the freak-out tents manned by medical personnel and members of the Hog Farm.

Although surveys did not reveal the extent to which concertgoers used psychedelic drugs, anecdotal evidence suggests that their use was fairly common at Woodstock. Festival attendee Glenn Weiser, for example, writes, "Lots of people, including me, took psychedelic drugs at Woodstock, and, truth to tell, enjoyed themselves."[72] Other attendees quoted by Joel Makower in his oral history of the festival attest to the easy access concertgoers had to drugs, in particular to marijuana and LSD.[73] Accounts of the festival suggest that most of the drug taking was like that described by Weiser. Some concertgoers, however, experienced "bad trips" on LSD. Woodstock Ventures had taken a number of precautions just in

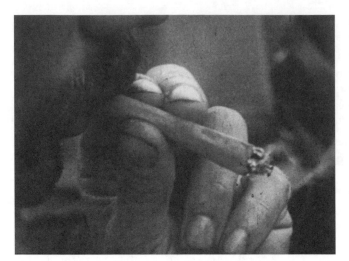

Marijuana was one of the psychedelic drugs present at the Woodstock Music and Art Fair. (Courtesy of Photofest)

case of such an eventuality. Although the size of the audience quickly made the size of the medical staff inadequate, there was a medical staff in place. It would later be enlarged, particularly when New York state governor Nelson Rockefeller declared the festival site a disaster area. The greatest contribution to the cause of assisting audience members through their bad trips, however, was made by members of the Hog Farm. Hog Farm members were stationed at the several freak-out tents that were set up around the festival site. The Hog Farmers, who had connections with Ken Kesey's Merry Pranksters[74] that went back several years before Woodstock, had accumulated considerable experience with bad reactions to LSD. They worked alongside medical personnel at the freak-out tents that were set up around the Yasgur property. Those having bad reactions to LSD were brought to the tents. Hog Farmers like Bonnie Jean Romney, Wavy Gravy, Lisa Law, and others used a psychological approach to help people through their bad trips. The medical personnel were more inclined to treat those who were freaking out with Thorazine and other drugs. The Hog Farmers' approach quickly won out, teaching medical personnel who had previously had little practical experience with how the psychedelic drugs affected people something new. As Lisa Law later recalled, "Your job was to help the next guy who was in the same condition you were in. And that also helped you get to the end of your trip, by helping that next guy. So instead of having all those Thorazined-out people who can't finish their trips—because on Thorazine, you can't finish your trip; you are cut off and it's not helpful to you—you are allowed to finish your trip."[75]

The use of psychedelics and the revolving nature of the audience—one did not simply sit in a seat in an auditorium or stadium for the duration of *this* concert event—played a role in attempts to reconstruct an accurate history of the festival. The performers' set lists, in particular, have been difficult to verify. Some performances were filmed or audio-recorded in their entirety, some were partially recorded, and some do not exist at all on film or audiotape. Recollections of performers, some of whom made unscheduled appearances or made last-minute changes to their sets (e.g., Joe Cocker) or had to jam for an extended period while adjustments or repairs were made to sound equipment (e.g., The Grateful Dead), and some of whom seemed to be too stoned even to remember the words to their own songs (e.g., John Sebastian) have provided some inaccurate information. Some of the compilers of set lists have relied on e-mails and other correspondence from concertgoers—in some cases, years after the fact—some of whom may have been in the same state described earlier by Glenn Weiser. Comedian Robin Williams has said in his monologues, "If you remember the '60s, you weren't really there." Those who were really there at Woodstock, participating in all the extracurricular activities, could probably be counted on to suffer from the same memory fuzziness jokingly described by Williams.

To help alleviate some of the fuzziness, Atlantic Records issued a two-album set of highlights from the Woodstock festival to accompany the 1970 Wadleigh–Maurice film *Woodstock: Three Days of Peace and Music*. The soundtrack album set included performances by artists such as John Sebastian, Canned Heat, The Who, Country Joe and the Fish, Joan Baez, Crosby, Stills, and Nash, the Paul Butterfield Blues Band, and others. Interspersed between the songs were stage announcements by Wavy Gravy, Chip Monck, and others. A second album set, *Woodstock Two*, was issued in 1971, and a package of both sets, along with additional, previously unreleased tracks, was issued on compact disc in 2001.

The film and audio recording created headlines in 1994, when near the twenty-fifth anniversary of Woodstock, Richie Havens sued Time Warner and three of its subsidiaries for a total of $50 million in damages for nonpayment of royalties and improper use of his image.[76]

THE LEGACY OF WOODSTOCK

Wavy Gravy has been quoted as saying, "Let's face it: Woodstock was created for wallets. It was designed to make bucks. And then the universe took over and did a little dance."[77] Wavy Gravy is right on both accounts. The festival was organized with the sole purpose of funding a recording studio. The festival, however, assumed a life of its own. Since the festival became a free event when the ticket booths didn't quite get into place in time and when the fences were torn down, Woodstock ended up losing a lot of money. It has been estimated that the Woodstock Music and Art Fair lost more than $1 million.

The Grateful Dead's Jerry Garcia has been quoted as saying, "The thing about Woodstock was that you could feel the presence of time travelers from the future who had come back to see it. You could sense the significance of the event as it was happening. There was a kind of swollen historicity—a truly pregnant moment. You definitely knew that it was a milestone; it was in the air."[78]

While it is possible to assume that the music of the Woodstock Music and Art Fair and the atmosphere of the festival were universally loved and admired by those associated in one way or another with the counterculture, they were not. Noted folksinger Judy Collins, who "was not invited, thank you very much," stopped by Woodstock on her way to Williamstown, Massachusetts, and stated that she was "horrified" with the mud, rain, and thousands of people. As Collins experienced the festival, the event itself was not as important as what it symbolized. She has been quoted as saying, "Woodstock is a mental attitude. If all the people who say they were at Woodstock were actually there, they wouldn't have fit into the state, let alone the site. But in a way they were all there."[79]

This is an aerial photo of the Woodstock Music and Arts Festival held on 600 acres of cow pasture leased from a farmer at White Lake in Bethel, Sullivan County, New York, in August 1969. The festival, billed as Three Days of Peace and Music, started on Friday, August 15 and ended Monday morning, August 18. More than 450,000 people attended. (AP/Wide World Photos)

The Yasgur's farm has changed hands several times in the decades since the historic music festival of 1969, with cable television pioneer Alan Gerry purchasing the site of the Woodstock festival in the late 1990s. Gerry's purchase was significant in that he was the only post-Yasgur owner of the site who actively welcomed anniversary concerts. The largest of the anniversary festivals, however, would not take place at the old Yasgur farm. The land had been parceled off so that by the early twenty-first century, less than fifty acres remained.

As the twentieth-fifth-anniversary festival of 1994 and the Woodstock 1999 festival approached, sociologists paid close attention. Sociological and demographical study of the audience and the entire gestalt of the original Woodstock Music and Art Fair had been haphazard and had taken place very much after the fact. Graduate students looking for material for theses and dissertations took the 1994 and 1999 events seriously: they did not want to miss an opportunity to study a gathering of the historical proportions of the 1969 festival. Ultimately, Woodstock '94 and Woodstock 1999 would reveal much about the newer generations of young people; however, to date it does not appear that any subsequent rock music festival will have the same historical significance, the same iconic status as *the* Woodstock.

At the time of the thirtieth anniversary of the festival, a short article in the conservative magazine *National Review* claimed, "Woodstock was marked by squalor, dehydration, and overdoses of drugs (and spurious drugs, sold by crooked dealers). The grim scene was glossed over, not just by the teenage baby boomers who attended, but by their elders. The media played up the luscious hippie chicks, not the filth."[80] Yes, there were rain, trash, a lack of food, unsafe drugs and bad trips, problems with the sound system, subpar performances from some of the musicians, an audience comprising, at least in part, of people who simply could not or would not fit into society. The *National Review* article, however, fails to acknowledge the fact that for many Woodstock attendees, a long weekend in August 1969 was the most significant time of their lives and a time in which a seemingly unattainable idealism prevailed. Whether the Woodstock Music and Art Fair was a validation of the ideals of the hippie lifestyle and rock music or an example of the depths to which American culture had descended depends upon one's political and social outlook. What cannot be argued, however, is that Woodstock defined an era and became a cultural icon whose influence continues to be felt over thirty years after it took place.

NOTES

1. It is true that much film was shot for the documentary *Woodstock: Three Days of Peace and Music*, but not all of the artists' sets were filmed and other documentation was sparse—after all, few people could have imagined the sociological importance of the Woodstock Music and Art Fair until the event was under way.

2. "Head shops" were stores that sold psychedelic drug-related paraphernalia.

3. The name of the group is given as "Diesel" in Rosenman, Joel, John Roberts, and Robert Pilpel, *Young Men with Unlimited Capital* (New York: Harcourt Brace Jovanovich, 1974). The Michael Lang-managed Train should not be confused with the more recent band (of *Drops of Jupiter* fame) of the same name.

4. Makower, Joel, *Woodstock: The Oral History* (New York: Doubleday Press, 1989), p. 25.

5. Spitz, Robert Stephen, *Barefoot in Babylon* (New York: Viking Press, 1979), p. 25.

6. Brooks, Tim, and Earle Marsh, *The Complete Directory to Prime Time Network and Cable TV Shows*, 6th ed. (New York: Ballantine Books, 1995), p. 799.

7. Roberts inherited $400,000 on his twenty-first birthday. The remainder was held in trust and was scheduled to be paid out in three equal payments of $1 million on his twenty-fifth, thirtieth, and thirty-fifth birthdays. Spitz, *Barefoot in Babylon*, p. 7.

8. Rosenman, Roberts, and Pilpel, *Young Men with Unlimited Capital*.

9. Makower, *Woodstock*, p. 23.

10. Spitz, *Barefoot in Babylon*, p. 13.

11. Rosenman, Roberts, and Pilpel, *Young Men with Unlimited Capital*, pp. 47–50.

12. Eventually, the recording studio idea would fall by the wayside.

13. Rosenman, Roberts, and Pilpel, *Young Men with Unlimited Capital*, p. 36.

14. The town of Wallkill, Orange County, New York, is not to be confused with the village of Wallkill, which is located in nearby Ulster County.

15. Rosenman, Roberts, and Pilpel, *Young Men with Unlimited Capital*, p. 37.

16. The town of Wallkill surrounds the city of Middletown, New York.

17. Lang, Rosenman, Roberts, and Kornfeld made their estimate of 50,000 to 100,000 people based on the 50,000 people who had attended the Monterey Pop Festival in 1967.

18. The dove and guitar logo, which became something of a popular culture icon of the day, was designed by artist Arnold Skolnick.

19. Rosenman, Roberts, and Pilpel, *Young Men with Unlimited Capital*, p. 102; Makower, *Woodstock*, p. 110.

20. Makower, *Woodstock*, p. 110.

21. Rosenman, Roberts, and Pilpel, *Young Men with Unlimited Capital*, p. 147.

22. Belmont, Bill, quoted in Makower, *Woodstock*, p. 129.

23. Manzarek, Ray, *Light My Fire: My Life with the Doors* (New York: G. P. Putnam's Sons, 1998), p. 234.

24. Rosenman, Roberts, and Pilpel, *Young Men with Unlimited Capital*, p. 93.

25. Spitz, *Barefoot in Babylon: The Creation of the Woodstock Music Festival, 1969*, p. 317.

26. Makower, *Woodstock*, pp. 8–10.

27. Rosenman, Roberts, and Pilpel, *Young Men with Unlimited Capital*, pp. 132–33.

28. Samuels, David, "Rock Is Dead (Woodstock 1999)," *Harper's Magazine* (November 1999).

29. Makower, *Woodstock*, pp. 214–15.

30. Weiner, Rex, and Deanne Stillman, *Woodstock Census: The Nationwide Survey of the Sixties Generation* (New York: Viking, 1979).

31. Sobran, Joseph, "A Nation of Loners," *National Review* 41/16 (September 1, 1989), pp. 28–29.

32. Weiser, Glenn, "Woodstock '69 Remembered," *Woodstock History.com*, http://www.advol.net/wood5.htm, accessed May 27, 2003.

33. What follows is not an exact chronology.

34. Richie Havens' guitar sound is a feature of his music that attracts the attention of many listeners. Havens used an unusual, low guitar tuning to an open chord that gave his instrument its unique tone color.

35. Rosenman, Roberts, and Pilpel, *Young Men with Unlimited Capital*, p. 151.

36. Spitz, *Barefoot in Babylon*, p. 414.

37. Spitz, *Barefoot in Babylon*, p. 416.

38. Unterberger, Richie, "Sweetwater," *All Music Guide*, http://www.allmusic.com, accessed December 22, 2003.

39. The Left Banke experienced business and personal-related difficulties following their top-10 1966 hit "Walk Away Renee." Mike Brown, the band's keyboardist, recorded with various other musicians using the name The Left Banke for these projects. That was the context in which Brown worked with singer Bert Sommer.

40. Melanie's "Lay Down (Candles in the Rain)" was inspired by her experience at the Woodstock festival.

41. According to a personal e-mail to the author from Ian Southworth (kashmir@ammoniterecords.demon.co.uk), a representative of Hartley's current record company (Kashmir Records), the band's performance was filmed, but the segment simply has never been released.

42. Ian Southworth (kashmir@ammoniterecords.demon.co.uk), a representative of Keef Hartley's current record company (Kashmir Records), in a personal e-mail to the author.

43. Ian Southworth (kashmir@ammoniterecords.demon.co.uk), a representative of the company (Kashmir Records), supplied this partial set list in a personal e-mail to the author.

44. Milward, John, "Field of Dreams," *Rolling Stone* (August 11, 1994), p. 36.

45. Powers, Jim, "The Incredible String Band," *All Music Guide*, http://www.allmusic.com, accessed December 22, 2003.

46. Derogatis, Jim, "Incredible String Band," *Yahoo! LAUNCH*, http://launch.yahoo.com, accessed January 13, 2004.

47. Canned Heat earned this title with their good-time, bouncy rhythmic approach to blues-rock.

48. "Going up the Country" was Canned Heat's biggest hit, reaching number 11 on the *Billboard* pop singles charts in winter 1968–69.

49. Weiser, "Woodstock '69 Remembered."

50. Weiser, "Woodstock '69 Remembered."

51. Max Yasgur's brief speech to the crowd was included on the audio recording of festival highlights, as well as in the documentary film. It has also been widely transcribed in several Woodstock-related books.

52. Weiser, "Woodstock '69 Remembered."

53. Manzarek, *Light My Fire*, p. 236.

54. *Grateful Dead: The Illustrated Trip* (New York: DK, 2003), p. 101.

55. Makower, *Woodstock*, pp. 234–35.

56. Makower, *Woodstock*, pp. 261–62.

57. Raised matches and lighters frequently greeted performances of "Light My Fire" by The Doors as early as 1967.

58. George Wein with Nate Chinen, *Myself among Others* (Cambridge, Massachusetts: Da Capo Press, 2003), p. 284.

59. Rosenman, Roberts, and Pilpel, *Young Men with Unlimited Capital*, p. 153.

60. Whitburn, Joel, *The "Billboard" Book of Top 40 Hits*, 6th ed. (New York: Billboard Books, 1996), p. 133.

61. This song title is sometimes given as "Barry's Caviar Dream." The only registered composition by Barry Melton with a title similar to this is his "Barry's Song."

62. Both "The 'FISH' Cheer" and "I-Feel-Like-I'm-Fixin'-to-Die Rag" are also preserved on the Woodstock audio recording and in the documentary film.

63. Schmid and de Lange cite *Woodstock Master Tapes for Sale*, http://www.digibuilders.com/jobs/woodstock/index.html as the source for this listing.

64. Keyboard player-singer Al Kooper had founded the group in 1968 but had been replaced by the time Blood, Sweat, and Tears achieved stardom in 1969.

65. Schmid and de Lange cite *Woodstock Master Tapes for Sale*, http://www.digibuilders.com/jobs/woodstock/index.html as the source for this listing. Other previously published set lists do not include the song.

66. Winter's performance of "Mean Town Blues" has been confirmed by several verified releases of recorded material from the Woodstock festival. The apparent original source for information on the remainder of Winter's set is the Web site *Woodstock Master Tapes for Sale*. To the extent that these tapes are authentic, they represent confirmation of Winter's entire Woodstock set.

67. Schmid and de Lange.

68. Wenner, Jann, "British Groups 'Smash' at Monterey," *Melody Maker* 42 (June 24, 1967), pp. 8–9.

69. Henderson, David, "Jimi Hendrix Deep within the Blues and Alive Onstage at Woodstock—25 Years after Death," *African American Review* 29/2 (1995): 213+.

70. Morrison, Joan, and Robert K. Morrison, *From Camelot to Kent State: The Sixties Experience in the Words of Those Who Lived It* (New York: Times Books, 1987; Updated ed. New York: Oxford University Press, 2001), p. 200.

71. Henderson, "Jimi Hendrix Deep within the Blues and Alive Onstage at Woodstock—25 Years after Death."

72. Weiser, "Woodstock '69 Remembered."

73. Makower, *Woodstock*.

74. The author of *One Flew over the Cuckoo's Nest*, Ken Kesey surrounded himself with young people who publicly experimented with LSD in the early 1960s before the drug was made illegal. This group was known as the Merry Pranksters. Interestingly, The Grateful Dead (when they were known as the Warlocks) was for a time the house band for these acid parties.

75. Lisa Law, quoted in Makower, *Woodstock*, p. 265.

76. Verna, Paul, "Richie Havens Seeking Woodstock Royalties," *Billboard* 106/30 (July 23, 1994), pp. 12+.

77. Graves, Tom, "Peace, Love, Music: From the Peace-Jubilee of 1869 to Woodstock," *American History* (January–February 1996), p. 48.

78. *Grateful Dead: The Illustrated Trip* (New York: DK, 2003), p. 101.

79. Gates, David, "Twenty-Five Years Later, We're Living in Woodstock Nation," *Newsweek* 124/6 (August 8, 1994), p. 38+.

80. "Forever Woodstock," *National Review* 51/16 (August 30, 1999), p. 14.

3

Woodstock '94: The Twenty-Fifth Anniversary Festival and A Day in the Garden

BACKGROUND AND A DAY IN THE GARDEN 1994

The twenty-fifth anniversary of the Woodstock Music and Art Fair represented the first major anniversary; however, an attempt had been made in 1989 to celebrate the twentieth anniversary. As the event was being planned, it was greeted with charges of commercialism,[1] the same charges that eventually would be leveled against Woodstock '94. The twentieth anniversary was derailed by the Bethel, New York, town government. When the concert finally took place, it was a spontaneous event. Louis Nicky, who now owned the Yasgur property, couldn't get the necessary permits to hold a commercial concert and then died just days before the event was scheduled to take place. Thousands of rock fans came for the concert anyway.[2] Since permits had not been obtained, tickets could not be sold, so free-will donations were taken up from the crowd. Money that was collected was presented to Bethel town supervisor Allan Scott to cover any expenses incurred by the town.[3]

In 1990, June Gelish owned the former Yasgur farm and wanted to mount a festival to celebrate the twenty-first anniversary of Woodstock. Bethel, New York, town supervisor Allan Scott again attempted to thwart the concert. Scott obtained a temporary restraining order to prevent the concert based on the zoning of the land. In an unexpected and somewhat bizarre move just prior to the scheduled start of the anniversary festival, Gelish (who up to that point had been actively trying to have the anniversary event on her land) charged the people who had already arrived with trespass.

Members of the so-called Rainbow Family continued to hold relatively small gatherings in 1991–93, despite the objections of landowner June Gelish. Some of the Woodstock pilgrims felt that "the public had established an easement on the property because of their continual use for more than 20 years, without asking permission from any owner."[4] In 1993, Gelish spread chicken manure over the entire site in an attempt to squelch the gathering. Ironically, Gelish's move angered not only Woodstock pilgrims but also neighboring farmers. Approximately 2,000 audience members showed up anyway. As various groups began planning for the twenty-fifth-anniversary festival, the National Multiple Sclerosis Society secured the rights from Gelish to hold a festival on the site of the original Woodstock festival.

Robert Gersch, head of the New York Chapter of the National Multiple Sclerosis Society, originally planned to sell 40,000 tickets to A Day in the Garden festival in 1994. Prices for tickets and packages were to range from $150 to $5,000.[5] Incidentally, the festival's name, A Day in the Garden, was chosen because of Joni Mitchell's references to "the garden" in her song "Woodstock." For a time, the planned festival was also known as Bethel '94. Woodstock Ventures was successful in ensuring that Gersch and the Multiple Sclerosis Society could not use the word "Woodstock" in the description of their charitable music festival. This was done to avoid confusion: the official Woodstock Ventures-produced anniversary festival would take place miles away from the former Yasgur farm.

By early August 1994, longtime concert promoter Sid Bernstein, who was working on the Bethel '94, or A Day in the Garden, festival, had scaled back the plans considerably. Due to laws that had been enacted after the 1969 Woodstock Music and Art Fair, gatherings of over 10,000 were severely limited by Bethel, New York's, mass-gathering permit. Bernstein had decided to limit ticket sales to less than 10,000 so as to avoid having to obtain the permit.

A Day in the Garden festival contrasted greatly with Woodstock '94. It must be remembered that the 1969 Woodstock Music and Art Fair had been designed as a commercial venture, in spite of the antiestablishment, anticommercialism aura that developed around it. Woodstock '94 was once again designed as a large moneymaking venture and suffered from the trappings of commercialism. The spirit that had arisen out of the original 1969 festival (once it became a free event and a true "happening") seemed to be best captured by A Day in the Garden.

A Day in the Garden 1994, however, eventually had to be canceled as an official event, due primarily to a massive $80 million lawsuit filed against the festival by Woodstock Ventures and PolyGram Entertainment. That, however, did not prevent approximately 12,000 people from showing up and a spontaneous festival from taking place. This spontaneous event may have captured the Woodstock spirit better than any of the other post-1969 Woodstock-related events, for if it had not been for a touch of the communal, let's-do-it-no-matter-what-it-takes spirit that came down from the original Woodstock festival, A Day in the Garden 1994 never would have taken place. This spontaneous event in Bethel, New York, was described by Dave Pirner of Soul Asylum as "very music oriented, very much the kind of thing I want to do." Pirner said, "Bethel was great. It had a real folk element to it, which is kind of what I'm trying to find right now in my life."[6] Pirner's interview makes it clear that it was not just the folk-oriented music of A Day in the Garden that struck a positive chord, but also the folklike, communal atmosphere.

The former Yasgur farm changed ownership after A Day in the Garden 1994.

The new owners, Jeryl Abramson and Roy Howard,[7] allowed pilgrims to the site to gather for the 1996 anniversary. As we shall see in the next chapter, however, a more official, concerted, and controversial effort to commemorate the site of the Woodstock Music and Art Fair would take place when cable television magnate Alan Gerry purchased the site in 1998.

WOODSTOCK '94

As plans were being made for the official, Woodstock Ventures-produced twenty-fifth anniversary festival, it became clear that the site of the original Woodstock would not be available for a massive gathering of music fans. The promoters, who included Michael Lang, Joel Rosenman, and John Roberts of the original Woodstock team, decided to try again for one of the locations that had not panned out twenty-five years before: the 840-acre Winston farm in Saugerties, New York, approximately sixty miles northeast of the site of the 1969 festival. Perhaps remembering all the difficulties that had been encountered in 1969, planning for the 1994 event (sometimes called Woodstock II) was done considerably more ahead of time. Lang, Rosenman, Roberts, and their associates from Metropolitan Entertainment filed the necessary applications for permits with Saugerties officials, and on March 31, 1994, the two permits that would allow the twenty-fifth-anniversary festival to go forward were approved.

At the original Woodstock festival, an adequate number of ticket booths could not be put in place due to intense traffic problems. Fences were torn down by the overwhelming number of people who showed up for the 1969 event. These circumstances caused Woodstock Ventures to declare the festival a free event and resulted in huge financial losses. In sharp contrast, the twenty-fifth-anniversary festival had relatively high ticket prices. Also, in sharp contrast to the ragtag way in which Woodstock Ventures hired food concessionaires and other crew personnel, the twenty-fifth-anniversary festival had massive corporate sponsorship by major companies, both in the area of food and beverages and in other areas. The high prices for tickets and highly visible corporate sponsorship caused numerous pundits sarcastically to label the 1994 event "Greedstock."

Many aspects of the festival reflected the lessons learned from the ragtag mistakes of 1969. For one thing, Ticketmaster, a well-organized enterprise, handled ticket sales. For another, since the three principals who had been part of the first Woodstock and were still on hand in 1994—Lang, Rosenman, and Roberts—were twenty-five years away from the youth market of Generation X, their new business partner, John Scher of PolyGram, had organized market studies to see what performers the young people of 1994 wanted to see at *their* Woodstock.

Basic logistical planning was also considerably more complex than it had been for the 1969 event. With the knowledge that the 1969 festival had been marred by rain, the promoters made contingency weather plans. Fire prevention was also a major concern, in part because of 1994 standards for large gatherings, themselves brought on by the more litigious atmosphere of 1994 as opposed to 1969.

The fire-prevention and weather-related planning was later detailed in a lengthy article in *Fire Engineering* magazine.[8]

Technology had changed considerably over the quarter century since the 1969 Woodstock festival. For one thing, cable television had emerged as an important commercial medium. For Woodstock '94, cable production company Ramp, Inc. produced hours of pay-per-view cable television coverage of the festival. Cable network MTV also broadcast live from the festival, but due to Ramp's pay-per-view arrangements, MTV could not show performances. The network's interviews and performance-less broadcasts from the scene did not seem to sit very well with their audience or with television critics: *People* magazine labeled the music network's coverage among the "Worst of Tube" for the week of the festival.[9] Interestingly, though, MTV's free coverage seems to have cut into the pay-per-view subscription base that Ramp, Inc. had originally envisioned.[10]

The other very visible, technology-related aspect of the twenty-fifth anniversary festival was Apple Computer's technology pavilion. The interactive computer applications and hardware that were on display generated interest among the press. This display had been anticipated even at the time the early zoning approvals were secured at the end of March 1994. Press releases and interviews at that time already emphasized that virtual reality computer technology would be on display for festival attendees to try. Comparison of the presence and the use of computer-based technology at the 1969, 1994, and 1999 Woodstock festivals says a great deal about the progress that was made within that time frame in the technology and, perhaps more importantly, shows how quickly and to what extent the different generations put the technology to practical use. For example, there simply was not computer technology at the 1969 festival. Woodstock '94 found organizers using computers on a regular basis in their business work and relied on computers in the actual concert production. The presence of the technology display, however, suggests that virtual reality and mass communications with computers were still something of a novelty. Within five years, Woodstock 1999 attendees would be making travel plans via e-mail, keeping track of the evolving roster of artists scheduled to appear on the Internet and through e-mail discussion lists, and eventually developing Web pages to chronicle the festival through electronic journaling in order to tell what they saw as the truth about the infamous violence that took place at *their* Woodstock.

For the 1969 festival Woodstock Ventures had relied heavily on Joel Rosenman's inheritance for funding. For the 1994 event, however, Rosenman, Roberts, and Lang took a $1 million investment and combined it with media giant PolyGram's $34 million,[11] along with other corporate sponsorship. Joel Rosenman was quoted as saying, "Philosophically, it's always bothered me that Woodstock worked in all respects but as a business venture."[12] The combination of Woodstock Ventures, PolyGram, and other sponsors like Pepsi, Häagen-Dazs, and Apple Computer, appeared to provide everything needed from a financial standpoint to make sure that Woodstock '94 succeeded where the 1969 festival had not. At the time of the festival, it was estimated that PepsiCo had paid approximately $2 million as part of its sponsorship agreement with Woodstock Ventures.[13] According to advertising industry experts who reviewed the workings of Woodstock '94 five years later, the actual figure was closer to between $5 and $6 million.[14]

It was not just computers, soft drinks, and ice cream that sported the new Woodstock logo of two birds on a Fender guitar neck. There was an official condom of the Woodstock '94 festival, as well as other merchandise, some of which could be purchased on the QVC shopping network. While the overtly commercial nature of the Woodstock enterprise would generate negative commentary, the sponsorship fees and other investments made it possible for the producers to mount a major event of a musical scope that would have been impossible for a Woodstock 1969–type operation.

Due in large part to this massive corporate sponsorship and the marketing of Woodstock as a brand, another aspect of Woodstock '94 had changed significantly from the 1969 festival: artists' fees. Instead of the approximately $15,000 top price paid for acts at the Woodstock Music and Art Fair, Woodstock '94 reportedly had an upper limit set at $350,000: far in excess of what a cost-of-living or inflation-adjusted increase might have warranted.[15] Although some concertgoers may have been a little jaded by the size of the purses their heroes would take home, the fact is that the hefty "most-favored nation" type of fee allowed the promoters to secure some major acts that probably would not otherwise have played the festival.

Despite the massive corporate sponsorship of the Woodstock '94 festival and the apparently tighter organization of the event compared with the 1969 festival, there were problems. Among the problems over which technology, hindsight, and better planning had no control was the weather. Saturday's performances were marred by significant rainfall. Unfortunately, this had also been true at the 1969 Woodstock Music and Art Fair and would also be true at Woodstock 1999. Among the problems that logic would have suggested could have been controlled was the use of toilet facilities. Portable toilets had caused headaches in 1969, and the organizers of Woodstock '94 undoubtedly thought that the 2,800 Port-O-San portable toilets they had secured would make for improvement. They had not anticipated that so many festival attendees would pitch their tents in unauthorized locations, which made it difficult for work crews to empty the portable toilets. As was the case with

Woodstock '94 revelers in the mud. (CORBIS)

rain, sanitation would also present serious problems at all three Woodstock festivals—Woodstock 1999, however, would eventually prove to be the worst.

Musicians also noticed the poor living conditions that festival attendees had to survive, due to the rain, mud, and poor sanitation. Billie Joe Armstrong of Green Day told *Rolling Stone* magazine, "Going into it [Woodstock '94], I thought that the nostalgia reasons behind the show were kind of a joke." Armstrong said that once the festival was under way, "it was the closest thing to total chaos I've ever seen in my life. . . . Technically it was a human disaster. Everybody was living like dogs, pretty much."[16]

The conclusion of the Woodstock '94 festival would also expose some of the inadequacies of planning. Ticketmaster had initially told ticket buyers that buses back to Manhattan would be available on Sunday evening after the conclusion of the festival. Later, people would be told that buses would not be available until Monday, which created difficulties for festival attendees who did not learn of the change of plans until the last minute. Shuttle service to the parking areas was inadequate, which caused long lines to form, particularly as the festival wound down.

Given these problems, it might be surprising for the reader to learn that the actual attendance of Woodstock '94 was only about half to three-quarters of the attendance of the 1969 Woodstock Music and Art Fair. Festival organizers Woodstock Ventures and PolyGram estimated the crowd at approximately 250,000 (some estimates put the crowd closer to 350,000 by Saturday evening),[17] but "they admitted that only about 200,000 tickets had actually been sold," according to Karen Schoemer and Patrick Rogers of *Newsweek*.[18] In fact, in the days leading up to the festival the minimum number of people in a group required to buy the discount-priced car pool tickets was changed from four to two in an effort to generate additional sales. In the end, Woodstock '94 became a free festival on its first day: Woodstock '94's fences proved to be nearly as porous as those of the 1969 festival. Although there were not nearly as many attendees who experienced the event without tickets as there had been at the 1969 festival, the fact that some 50,000 or more people apparently attended for free was probably at least partially responsible for this edition of Woodstock losing money.

Just who constituted the Woodstock '94 audience? Reports suggested that it was young, mostly male, and overwhelmingly white—in other words, very similar to the 1969 festival. In fact, the racial homogeneity of the audience was the subject of some media commentary. *National Review* writer Todd Seavey, for example, made a special note of this in his entirely negative article about the festival.[19] Some among these white Generation Xers questioned the values of their generation after seeing how many attendees seemed to fit right in with the world of commercialism and consumerism around them. Link Byfield, for example, pondered how his generation had managed to become just so many "feckless phonies."[20] *Newsweek* reporter Karen Schoemer concurred, writing, "It might have been a hell of party, but no one in his or her right mind is going to want to hold this up as a defining moment of the generation [Generation X] in the years to come. It's too embarrassing."[21]

Newsweek's Karen Schoemer was reacting, however, both to the embracing of consumerism by many in the audience and to the actions of other festival attendees who protested the commercialism through violence. Apparently viewing the media as part of this commercial culture at Woodstock '94, concertgoers "trashed" at least two television news trucks and caused a total of nearly $40,000 damage.[22] When this and a few other incidents took place, like the Saturday "liberation" of several concessions stands by audience members, security personnel reportedly abandoned their posts. Other than a few incidents, however, the protests and debate over commercialism mostly were verbal, and, by and large, they were leveled not so much at the individual concessionaires as at the promoters of the festival. Although not quite as peaceful as the 1969 Woodstock Music and Art Fair, Woodstock '94 was a far cry from the openly violent Woodstock 1999.

Another major difference between the 1969 festival and Woodstock '94 was the media coverage. As *Rolling Stone* reporter John Milward wrote, "The original Woodstock festival caught the mass media by surprise; that didn't happen in 1994, as some 1,800 journalists from 41 countries were on hand with 32 satellite dishes."[23] As mentioned previously, MTV was also on hand to do live reports, even though the music network contractually could not show performances.

Although the twenty-fifth anniversary festival featured some performers who had been active at the time of the original event (Bob Dylan, The Band, Santana, Joe Cocker, Country Joe McDonald, and Crosby, Stills, and Nash), the festival also featured acts whose primary commercial impact was in the 1970s, 1980s, and 1990s. The complete roster of performers included the following: Melissa Etheridge; Crosby, Stills, and Nash; Metallica; Nine Inch Nails; Salt-N-Pepa; Arrested Development; Aerosmith; The Allman Brothers Band; The Band; Blind Melon; Johnny Cash; Blues Traveler; James; Candlebox; Jimmy Cliff's All-Star Reggae Jam; Collective Soul; The Cranberries; Sheryl Crow; Cypress Hill; Peter Gabriel; Green Day; Jackyl; King's X; Live; The Neville Brothers; Porno for Pyros; Orleans; Primus; Red Hot Chili Peppers; the Rollins Band; Todd Rundgren; Traffic; Spin Doctors; the Sisters of Glory; The Violent Femmes; W.O.M.A.D.; Youssou N'Dour; Zucchero; the Paul Rodgers Band (which included Slash, Jason Bonham, Neal Schon, and Andy Fraser); Country Joe McDonald; Bob Dylan; and Joe Cocker.

This lineup stressed diversity, both in terms of the longevity of the careers of the performers up to this point and the ages of the performers, and in terms of musical style. In fact, it could be argued that Woodstock '94 offered the greatest amount of musical variety of any of the three Woodstock festivals. It certainly offered more performers and more variety than the 1969 festival, and Woodstock '94 was certainly more balanced stylistically than the punk and rap-heavy Woodstock 1999. Although some of the performers have continued making the charts, if not the headlines, in the decade since Woodstock '94, some have not. It might be helpful, then, to overview some of the artists and their styles.

Perhaps one of the most eclectic assemblages at Woodstock '94, W.O.M.A.D., or the World of Music, Arts and Dance, consisted of several world musicians. The confederation, associated with Peter Gabriel, still existed in 2004. At Woodstock '94, the various W.O.M.A.D. performers brought a world music style to the proceedings, filling the kind of role that Ravi Shankar's ensemble had done at the 1969 Woodstock Music and Art Fair. African singer Youssou N'Dour also added significantly to the world music feel at Woodstock '94. N'Dour had established an impressive résumé by the time of his Woodstock '94 appearance, highlighted by his 1986 performances on Paul Simon's *Graceland* and Peter Gabriel's *So* and his own 1990 album, *Set*, which achieved considerable critical success. Like the W.O.M.A.D. performers, N'Dour has continued to perform and record into the twenty-first century.

The Italian pop singer Zucchero (stage name for Adelmo Fornaciari) never really saw his career take off in the United States but had been a favorite in Europe since the mid-1980s with his unique blend of mainstream Italian pop and electric blues music. Zucchero's appearance at Woodstock '94 further enhanced the international flavor of the festival; neither the 1969 Woodstock Music and Art Fair nor Woodstock 1999 featured any equivalent to Zucchero.

The well-established acts included Country Joe McDonald, who had appeared at the 1969 festival and whose "I-Feel-Like-I'm-Fixin'-to-Die Rag" is still remembered in the context of protest against the U.S. involvement in the Vietnam conflict in the mid-1960s. Joe Cocker, another Woodstock Music and Art Fair performer, had enjoyed bursts of popularity in the 1970s, 1980s, and 1990s, so he did not represent so much a nostalgia act as did McDonald.

Although Bob Dylan lived fairly close to the site of the 1969 Woodstock festival, he did not perform there. Dylan made significant contributions to American music in the 1960s through the 1990s, so, even more than Joe Cocker, he did not represent so much nostalgia for the spirit of the 1969 festival, as an American icon. Johnny Cash, an artist whose country style was not represented at the 1969 festival, was in the same iconic category as Dylan.

Another veteran act, The Allman Brothers Band, brought a southern rock touch to Woodstock '94. The group had virtually defined that style in the early 1970s. Since several members of the original group and subsequent incarnations had died, including co-founder Duane Allman, and since the group had disbanded and reformed several times in the 1980s, Woodstock '94 represented something of a return to glory for what was now primarily a vehicle for Gregg Allman. Stylistically very different from Gregg Allman's outfit, the British band Traffic's appearance at the festival represented another reunion, this time of keyboardist Steve Winwood's late 1960s–early 1970s band.

A number of singer-songwriters took the stage at Woodstock '94, including Melissa Etheridge and Sheryl Crow. The Berklee College of Music–trained Etheridge created a sensation among music critics with her 1988 album *Melissa Etheridge*. Her 1993 album *Yes I Am*, and her acknowledgment that she is gay found Etheridge not only making the *Billboard* album charts just before the Woodstock '94 festival but also making headlines. Crow, who had worked as a grade school music teacher, enjoyed greater exposure as a result of her appearance at the festival. Crow's song "All I Wanna Do," which made its chart debut right around the time of Woodstock '94, held the number 2 spot on the *Billboard* pop singles charts for an unusually long six weeks and reached number 1 on the magazine's adult contemporary chart.

One intriguing group that was put together in 1994 was Sisters of Glory. Thelma Houston, CeCe Penistron, Phoebe Snow, Mavis Staples, and Lois Walden had all made significant contributions to soul and gospel music as either soloists or members of other vocal groups. As such, Sisters of Glory was a kind of super-group of the gospel-soul genres. They were not, however, the only supergroup to perform at Woodstock '94. Although their work together was not constant from 1969 to 1994, Crosby, Stills, and Nash still retained their supergroup status at the festival. The version of The Band that performed at Woodstock '94 differed significantly in personnel from the group of the same name that appeared at the 1969 festival. The 1994 version of the group included some members of the original ensemble but was truly an all-star band, as discussed later. Jimmy Cliff's All-Star Jam featured reggae performers of major importance, including Cliff himself.

While Woodstock 1999 would feature a heavy dose of rap, the genre was also represented, in significantly more muted form, at Woodstock '94. Arrested Development, a rap group that originated in Atlanta, Georgia, had made a splash with their 1992 debut recording *Three Years, Five Months and Two Days in the Life of . . .* The group combined elements of hip-hop, soul, and blues. Arrested Development was influenced by both the music and the lyrics of Sylvester Stewart, leader of Sly and the Family Stone. This provided the rap group with a link to the 1969 Woodstock Music and Art Fair. Arrested Development never matched the success of their first album, but they were still popular when they appeared at Woodstock '94. The group, however, would break up in 1996. Salt-N-Pepa, "the first all female rap crew,"[24] was much better known than Arrested Development, based largely on the fact that they had been recording for eight years at the time of Woodstock '94. The Los Angeles–based rap trio Cypress Hill also brought the genre—and some of the rowdiness often associated with it—to the Woodstock '94 stage.

Porno for Pyros was another of the newer acts that appeared at the festival. Although band member Perry Farrell was known for his work with Jane's Addiction, Porno for Pyros had made its debut in 1993. The band broke up approximately two years after their Woodstock '94 performance.

The Red Hot Chili Peppers combined elements of rap, funk, and rock and had enjoyed a period of high visibility in the year before Woodstock '94. They were certainly one of the most notorious groups of the day, often appearing nearly naked in photographs and in their performances and playing music of high energy and controversy. The Chili Peppers continued their career and would later play a prominent role in the fiasco at the end of the Woodstock 1999 festival.

Primus, a trio fueled by bass player Les Claypool, brought an intriguing mix of what has been called "post-punk Rush spiked with the sensibility and humor of Frank Zappa"[25] to the Woodstock '94 stage.

King's X was another rock trio that performed at Woodstock '94. The band's style included vocal harmonies reminiscent of the Beatles, combined with elements of art rock and heavy metal. King's X appeared on the opening day of the festival in what *All Music Guide* critic Greg Prato describes as a "show-stopping performance."[26]

Largely as a result of the musical impact of Kurt Cobain's band Nirvana in the late 1980s and early 1990s, the Seattle grunge style had made significant inroads in the rock world by the time of the Woodstock '94 festival. Candlebox, a Seattle group, brought a post-Nirvana version of the grunge genre to the Woodstock stage. The group was at the height of their popularity at the time of their appearance but, like several other Woodstock '94 performers, would fade quickly from view within a few years of the festival.

Todd Rundgren, probably best remembered for his number 5 hit "Hello It's Me" (1973), represented mainstream pop at the festival. Orleans, a band best remembered for their hits "Dance with Me" (1975) and "Still the One" (1976), also represented mainstream, adult-contemporary rock. The long-standing New Orleans group The Neville Brothers represented mainstream rhythm and blues. Another prominent 1970s and 1980s musician, singer, guitarist, and songwriter Paul Rodgers, had been one of the principals of the groups Free and Bad Company (among other bands). Rodgers, who proved the commercial potential of a hybrid brand of British blues, hard rock, pop, and heavy metal, had influenced several 1980s and 1990s rock bands. He assembled something of an all-star band at Woodstock 1994. The Rodgers group included Slash (formerly lead guitarist of Guns N' Roses), drummer Jason Bonham (son of famed Led Zeppelin drummer John Bonham), guitarist Neal Schon (formerly of Santana and Journey), and bass player Andy Fraser (a former member of John Mayall's Bluesbreakers and Free).

While Paul Rodgers represented a link to early British electric blues, the American group Blues Traveler was a sort of retro electric blues outfit. Unfortunately, the group has experienced several setbacks and tragedies, including singer John Popper's serious automobile accident in 1992 and angioplasty in 1999 and bassist Bobby Sheehan's unexpected death in 1999. The band has continued, however, to perform into the twenty-first century and at the time of their Woodstock '94 appearance enjoyed popularity as a live "jam" band.

The influence of electric blues was also felt at Woodstock '94 in the music of the Spin Doctors. Although the group had become something of an MTV sensation in 1992, the Spin Doctors' recording career was not going particularly well at the time of their Woodstock performance. The group was another of those that virtually disappeared within a couple of years of Woodstock '94.

Blind Melon's style also owed a debt of gratitude to the rock music of the 1970s. The group had made a name for itself as a live band for several years leading up to the Woodstock '94 festival, often opening for some of the leading seasoned and newer big-name rock acts. After winning Grammy awards for Best New Artist and Best Rock Performance, however, singer Shannon Hoon was suffering from the effects of substance abuse. Blind Melon's Woodstock appearance, in fact, came just after part of the band's then-current tour had to be canceled due to Hoon's drug-related problems. Unfortunately, the singer would die from drug-related causes a little more than a year after Woodstock '94.

While they were not particularly well known yet at the time of their Woodstock '94 performance, The Cranberries, a band formed in Ireland in 1990, were starting to make some pop headway with their 1993 album *Everybody Else Is Doing It, So Why Can't We?* and their 1994 album *No Need to Argue*. James, another group from the British Isles, brought a folk-pop, alternative stylistic blend to Woodstock '94.

The Violent Femmes had been recording songs of "teen angst"[27] since 1983 and continued to be a popular cult band throughout the 1980s. For several years before Woodstock '94 their output had slowed. In addition to appearing at the festival, however, The Violent Femmes made a return of sorts with the album *New Times*.

Heavy metal, hard rock, and industrial music were also well represented at Woodstock '94. Metallica, which had been creating some of the most influential metal music around from 1983 up to and well beyond the time of Woodstock '94, was one of the more highly anticipated bands at the festival. Aerosmith had been leaders in the hard rock genre since the early 1970s. Lead singer Steve Tyler and company had scored *Billboard* pop top 10 hits in the 1970s, 1980s, and 1990s and were another of the truly major, big-name bands that graced the stage at Woodstock '94. Nine Inch Nails, which in the recording studio is a solo vehicle for multi-instrumentalist, singer-songwriter Trent Reznor, performed as an ensemble at Woodstock '94. At the time of the festival, Reznor/Nine Inch Nails had a reputation built largely on live shows and on the 1989 *Pretty Hate Machine* album. Although the "band" did not release an album between 1989 and 1994, it had a substantial fan base at the Woodstock performance, largely on the strength of *Pretty Hate Machine* and the popular 1994 album, *The Downward Spiral*.

Punk rock was well represented by the hot new trio Green Day. Billie Joe Armstrong, Mike Dirnt, and Frank Wright had worked together since 1989 but achieved their commercial breakthrough on the *Billboard* airplay charts in May 1994. Green Day would play a much-publicized role in some of the (rather mild compared to what would transpire at Woodstock 1999) controversy that arose from the Woodstock '94 festival.

Woodstock '94 officially began on Friday, August 12, 1994, and lasted through Sunday, August 14. Despite some of the difficulties encountered by the promoters and audience at the festival, it was an event that focused on music. In terms of diversity of styles and the well-organized way in which the performances took place on two stages, not to mention the spectacular light shows that accompanied some of the performances, Woodstock '94 was a highly successful example of a multiday, outdoor rock festival, despite the charges of commercialism, the poor sanitation, and the rain and mud. Some of the acts were better received than others, and some had more broadly based crossover appeal than others, but for the most part the ordering of the performance bill worked well.

The crowd grew restless, however, during the approximately three hours the W.O.M.A.D. performers were onstage. Although listed as one band, the collection included several different groups and solo performers. One review that has been posted on the Internet by reputed concert attendee Ram Samudrala describes Geoffrey Oryema's performance as "truly brilliant."[28] The reviewer notes, however, that all of the W.O.M.A.D. troupe, which included Oryema, Xalem, the Justin Trio, and Hassan Hakmoun, were generally poorly received as the bulk of the audience was awaiting the punk band Green Day.

Green Day's performance was marred by singer Billie Joe Armstrong dropping his pants and telling the crowd to shout, "Shut the fuck up," which led to his mother later sending him a "hate letter" that accused him of being "disrespectful and indecent."[29] In addition, in the middle of an onstage mud fight, which had been encouraged by the band, a security guard tackled bass player Mike Dirnt (the security guard apparently thought that Dirnt was a fan who had jumped onstage) and smashed the musician's front teeth. All of this was seen on the pay-per-view broadcast of the festival. Incidentally, Billie Joe Armstrong's stage deportment would eventually prove to be rather tame, at least by Woodstock 1999 standards, and the mud fights would continue throughout the rest of the festival.

All accounts of Woodstock '94 suggest that Bob Dylan performed one of the most memorable and perhaps one of the most unusual sets of the entire festival. Although he performed many of his best-known songs of the 1960s like "All Along the Watchtower," "Highway 61," "Masters of War," "Don't Think Twice, It's Alright," and others, he did not say a word to the audience between numbers. Other musicians on the Woodstock '94 bill included a great deal of stage banter with the audience, but not Bob Dylan. Dylan got his biggest reaction from the crowd during his song "Rainy Day Women #12 and 35," which includes the famous refrain "Everybody must get stoned."

Speaking of getting stoned, the drugs of choice of the late 1960s, LSD and marijuana, certainly had been very much in evidence at the 1969 Woodstock Music and Art Fair. Like their colleagues of a quarter century before, the medical team of Woodstock '94 also found themselves occupied with helping young people through bad LSD trips. In addition to marijuana and LSD, however, the new drugs of choice for the Woodstock '94 crowd were ecstasy and other so-called designer drugs associated with the rave subculture.

The Band was one of the acts that gave a memorable performance at the 1969 Woodstock Music and Art Fair. Woodstock '94 also featured the group, which by this point had a much different membership. The 1994 edition of the group resembled more of an all-star rock group and included such nonoriginal personnel as Bob Weir of The Grateful Dead, Jorma Kaukonen and Jack Casady of the Jefferson Airplane, Bruce Hornsby (who had been with The Grateful Dead but is probably best remembered for his work with the group Bruce Hornsby and the Range), Roger "Jim" McGuinn of The Byrds, Country Joe McDonald, John Sebastian, and others. Bassist Rob Wasserman was another musician who appeared with The Band. After the group's performance, Wasserman tripped over a tent rope and broke his arm. This incident resulted in one of the several lawsuits that eventually were leveled against Woodstock Ventures.

One of the interesting observations from a reputed Woodstock '94 attendee was that the vast majority of the acts he saw actively promoted peace, both in their songs and in their stage banter. According to the music fan's Web site, however, Cypress Hill, in addition to actively encouraging marijuana smoking among the crowd, was "one of the few bands actually promoting aggression."[30] If this was the case, and the observation of other attendees suggests that it was, then Woodstock '94 contrasted greatly with Woodstock 1999, an event at which charges of inciting the crowd easily could be leveled at several acts.

Although it was not meant to be violent, the crowd surfing and mosh pit near the Woodstock '94 stages could be dangerous. Some concertgoers sustained injuries while moshing; however, the activity seemed to have been enjoyed by numerous fans with little or no incident. Anonymous reports from the site suggest that Primus generated the most intense moshing and slamming by the greatest number of festival attendees.[31] Generally, this type of activity is associated with hard-core music. At Woodstock '94, however, even performers whose music would not normally be considered mosh-friendly or mosh-inspiring, like Bob Dylan, generated at least a small amount of crowd surfing and moshing.

Woodstock '94 included several audio and visual tributes to the rock greats of the late 1960s who had died at young ages, Jimi Hendrix, Janis Joplin, and Jim Morrison. Probably most notable was the Red Hot Chili Peppers' performance of "The Star-Spangled Banner" in tribute to Hendrix and Melissa Etheridge's performance of "Piece of My Heart," one of Joplin's best-known recordings and a song that the late singer had included in her 1969 Woodstock set. Blind Melon's Shannon Hoon, whose brief career included some of the same sort of drug addiction problems from which Janis Joplin had suffered, also paid tribute to Joplin. It seems as though these tributes were made even more meaningful to the crowd by the suicide only a few months before Woodstock '94 of Nirvana's Kurt Cobain, who was seen by some members of Generation X as being the Jim Morrison of their generation.[32]

In keeping with one of the trends of the mid-1990s, Woodstock '94 also included a festival within a festival titled Ravestock. Announced only two weeks before the actual start of Woodstock '94, Ravestock began at midnight Saturday morning and ran approximately 6½ hours. Ecstasy and other designer and rave drugs were in abundance, and the music had a definite techno, dance nature to it. The Orb, Deee-Lite, and Orbital were among the musicians who entertained at the rave.

All in all, Woodstock '94 was about rock music in its various guises; there was not the focus on causes or the validation of a counterculture lifestyle such as had turned out to be the case at the 1969 Woodstock Music and Art Fair. There were a few exceptions, however, as noted by *Rolling Stone* writer John Milward:

> Woodstock '94, like its namesake, was also a whale of a rock show, but it's perhaps folly to look for deeper meaning. Sure, Greenpeace was on hand to preach concern for the environment, but in the context of farm-land polluted by piss and littered with plastic Pepsi bottles, nobody could pretend that the event was kind to the earth. Similarly, with a bill lacking more socially aware

superstar bands like R.E.M. and U2, the wide-ranging roster at Woodstock '94 added up to little more than a marathon arena-rock concert.

Peter Gabriel, consequently, was the only artist fit to put a thoughtful benediction on Woodstock '94. Playing a set that included an appearance by Youssou N'Dour, Gabriel did nothing that he hadn't done in hundreds of arenas, but his politically aware perspective soothed the savage, waterlogged beast.[33]

Gabriel had included "Biko," a song about a martyred South African fighter against apartheid, in his set. Votive candles were distributed to the crowd, and these were lit during the song. Milward's report notes, somewhat sarcastically, "The shimmering sea of light, not coincidentally, also played well to the television cameras."[34] So, even the one moment that seemed to be concerned with a political/social cause seemed to have been constructed for a commercial reason: the concert film that was being shot.

One unfortunate aftermath of Woodstock '94 was the several lawsuits that arose out of the festival. In addition to bass player Rob Wasserman's lawsuit over the broken arm he sustained when he tripped over a tent rope, concessionaires took Woodstock Ventures to court. Vendors claimed that the promoters had promised to donate a portion of the festival's profits to them. When the vendors who represented charitable organizations were not paid, many expressed anger. Susan Acosta filed a lawsuit against the festival in spring 1995,[35] thereby extending the accusations of greed on the part of Woodstock '94 promoters well into 1995.

Woodstock Ventures also ran into legal difficulties with officials of Dutchess County, New York, near which the Saugerties festival site was located. The county demanded that Woodstock Ventures pay for environmental damages that had occurred as a result of the festival. In part, this was a result of the problems with raw sewage that were described earlier. The environmental damage that occurred at the Winston farm was a particular embarrassment to Woodstock '94 promoters, since they had touted the festival's emphasis on protection of the environment.[36]

Newsweek reporters Karen Schoemer and Patrick Rogers described the sanitation problems, mud, and debates over commercialism that, aside from the music, defined the festival. According to the reporters, however, "In the end, what Woodstock '94 proved had nothing to do with myth-making or generations or defining cultural moments. All it showed was that if you put a load of mostly middle-class kids on a field with a bunch of bands they love, they'll be patient and well behaved despite rain, stink, and bad pizza."[37] Although other reporters and commentators did not use exactly this same language, conclusions about the significance of Woodstock '94 were consistent. Looking back on the festival with the advantage of being able to compare three Woodstock events, it appears that Woodstock '94 may not have defined a generation the same way that the 1969 and the 1999 festivals did, but as an outdoor rock festival, it succeeded musically and technically perhaps better than the other two events.

In reviewing reactions of attendees to the three Woodstock festivals, one of the main contrasting features that played into the differences between the 1969 and the other two in terms of defining a generation was perhaps due in part to the relative technical proficiency of the producers of the latter events when compared with the 1969 festival. Woodstock '94 (and Woodstock 1999) utilized two main stages and had a fairly constant flow of musical activity, unlike the 1969 festival, with its one main stage and relatively long stagnant periods. This is one of the important factors in terms of the relative amounts of communal spirit that arose at the festivals. At Woodstock '94, one could move from stage to stage (or even check out the technology display) and be much more selective about the types of music to which one listened. At the 1969 festival, audience members who wanted to hear music on "a" main stage—in this case *the* main stage—had to at least experience a range of styles and, probably, interact with other concertgoers with different tastes from one's own.

A year after Woodstock '94, *Billboard* contributor Melinda Newman wrote an article reassessing the successes and failures of the festival. Newman noted that several acts whose recordings were distributed by PolyGram, namely Sheryl Crow, Melissa Etheridge, The Cranberries, and Blues Traveler had "gone on to reach new sales heights following their Woodstock '94 appearances." Even artists not affiliated with PolyGram, which co-produced the festival with Woodstock Ventures, "saw significant sale increases after Woodstock '94, including Live, Collective Soul, Nine Inch Nails, Candlebox, and Green Day."[38] One of the more significant contributions of the festival, according to Newman, was that radio program directors suddenly realized that there were many bands that were popular with audiences whose music was being virtually ignored by the radio industry. Newman notes, however, that PolyGram was disappointed in the festival, especially from a commercial standpoint: jammed phone lines at Ticketmaster and the bad weather combined to limit attendance.

In conclusion, it can be said that Woodstock '94 was an uneven success: as a business venture it did not live up to its expectations. It did not define an era in American popular culture or a generation nearly as dramatically as the 1969 Woodstock Music and Art Fair or Woodstock 1999. As a mammoth outdoor pop music festival, however, it was major success. Since the festival's success primarily lies outside being symbolic of an era, it seems unlikely that Woodstock '94, despite its musical successes, will be viewed in hindsight with the same kind of iconic status as its 1969 and 1999 cousins.

NOTES

1. Azerrad, M., "Now They Spell It 'Wood$tock,' " *Rolling Stone* n549 (April 6, 1989), p. 17.

2. Estimates were eventually placed at approximately 22,000.

3. Woodstock Nation Foundation *For Perpetual Free Assembly*. http://www.woodstocknation.org/history.htm, accessed May 27, 2003.

4. Woodstock Nation Foundation *For Perpetual Free Assembly*.

5. Solomon, Jolie, and Robin Sparkman, "The Faithful Brace for Battle at Rock Music's Sacred Site," *Newsweek* 122/10 (September 6, 1993), p. 61.

6. Dunn, Jancee, "Soul Asylum," *Rolling Stone* n695 (November 17, 1994), p. 55.

7. The ownership of the site was in dispute several times after Max Yasgur's death. For a time in 1996–97, it seems that there was a question as to whether June Gelish or Jeryl Abramson and Roy Howard owned the property.

8. O'Rourke, John J., and John J. Murphy Jr., "Woodstock '94: Fire Planning for Large Public Events," *Fire Engineering* 148/1 (1995), pp. 74+.

9. "Worst of Tube," *People* 42/26 (December 26, 1994), p. 16.

10. Applefeld, Catherine, "Music PPV Proves Disappointing." *Billboard* 107/42 (October 21, 1995), pp. 16+.

11. Newman, Melinda, "Woodstock '94: Mixed Aftermath," *Billboard* 107/33 (August 19, 1995), pp. 1+.

12. Milward, John, "Field of Dreams," *Rolling Stone* n688 (August 11, 1994), p. 36.

13. Farley, Christopher John, and David E. Thigpen, "Woodstock Suburb," *Time* 144/8 (August 22, 1994), p. 78.

14. Friedman, Wayne, "Woodstock Revisited Finds Few Sponsors," *Advertising Age* 70/27 (June 28, 1999), p. 4.

15. Milward, "Field of Dreams."

16. Foege, Alec, "Billie Joe of Green Day," *Rolling Stone* n695 (November 17, 1994), p. 24.

17. Milward, John, "Joy in Mudville," *Rolling Stone* n691 (September 22, 1994), p. 61.

18. Schoemer, Karen, and Patrick Rogers, "By the Time They Got to . . . ," *Newsweek* 124/8 (August 22, 1994), p. 64.

19. Seavey, Todd, "Once Is Enough," *National Review* 46/17 (September 12, 1994), p. 27.

20. Byfield, Link, "Why Doesn't Someone Do Us a Favour and Drop a Bomb on Woodstock '94?" *Alberta Report* 21/34 (August 8, 1994), p. 2.

21. Schoemer, Karen, "Talking 'bout Our Generation," *Newsweek* 124–25/26–1 (December 26, 1994–January 2, 1995), p. 33.

22. Donohue, Steve, "No Love for TV at Woodstock," *Electronic Media* 18/31 (August 2, 1999), p. 35.

23. Milward, "Joy in Mudville."

24. Erlewine, Stephen Thomas, "Salt-N-Pepa," *All Music Guide*, http://www.allmusic.com, accessed March 22, 2004.

25. Erlewine, Stephen Thomas, and Greg Prato, "Primus," *All Music Guide*, http://allmusic.com, accessed April 12, 2004.

26. Prato, Greg, "King's X," *All Music Guide*, http://allmusic.com, accessed April 14, 2004.

27. Ankeny, Jason, "Violent Femmes," *All Music Guide*, http://allmusic.com, accessed March 22, 2004.

28. Samudrala, Ram, *Woodstock 1994 Concert Review*, http://www.ram.org/music/woodstock/woodstock.html, accessed March 7, 2004.

29. Mundy, Chris, "Green Daze," *Rolling Stone* n700 (January 26, 1995), p. 40.

30. *Woodstock 1994 Concert Review*, http://www.ram.org/music/woodstock/woodstock. html, accessed March 7, 2004.

31. *Woodstock 1994 Concert Review.*

32. Interestingly and ironically, Hendrix, Joplin, Morrison, and Cobain were all part of what some people have somewhat morbidly called "the 27 club"; all four died when they were twenty-seven years old.

33. Milward, "Joy in Mudville."

34. Milward, "Joy in Mudville."

35. Steinberg, Jacques, "Love, Peace, Money, Lawsuits," *New York Times*, May 12, 1995, p. B1.

36. "Arborcidal Maniacs," *New York* 27/35 (September 5, 1994), p. 14.

37. Schoemer and Rogers, "By the Time They Got to . . . ," pp. 64+.

38. Newman, "Woodstock '94: Mixed Aftermath," p. 1.

Woodstock 1999 and A Day in the Garden

WOODSTOCK 1999

Woodstock '94 could be described as having been all about the music of the mid-1990s generation. The 1969 Woodstock Music and Art Fair had been all about peace, love, understanding, and music. The thirtieth-anniversary concert, Woodstock 1999, was anything but. Woodstock 1999 featured a fair number of musicians known for their violent and sometimes brutal lyrics and performances, and by the end of the festival, violence and brutality became not just part of the show but part of the audience's experience as rapes, riots, and looting generated headlines across the country.

The principal organizers of Woodstock 1999 were the omnipresent Michael Lang, John Scher of the Metropolitan Entertainment Group, and Ossie Kilkenny, an Irish rock entrepreneur who managed Irish and English acts like U2 and Oasis. Lang, in particular, had high hopes for the festival as the July 23, 1999, opening approached. Lang described the ideal conditions he hoped for to *Harper's Magazine* reporter David Samuels:

> The temperature would be between seventy-five and eighty degrees. Light showers in the late afternoon . . . no bad traffic jams. I have a lot of faith in the production being together. And people would be connected in a meaningful way—in a vulnerable, connected way, feeling like it's their space.[1]

Lang, Scher, and Kilkenny certainly had a considerable amount of experience producing rock music festivals. Lang, in particular, had seen the 1969 Woodstock Music and Art Fair go from being a festival designed to fund a recording studio, to a free event that ended up capturing the imagination of more than one generation of Americans. He had also been part of the Woodstock '94 team and had seen that any overt show of commercialism would elicit negative comparisons with the peace, love, freedom, and understanding of the original Woodstock festival. As the start of the 1999 festival approached, media coverage suggested that plans and preparations were moving along smoothly and that the festival might well re-create the spirit of 1969. In fact, *New York Times* reporter Paul Zielbauer titled his report on the final preparations for Woodstock 1999, "Woodstock Arrives and Mood Is Mellow."[2]

There were certainly some specific things that the producers had learned from earlier shows. One significant change from the Woodstock Music and Art Fair, for example, was that the food concessions for Woodstock 1999 were handled by an experienced enterprise, Ogden Corporation, which was one of the nation's largest concessionaires for outdoors events. The downtime of the 1969 festival was avoided by having two main stages at Woodstock 1999, with a smaller emerging artists' stage also available as a performing venue.

All was not well, however, even at the start of Woodstock 1999. For one thing, Lang, Scher, and Kilkenny selected the former Griffiss Air Force Base in Rome, New York, as the site for the festival. Not only was the former military installa-tion on the U.S. Environmental Protection Agency's list of the most toxic sites in America—a fact not known by many concertgoers at the time of the festival—but the setting left much to be desired aesthetically. *Rolling Stone* reporter Kurt Loder, for example, described Griffiss Air Force Base as a "bleak and unwelcoming site."[3] It certainly lacked the bucolic nature of the Yasgur farm (Woodstock Music and Art Fair, 1969) and the Winston farm (Woodstock '94).

Woodstock 1999's lineup of acts was impressive enough and featured a mixture of hard rock, heavy metal, pop, rap, country, funk, world music, soul, punk, and other styles. The following acts appeared at the festival: the Brian Setzer Orches-tra, James Brown, Buckcherry, Bush, The Chemical Brothers, Collective Soul, Elvis Costello, Counting Crows, Creed, Sheryl Crow, the Dave Matthews Band, DMX, Everclear, Everlast, G. Love and Special Sauce, Godsmack, Guster, Bruce Hornsby, Ice Cube, Insane Clown Posse, Jamiroquai, Wyclef Jean, Jewel, Kid Rock, Korn, Limp Bizkit, Lit, Live, Los Lobos, Megadeth, Metallica, moe, Alanis Morissette, Willie Nelson, Mike Ness, The Offspring, Oleander, Our Lady Peace, Paliament/Funkadelic, Mickey Hart's Planet Drum, Rage against the Machine, the Red Hot Chili Peppers, The Roots, Rusted Root, Sevendust, and the Tragically Hip.[4] Other acts scheduled to perform had to cancel their sets for one reason or another, including soul singer Al Green.

In addition to the performers and the festival organizers, plenty of other per-sonalities took to the stage at Woodstock 1999. The first day of the festival in-cluded an announcement from a member of the Oneida Nation of Native Americans who reminded concertgoers that they were on Oneida land and asked them to have a good time but to be careful. In contrast to the 1969 Woodstock Music and Art Fair, at which Swami Satchadinanda proclaimed a reverent Hindu blessing on the proceedings, the Oneida speaker's announcement concluded with his pronouncing the festivities "phat," to use a colloquialism of the late twentieth and early twenty-first centuries. This kind of irreverence seemed to pervade the entire Woodstock 1999 festival. Another highly visible personality at Woodstock 1999 and one who had figured prominently into the 1969 festival was Wavy Gravy. The head of the Hog Farm commune made stage announcements and introductions several times throughout the 1999 festival. Wavy Gravy also caught the spirit of irreverence, appearing at times dressed in a clown costume.

The festival official began around noon on Friday, July 23, 1999. It was an auspicious beginning, too, with soul-funk legend James Brown kicking off the event. Despite Brown's standing in the history of American popular music of the previous forty years, fans were less than fully enthusiastic. This would be the first hint that one of the great myths of rock—that the music transcends generations—was indeed a myth. *Rolling Stone*'s Fred Goodman had exposed this myth at the 1998 A Day in the Garden festival. At the 1998 event, which had been held on the site of the Yasgur farm, fans of nostalgic acts like Ten Years After, Richie Havens, Melanie, and Donovan were worlds apart from the fans of such new acts as Dishwalla, The Flys, and Third Eye Blind.[5]

The young audience members received the Offspring and Korn much more enthusiastically than they had received James Brown. The Offspring and Korn represented hybrids of musical styles popular with Generation Xers: punk, rap, and heavy metal. Performers who generated the greatest amount of audience response throughout the festival would fit pretty much squarely in the punk, rap, or heavy metal categories or were hybrids of these styles. While the crowd seemed to be enthusiastic about Korn, not all of the rock critics agreed. *Rolling Stone* reporter Rob Sheffield, for example, described Friday's performers as "uninspiring," giving some praise to the Roots' set but downplaying the performances by DMX, Jamiroquai, The Offspring, Korn, Insane Clown Posse, and Bush.

Regardless of whether they were well received by the audience or panned by some of the critics, Korn's funky heavy metal performance signaled the beginning of intense moshing at the festival. The intensity level of the Woodstock 1999 mosh pit led to more than a few audience members being rushed out on disposable medical stretchers. As *Rolling Stone*'s Rob Sheffield described the scene in the pit and Korn's performance, "The brutality is the show."[6]

Korn and other newer groups were certainly more typical of the Woodstock 1999 performers than were acts like Willie Nelson. Although he was in his mid-sixties at the time of the festival, making him well over a generation older than most of the Woodstock 1999 attendees, Nelson's performance was generally well received by those who heard him. The crowd might have been relatively small and generally older than the norm, but they seemed to appreciate Nelson's set and his outlaw, nonconformist personality.

Sheffield also described the highly publicized sexual scene at Woodstock 1999, a scene that permeated the entire festival. Young women were encouraged throughout the festival to expose their breasts, and many did, due to the intensity of the pressure they felt. Sheffield described the situation as "sexual assault," adding that "it's about power, not pleasure."[7] David Samuels also described the sexual scene in terms that suggested its impersonal nature and frat-boys-on-spring-break atmosphere in his post-Woodstock 1999 feature article in *Harper's Magazine*.[8]

Another situation that cast a shadow over Woodstock 1999 from the first day was the amount of garbage that was generated. Lisa Law, who had been a key member of the Hog Farm commune that helped with security, treating concert-goers who were experiencing bad drug trips and feeding the masses at the 1969 Woodstock festival, was among those who went through the crowd asking the Generation Xers to clean up after themselves. David Samuels quoted one young male concertgoer who approached one of the golf carts making the rounds of the area with trash bags as saying, "I paid $150 to come here. You clean up my fuck-ing trash."[9] This represented quite a change from the spirit of the 1969 Wood-stock Music and Art Fair and again illustrated that although the music was still rock (or some variant thereof), generations can and will change.

Unfortunately, it wasn't just bagable trash that proved difficult for Woodstock 1999's crews to control; it was also raw sewage from some 2,000 portable toilets. The toilets could not be emptied quickly enough, and many continued to over-flow, creating a terrible stench. It was especially ironic that raw sewage was a prob-lem for all three of the Woodstock festivals: the 1969 event suffered primarily due to a crowd that was far in excess of what was expected, the 1994 event difficul-ties were caused by the large number of tents that were pitched in locations that hampered sanitation crews' access to the portable toilets, and the 1999 festival suf-fered from a general lack of service of the facilities in relationship to the size of the crowd. The irony is that the entire concept of the original Woodstock Music and Art Fair was built around the natural, bucolic surroundings. The Woodstock '94 festival continued the peaceful, rural theme when the site was chosen, but the sanitation problems contrasted with the entire Back to the Land Woodstock ideal. Woodstock 1999 remained the ultimate irony, as the festival suffered from poor sanitation and took place—unknown to the attendees—on one of the nation's worst toxic waste sites.

Heat was also a problem. The intense heat compounded the odor problems from the trash and from the raw sewage that leaked from the portable toilets. Due to the intense heat, "Water—not LSD—was the substance of choice for 1999's visitors, with refreshment stands running dangerously low on supplies of bottled water and soft drinks. Beer sales fizzled, vendors saying it was too hot for con-certgoers to drink alcohol."[10] Although the festival's organizers set up free water-dispensing stations and also set up tents with sprinklers, "over 1,000 people were treated for heat exhaustion and dehydration."[11] There simply was not enough free water to go around, and the bottled water was thought by many concertgoers to be too expensive.

Despite these problems, the music continued on the two main stages and on the emerging artists' stage. Again, depending upon one's point of view, critics and audience members did not always agree on how well the performances went. Even critics from the same publication disagreed on some of the acts. For example, Rob Sheffield compared Elvis Costello's set as having the effect of the embarrassment that accompanies one's drunken uncle showing up at a party,[12] while Kurt Loder called Costello's performance "cheery" and wrote that the singer-songwriter had the audience "smiling as they savored his lyrics and sinuous delivery."[13] Costello's understated anger, something for which he has been known throughout his career, greatly contrasted with the overt anger and calls to violence that would eventually become the real story of Woodstock 1999.

As demonstrated by the presence of a musician like the ever-eclectic Elvis Costello, there was much more than rap, punk, and metal music (and various combinations thereof) at Woodstock 1999. While those three styles predominated and received the lion's share of attention, particularly in light of the violence that some of the rap and punk rock acts were accused of inciting at the festivals, rockabilly and swing were present in the form of the Brian Setzer Orchestra. Setzer, who gained fame as the guitarist and lead singer of the retro-rockabilly band the Stray Cats in the early 1980s, had moved toward retro-big band swing in more recent years.

Outlaw country singer-songwriter Willie Nelson also added to the mix of styles in evidence at the festival. Many young people who attended Nelson's performance called out for him to light up a joint, or marijuana cigarette, as Nelson had for many years been an acknowledged user of the drug. While Nelson might not have lit up during his set, he, along with festival opener James Brown, was one of the few true musical legends at Woodstock 1999.

Also counted among the long-standing musical legends was George Clinton's Parliament/Funkadelic. Clinton had been a founding member of the a cappella vocal group The Parliaments in the mid-1950s. By 1967 Clinton had moved into a soulful funk style and was one of the acknowledged developers of funk in the early 1970s. A sort of second-generation funk was also heard in the performance of Jamiroquai.

The relatively heavy dose of world music that had been part of Woodstock '94 in the form of the W.O.M.A.D. aggregation of performers was for the most part absent from the 1999 edition of Woodstock. Mickey Hart, former drummer with The Grateful Dead, had put together a world percussion organization known as Mickey Hart's Planet Drum, a group that performed at Woodstock 1999.

One could argue that the role of The Grateful Dead at the 1969 Woodstock Music and Art Fair was that of a very popular live band that featured eclectic musical influences and that enjoyed an almost cultlike following. In some respects, the Dave Matthews Band played a similar role at Woodstock 1999. This group, led by South African native Matthews, merged jazz, rock, and classical music influences and enjoyed a strong fan base; perhaps they were not quite the Deadheads of the 1990s, but they were and continue to be a very loyal contingent of fans.

Another tie to The Grateful Dead could be found in keyboardist-singer Bruce Hornsby, who had toured from time to time with The Dead in addition to backing up Sheena Easton and making the singles and album charts with his group Bruce Hornsby and the Range in the late 1980s. Hornsby was not the only mainstream rock act at the festival. Counting Crows brought their blend of the styles of Van Morrison, The Band, and R.E.M. to Woodstock 1999.

Yet another, although somewhat oblique, tie to The Grateful Dead could be seen in the band Rusted Root. This band combined world music-style percussion with jams reminiscent of The Dead. *All Music Guide* critic John Bush referred to Rusted Root's live performance style as "entrancing."[14]

The 1990s singer-songwriters were not quite as much in evidence at Woodstock 1999 as they had been at the 1994 event. Most notable in this category was Sheryl Crow's appearance. Crow, who had also appeared at the Woodstock event five years previously, was one of the bigger solo stars at the 1999 festival. In fact, *All Music Guide* critic Steve Huey describes her as "one of the most popular mainstream rockers of the '90s" and as "a perennial favorite at Grammy time."[15] Jewel also represented the 1990s singer-songwriter movement.

In contrast to the extensive nationwide fan base of someone like Sheryl Crow, the Boston area trio known as Guster was more an East Coast regional favorite at the time of their Woodstock 1999 performance. Adam Gardner, Ryan Miller, and Brian Rosenworcel combined the unusual sound of acoustic guitars and bongo drums as they became well known on the college circuit in the late 1990s.

There were other unusual-sounding alternative bands at Woodstock 1999, including moe, which had gotten its start in Buffalo, New York, and the Tragically Hip, a long-standing alternative band originally from Kingston, Ontario, Canada.

The harder-core end of the late 1990s music scene, including punk, metal, rap, and various combinations thereof, was well represented by the Portland band Everclear (punk and grunge), Limp Bizkit (a combination of metal, punk, and hip-hop), Korn (funk and metal), DMX (the leading hard-core rap artist to emerge since the deaths of Tupac Shakur and the Notorious B.I.G.), Mike Ness (a much-tatooed punk musician late of the band Social Distortion), Godsmack (alternative metal with a Wiccan connection), Wyclef Jean (rap), Everlast (rap), Insane Clown Posse (highly theatrical metal and rap), former member of the controversial N.W.A., Ice Cube (hard-core rap), Sevendust (metal), and Kid Rock (a fusion of metal and rap), as well as the long-standing metal bands Metallica and Megadeth. The Roots, a hip-hop/rap group that had been recording since 1993, was of special note since they were one of the few such groups that specialized in live performances, not relying heavily on digital sampling like most rap-related acts.

Undoubtedly, however, the Red Hot Chili Peppers were the best-known hardcore band to perform at Woodstock 1999. The Chili Peppers had been together since 1983 and had been recording since 1984. Despite several death and musical-disagreement-related personnel changes, the band continued on. In fact, their Woodstock 1999 performance came hot on the heels of their highly successful reunion album *Californication*. If there was one band whose stage performance could easily incite a crowd, it was often the nearly nude onstage Red Hot Chili Peppers.

Other hard rock bands (although not exactly "metallic" in style) included Los Angeles club favorites Buckcherry and Collective Soul, a group that had also performed at Woodstock '94. For something a little different, Tom Rowlands and Ed Simons, known collectively as The Chemical Brothers, brought an electronic dance flavor to Woodstock 1999.

Post-Nirvana grunge was represented by the British band Bush, the Canadian band Our Lady Peace, and the highly popular American bands Creed, Lit, Oleander, Live, and The Offspring. G. Love and Special Sauce also represented post-grunge, although the somewhat eclectic band incorporated rap and rhythm and blues into the mix. Interestingly, most of the bands that had initially followed Nirvana's lead in the early 1990s and had appeared at Woodstock '94 were absent from the 1999 festival: for the most part that wave of grunge groups had run their course and were no longer headliners or, in some cases, even functioning bands any longer. The exception was Live, which appeared at both anniversary Woodstock festivals.

With this degree of eclecticism, Woodstock 1999 resembled a mix of special interest group musical collections. Adding to this was the fact that Woodstock 1999—by virtue of having two main stages and by virtue of the fact that it did not have lengthy stretches of downtime like the 1969 festival—had so many performers. In other words, the programming virtually guaranteed that at least some of the communal spirit of the Woodstock Music and Art Fair would be missing. At the 1969 festival, everyone had to share the same music—there was only one main stage—while at Woodstock 1999, one might try to plan one's day around catching the punk acts by going from stage to stage. Audience members attempted to do just that.

The use of two main stages at Woodstock 1999 caused difficulties for some concertgoers. This was especially true when a person left one of the stage areas to see an act at the other stage, only to find that the performance schedule had been rearranged. At times, performers who might logically have had an overlapping base of fans were scheduled at the same time on opposite stages. For example, the Brian Setzer Orchestra and Mike Ness, both of whom had rockabilly, western-swing roots and shared at least part of their fan bases, performed at overlapping times.

Given the diversity of musical styles, especially within the generally musically hard-core atmosphere surrounding the festival, the size of the audience for the various acts fluctuated somewhat—this aspect of the festival would tend to support the view of Woodstock 1999 as having a more specialized, special-interest audience generally than those who attended the 1969 festival, at which one was forced to commune with several musical styles. The response to the music also varied considerably around the former Griffiss Air Force Base, again supporting the special-interest group view of the festival. Another part of Woodstock 1999 that seems to have elicited varying responses was the Jimi Hendrix tribute. Critic Rob Sheffield panned the tribute,[16] but some members of the Generation X audience, many of whom had probably heard Hendrix's music and had heard of his influence without having firsthand appreciation of the guitarist-singer-songwriter's importance, were favorably impressed by the multimedia tribute. The spirit of Jimi Hendrix, however, was not present only in the official tribute. Several acts performed songs that Hendrix had played at the 1969 Woodstock Music and Art Fair, including Wyclef Jean, who performed "The Star-Spangled Banner,"[17] Everclear, who performed "Purple Haze," and the Red Hot Chili Peppers, who performed "Fire." The spirit of Jim Morrison was also present at Woodstock 1999: Creed performed The Doors' "Roadhouse Blues," complete with a guest appearance by former Doors guitarist Robbie Krieger.

Although the popular media portrayed Woodstock 1999 as a disaster, there were

Fires burn through trailers and debris at Woodstock 1999 after the three-day event on the former Griffiss Air Force Base in Rome, New York, early Monday morning, July 26, 1999. (AP/Wide World Photos)

dissenting opinions among those who attended and those who produced the festival. At his September 1, 1999, postfestival press conference, Michael Lang said, "I thought most of it [the festival] was a positive experience for everybody, although the last few hours on Sunday cast a shadow over everything. The plans for the most part worked well, and we've seen what worked and what didn't. We made a lot of improvements from Woodstock '94."[18] Lang acknowledged the problems with the fires and the rapes that took place, placing most of the blame for the events of Sunday on a few concertgoers "who were bent on causing trouble all weekend" and on some of the musical programming.[19]

Despite Michael Lang's downplaying of the events of Sunday at the festival's final set—a performance by the Red Hot Chili Peppers—there were at least four rapes, fences were torn down and burned, ATM machines were overturned and broken into, and the booths of numerous vendors were set on fire and destroyed. MTV covered the festival live but removed its crew as the rioting intensified. According to MTV on-air personality Kurt Loder, "It was dangerous to be around. . . . There were just waves of hatred bouncing around the place. . . . It was like a concentration camp. To get in, you get frisked to make sure you're not bringing any water or food that would prevent you from buying their outrageously priced booths. You wallow in garbage and human waste. There was a palpable mood of anger."[20]

Some commentators blamed the Red Hot Chili Peppers for inciting the riot; however, much earlier in the festival, Everclear had used the stage as a profane venue for lashing out at anyone who had ever wronged them. Some attendees saw this as the start of the breakdown of order at Woodstock 1999, but the Chili Peppers and Everclear were not the only musicians who incited the crowd. Limp

Bizkit's Fred Durst told the crowd to smash things and told his audience that "there are no rules." Durst was reacting to singer Alanis Morissette, who earlier had asked the increasingly agitated crowd to "mellow out." Morissette was clearly in the minority among performers who in some way addressed the mood. *Rolling Stone*'s Kurt Loder linked the increase in violence at the festival with this performance by Limp Bizkit.[21] Perhaps significantly, this band seemed to be a particular favorite of many of the Woodstock 1999 generation: audience members were all too ready to carry out lead singer Fred Durst's sung and spoken directives. It should be noted that at least one of the mosh pit rapes that occurred at Woodstock 1999 took place during Limp Bizkit's set. Festival producers noticed the upturn in violence in the mosh pit area that occurred when Durst made his remarks. As a consequence, they pulled the plug on the band in the middle of their set.

The Karl Marx–inspired band Rage against the Machine's songs advocated the overthrow of traditional capitalistic society. Rage against the Machine's communistic political stance has caused some consternation between rock journalists and young fans of Rage against the Machine. Kurt Loder, in his article on the festival for *Rolling Stone*, suggested that the young people who cheered the band did not understand the true messages of the band.[22] Members of the audience who considered themselves fans of Rage against the Machine, however, argue that they do understand the communistic political and social messages of the band. This gulf between the official rock journalistic establishment, represented by Loder, and members of Generation X illustrates once again one of the truths that *Rolling Stone*'s Fred Goodman had claimed to have learned at the 1998 A Day in the Garden festival: that contrary to the conventional "wisdom" that has been widely espoused for years, rock music truly does not transcend or connect the generations.[23]

The lyrics and stage rants of musicians like the Red Hot Chili Peppers, Everclear, Rage against the Machine, Limp Bizkit, and others contrasted greatly with the performances at the 1969 Woodstock festival. One of the inspired decisions made by the original Woodstock Ventures was to make the first festival a musical—as opposed to a political—event. The one overtly political rant of the Woodstock Music and Art Fair had been Abbie Hoffman's stage announcement concerning the fate of White Panther Party founder John Sinclair, and that declamation was cut short by Who guitarist Pete Townshend's either accidental or intentional striking of Hoffman with his guitar. The other political messages of the 1969 festival had been delivered in a somewhat tongue-in-cheek manner, such as Country Joe McDonald's profane "FISH" cheer. The alternative hippie lifestyle was the counterculture message of the original Woodstock, while violent overthrow of society was the counterculture message of the close-of-the-millennium event.

Although the burning of concessions structures on the last day of the festival made headlines across the nation, one-on-one violence was also in evidence. Reporter David Samuels described one particularly horrifying scene in his *Harper's Magazine* feature article on the festival:

An hour later, I see a man about twenty-five years old, with marblewhite skin and perfectly proportioned limbs in which every last muscle is visible. His fellow concertgoers, returning from the rave with black balloons filled with nitrous oxide, give him a wide berth, because he is stark naked and obviously out of his mind. Standing in the middle of the runway, he whirs his arms over his head as if signaling to his fleet of invisible helicopters that it is time for them to land. As I stand and watch from a distance of twenty feet away, he walks up to two frat boys in T-shirts and starts talking excitedly about something. After less than a minute, the bigger of the two frat boys has heard enough. His eyes go wide, he looks down at the boy's exposed genitals, then draws his fist back and punches him hard in the face. Spat! I can hear the sound very clearly from where I am standing as the boy's nose bursts open, and then I hear Crack! as he hits the pavement face-down.[24]

Some festival attendees saw Woodstock 1999 and the fires that were set near the end of the event in a different light. A purported concert attendee who writes under the moniker "Green Mind" observed the following:

It wasn't until we slipped through the crowd of people heading towards the West Stage that we got the full extent of what was happening around us. We saw the smoke first and then the bonfires everywhere. It was like a primitive war zone inside the gates of the East Stage. . . . People were dancing around fires in huge groups of at least 50 per fire and were screaming, shaking, and singing really loudly but no one was getting hurt. . . . Having gone to Michigan State, which is affectionately known as Riot U., and I did see all the big riots. I saw the big Gunson Street riot, I saw the Munn Field Riot. . . . I was there at the Klu [sic] Klux Klan rallies where we counter-protesters (the anti-KKK people) got into fights with the police while the Klan got away scott free. . . . I've seen riots in the American sense (where no real shots are fired) and seeing what occurred at Woodstock, I wouldn't even classify it as riot at the point I left at 10:50 P.M., just a lot of people dancing around fires.[25]

"Green Mind" was describing the scene at approximately the time Megadeth was taking the stage, after what the popular press described as the riots that were raging during the Red Hot Chili Peppers' set. The writer did not seem to have seen the lighting tower torn down or witnessed the vendors' stands being destroyed. The bonfires he describes seem to have been the result of the arson of those concessions vendors' stands.

One of the few bright spots totally devoid of the violence that marred the rest of Woodstock 1999 was the Kidstock festival of children's music that was part of the festival. Organized by Beth Kohn, the festival was originally designed to be a traveling show, simply named in tribute to Woodstock. Kohn worked with Woodstock Ventures' Michael Lang, John Roberts, and Joel Rosenman to make the traveling festival part of the larger festival.

REACTIONS TO THE VIOLENCE OF WOODSTOCK 1999

Assessments of the festival by the media tended to focus on the riots, rapes, and looting and on the violence the young people of 1999 are exposed to on television and in rap, heavy metal, and punk (and various combinations thereof) music. Members of Generation X tended to place the blame on the poor setting and facilities and on what many saw as the greed of the festival's promoters and concessions vendors. The promoters themselves tended to describe the violence as the misdeeds of a few that reflected poorly on what was an otherwise successful rock festival.

As Christopher Caldwell, senior editor at *The Weekly Standard*, wrote in the *National Review*, even though Woodstock 1999 was far removed from the original Woodstock festival, "there was political protest at Woodstock '99." Caldwell, however, quotes concertgoer Don Waslelewski as pinpointing the source of the protest, which eventually spawned the riots and looting, as the festival promoters. Waslelewski stated, "I blame Michael Lang. He totally overpriced everything. He forgot what Woodstock is all about. It's 95 degrees outside and the guy is selling water for $5 a pop."[26]

When the rioting had broken out, Allen Salkin, investigative reporter for the *New York Post*, went onstage to question festival co-producer John Scher about what was transpiring. According to Salkin, "He [Scher] grabbed me and started throwing punches saying, 'don't you tell me I made a mistake, who the hell are you? It's no big deal, there are just a couple of kids out of control.' "[27] Salkin further alleged that the garbage that accumulated around the festival site, the layout, the sleep deprivation that many members of the audience endured, and the high prices for concessions items all sowed the seeds of the disaster. Alison Stateman, managing editor of *Public Relations Tactics*, studied the attempts by Scher and his fellow festival producer Michael Lang to minimize the riots. Stateman quotes sources that had witnessed earlier concert disasters as saying that Lang and Scher's attempts to explain the riots as the misdoings of a few intent on violence were misleading.[28] The third part of the Woodstock 1999 production triumvirate, Ossie Kilkenny, seemed to be less optimistic about the outcome of the festival than Lang and Scher when he stated in an interview, "Did we get anything across to people? I don't think that we did. Which is an amazing admission to make, after bringing 200,000 people together in one place and spending $38 million."[29]

As reported by Kelly Barbieri of *Amusement Business* magazine, Sonicnet.com conducted a study of the Woodstock 1999 festival, looking for the reasons behind the riots and rapes. Although festival co-producer John Scher alleged that

Sonicnet.com went into the investigation with a preset, anti-Woodstock 1999 agenda, it should be noted that the on-line company placed much of the blame for the violence on festival producers, city of Rome, New York, officials, and the hundreds of security guards hired for the event.[30] The report alleged that guards were given the answers to exam questions that were used in determining their suitability for employment at the festival. Sonicnet.com also raised concerns that concertgoers were not aware of the fact that the former Griffiss Air Force Base where the festival was held was considered by the Environmental Protection Agency to be one of the most toxic locations in America.

Sonicnet.com and the sources cited by Alison Stateman in *Public Relations Tactics* were not the only prominent sources that placed at least some of the blame for the violence on the producers of the festival. For example, in his report on Woodstock 1999, *Rolling Stone* reporter Rob Sheffield wrote, "The promoters were outrageously clueless about the physical toll that the Griffiss Air Force Base would take on the kids who paid to party there."[31] Sheffield also blamed the "sheep mentality" that inspired the mob violence, excessive drug taking by audience members, and the overly commercial nature of the entire Woodstock 1999 enterprise.

David Samuels captured the media-saturated commercial nature of Woodstock 1999 when he wrote that the festival was "a prepackaged Information-Age happening, streaming from this room [the press tent] and the video trailers parked out back into millions of brains in multiple formats, with pay-per-view, MTV, newspapers, magazines, local and national news, and the Internet adding value to the Woodstock brand and making the promoters, artists, record companies, and associated vendors happy."[32] The reader might note that notably missing from the *Harper's Magazine* contributor's assessment of who had to be kept happy was the audience.

As *Harper's Magazine* contributor David Samuels wrote, the attendees of Woodstock 1999 mentioned that they were most excited to see some of the "brand-name touring acts like the Red Hot Chili Peppers, Dave Matthews, or Korn without any greater enthusiasm than they show for the videos of these same groups, which they also like." Samuels, who attended the festival, describes the Generation Xers as "sullen." He writes that many of the young women, in their "dirty-girl allure," appeared to be "lost in a haze of sexual discomfort that makes me feel like the worst moments of my adolescence have been captured in some highly concentrated form and sprayed out over the runway like cheap perfume." In assessing Woodstock 1999, Samuels concludes that the festival "really has nothing to do with the original Woodstock at all."[33]

Amusement Business writer Ray Waddell wrote, "The wake of Woodstock '99 has been ugly. Too much ink has already been spilled regarding this festival, so I'll keep it to a minimum. You can't blame totally out of control behavior on high-priced hot dogs. What you can blame it on is a disturbing trend of spoiled, thuggish punks seeking attention and letting the mob mentality rule."[34]

Billboard magazine's Melinda Newman wrote, "Woodstock '99 was the defining moment of the year for many . . . the 30th anniversary event this summer tarnished the name sufficiently enough to make it doubtful that the organizers' plan to hold a Woodstock festival every five years will be realized." Newman continues by observing that "the ugly tone of some of the music, combined with the violent actions by some of the crowd, made for a disturbing commentary on disaffected youth and the mean-spiritedness that permeates many of our movies, music, and videos now."[35]

Press coverage of Woodstock 1999 was considered to be suspect not only by the attendees and producers who considered the majority of the problems to have been caused by the actions of a few troublemakers and to have been blown out of proportion by reporters but also by some in the press itself. Contrary to the picture of the press as being overly critical, as suggested by the festival's promoters, some of the concerns that were raised by those who study the press were with a possible profestival bias. For example, the *Columbia Journalism Review* reported on articles one Gary Graft (Gary Graff) wrote for the Oakland Press. According to the *Review*, the same Gary Graft wrote special features on the festival for Woodstock.com, the festival's official Web site. As the *Columbia Journalism Review* concludes, "Graft's story on the episode seemed evenhanded enough, but could a reader be sure?"[36]

Conservative media, like the *National Review*, gloated over the rapes, looting, and general misbehavior that took place at Woodstock 1999. According to the magazine, "The only virtue of Woodstock '99 is in showing how harmful the spirit of Woodstock '69 always was."[37] David Samuels' feature article in *Harper's Magazine* comes to a similar conclusion: "Thirty years ago something vital and lasting—an idea of the good life and how to live it, what marriage meant, what to eat, what family and community were for, and of who was supposed to take care of the kids when the parents both work—broke apart, and now, thirty years later, that sense of connection, or some overarching narrative frame for our lives, still hasn't been repaired or replaced."[38]

The violence that marred Woodstock 1999 as well as the commercial nature of the enterprise and the contrast between the sociological makeup of the audience as compared with the original Woodstock festival have also been the source of black humor. Top 10 lists, based on Dave Letterman's famous such lists on his late-night television program, can be found on the Internet and on e-mail joke lists. One such Internet list of the Top Ten Differences between the 1969 Woodstock Music and Art Fair and Woodstock 1999 includes the following: "#10, 1969. . . . Ignited a Generation, 1999. . . . Generated an Ignition; #9, 1969. . . . Three days of Peace, Love, and Music, 1999. . . . 3 Days of Pay Per View for $89.95; and #8, 1969. . . . 'I was there, man . . . ,' 1999 . . . 'My client refuses to answer on the grounds it may incriminate him.' "[39] Within days of the festival, *The Economist* magazine published similarly dark-humored lyrics set to the tune of Bob Dylan's "The Times, They Are A-Changin'." *The Economist*'s "Woodstock, 1999" referred to the overturning of ATMs, the overly commercial nature of the festival, the fires that were set, the rain that plagued the festival, and the differences in the nature of the Woodstock 1999 crowd compared with that of the original 1969 festival.[40]

Some Woodstock 1999 attendees have attempted to portray the festival in a very different light from that which the media image. One purported attendee, who uses the alias Green Mind, has set up the Web site *Woodstock Journal 1999*, which records his activities and day-to-day reactions to the festival. According to the mission statement on the author's Web site, "Green Mind's Woodstock 1999 Journal and the other sites in the Woodstock 1999 Truth Network Webring are devoted to getting out the message that there was both good and bad at Woodstock 1999. We all attended the event and are independent of any national publication. It is our goal to make sure a true picture of Woodstock 1999 is presented as opposed to just the biased picture of violence portrayed by the media!"[41] Green Mind's journal and those of other Truth Network Webring members provide real-time, first-person accounts of many sociological aspects of Woodstock 1999, including (1) the types of drugs concertgoers used, including ephedrine, ecstasy, marijuana, and others; (2) the importance of the Internet in making travel arrangements and making sense out of the evolving nature of the festival's actual lineup and rumored lineup of performers; (3) the frat-boy nature of some of the festival's attendees; and (4) that male concertgoers were already trying to get female concertgoers to show off their breasts on the caravan to the festival but that the intensity of sexual pressure increased throughout the festival, sometimes incited by the onstage musicians. Although Internet sources can easily provide information of dubious quality, it should be noted that the establishment and maintenance of the Webring suggest the sense of ownership that Woodstock 1999 attendees have for "their" Woodstock.

The use of Webrings, blogs, and other such electronic communications forums also illustrates the extent to which society had changed technologically from 1969 to 1994 to 1999. First-person remembrances of attendees of the 1969 festival were published in books that began to appear years after the event—in the case of Joel Makower's oral history book, twenty years after the first Woodstock festival. The audiotaped oral Woodstock history project undertaken at Youngstown State University relied on memories twenty-five years after the 1969 festival. While graduate students in sociology attended Woodstock '94 looking for thesis and dissertation material, computer technology, especially involving the Internet, was still novel enough that a display of interactive computer technology generated considerable attention at the 1994 event.[42] By 1999, the Internet was used to make travel arrangements and to publish first-person accounts of the festival to the entire wired world by purported attendees almost instantly.

Not only did the Woodstock 1999 festival generate humor and considerable controversy, particularly after the looting, arson, and rapes were reported, but attempts by the New York State Police to identify the perpetrators of those crimes also generated controversy and press coverage. The police organization digitized copyrighted photographs of rioters that had been published by several news organizations and published them on the State Police Web site. News organizations such as the Associated Press, the New York Press Association, the *New York Daily News*, the *New York Times*, and Syracuse Online complained that the actions by New York State Police violated copyright laws and compromised the freedom of the press.[43] The police removed the photos from the Web, but officials insisted that their actions were not due to the complaints that had been lodged by news organizations. According to the State Police, the photos were removed because they proved not to be helpful in identifying the rioters.

A DAY IN THE GARDEN 1998 AND 1999

Although the Woodstock 1999 festival that took place in Rome, New York, proved to be something of an antithesis of the original hippie-era Woodstock Music and Art Fair, a much smaller and significantly more peaceful and less commercially oriented minifestival took place at the site of Max Yasgur's farm. Dubbed "A Day in the Garden," from a line in Joni Mitchell's song "Woodstock," this event largely featured performers who played at the original Woodstock festival of 1969. Approximately 13,000 people attended A Day in the Garden.[44]

The owner of the site, cable television pioneer Alan Gerry, had staged a weekend festival in August 1998, which had attracted as many as approximately 73,000 people.[45] The 1998 event included performers from the late 1960s Woodstock era, such as Joni Mitchell, Pete Townshend of The Who, Donovan, Richie Havens, Lou Reed, and Ten Years After. New bands, like the Goo Goo Dolls, Third Eye Blind, and Marcy Playground, however, "proved to be the bigger draw," according to *Business Week* reporter Anthony Bianco.[46] Other artists who appeared at the 1998 A Day in the Garden Festival included Dishwalla, The Flys, and Joan Osborne. *Rolling Stone* rock critic Fred Goodman especially praised the sets by Pete Townshend, Joan Osborne, and Marcy Playground. Goodman, however, found sets by Melanie, Donovan, Richie Havens, and Ten Years After to be little more than nostalgia. He also pointed out one of the more interesting "discoveries" of the 1998 A Day in the Garden festival, that "the notion that rock transcends generations" is false.[47] As discussed, this generational difference would become even more evident at the Woodstock 1999 festival, which was seen by some as something of an indictment of the so-called Generation X.

Since 1999 was the year of the official thirtieth-anniversary festival, Woodstock 1999, the year's A Day in the Garden festival was a considerably smaller event than the 1998 festival on the site of the old Yasgur farm had been. A Day in the Garden 1999 drew approximately 13,000, according to the *Music Festival Home Page*.[48] Although the 1999 festival opened with the newer band Jake's Blues, followed by Donna Andreeff and Winnie Bergner's relatively new group, Anatara, the majority of the performers had been connected with the Woodstock Music and Art Fair of 1969.

Woodstock alumni who performed at the 1999 festival on the site of the Yasgur farm included the following: Country Joe McDonald, who performed "Not So Sweet Martha Loraine," "I-Feel-Like-I'm-Fixin'-to-Die Rag," and other songs; Melanie, who performed "Birthday of the Sun," "Beautiful People," and "Look What They've Done to My Song Ma"[49]; Rick Danko and Garth Hudson of The Band, who performed "Ophelia," "Chest Fever," and "Shape I'm In"; Leslie West, formerly of Mountain, who performed "For Yasgur's Farm," "Mississippi Queen," and "Theme from an Imaginary Western"; Richie Havens, who performed "All Along the Watchtower,"[50] "Blood on the Wire," "Freedom," and "Motherless Child"; Arlo Guthrie, who appeared with his children Sarah and Abe and sang "The House of the Rising Sun,"[51] "The Sinking of the Ruben James," "Coming into Los Angeles," and "City of New Orleans"; David Crosby, who with his then-current band CPR performed "Long Time Gone," "Wooden Ships, "Almost Cut My Hair," and "Ohio," as well as several newer CPR songs; and Johnny Winter, who performed "Got My Mojo Workin'," "Black Jack Game," and his brother Edgar's hit song "Frankenstein."

NOTES

1. Samuels, David, "Rock Is Dead (Woodstock 1999)," *Harper's Magazine* (November 1999).

2. Zielbauer, Paul, "Woodstock Arrives and Mood Is Mellow," *New York Times* July 22, 1999, p. B5.

3. Loder, Kurt, "Tales from Satan's Playground," *Rolling Stone* n820 (September 2, 1999), p. 56.

4. *The Woodstock 1999 Truth Network Web Ring*, http://www.geocities.com/TheTropics/Bay/9641/wring.html.

5. Goodman, Fred, "Performance," *Rolling Stone* n796 (October 1, 1998), p. 32.

6. Sheffield, Rob, "Rage against the Latrines," *Rolling Stone* n820 (September 2, 1999), pp. 52+.

7. Sheffield, "Rage against the Latrines."

8. Samuels, "Rock Is Dead (Woodstock 1999)."

9. Samuels, "Rock Is Dead (Woodstock 1999)."

10. "Bands and Fans Feel the Heat at Woodstock Reunion," *Christian Science Monitor* July 26, 1999, p. 5.

11. "Bands and Fans Feel the Heat at Woodstock Reunion."

12. Sheffield, "Rage against the Latrines."

13. Loder, "Tales from Satan's Playground."

14. Bush, John, "Rusted Root," *All Music Guide*, http://www.allmusic.com, accessed April 2, 2004.

15. Huey, Steve, "Sheryl Crow," *All Music Guide*, http://www.allmusic.com, accessed March 30, 2004.

16. Sheffield, "Rage against the Latrines," pp. 52+.

17. Although Wyclef Jean might be better known as a rapper in his work as a member of the Fugees and as a solo artist, he also plays guitar.

18. *Michael Lang Answers Questions about Woodstock '99*, http://members.aol.com/Mary1NYS/Lang2.html, accessed October 23, 2003.

19. *Michael Lang Answers Questions about Woodstock '99*.

20. *USA Today* July 27, 1999, quoted in "Woodstock 1999," *Wikipedia*, http://en.wikipedia.org/wiki/Woodstock_1999.

21. Loder, "Tales from Satan's Playground," pp. 56+.

22. Loder, "Tales from Satan's Playground."

23. Goodman, "Performance."

24. Samuels, "Rock Is Dead (Woodstock 1999)."

25. Green Mind, *Woodstock 1999 Journal: July 25, Part 2*, http://www.geocities.com/TheTropics/Bay/9641/july25b.html, accessed January 29, 2004.

26. Caldwell, Christopher, "When in Rome. The Horrid Spirit of Woodstock," *National Review* 51/16 (August 30, 1999), p. 29.

27. Stateman, Alison, "Bonfire of the Inanities," *Public Relations Tactics* 6/10 (October 1999), pp. 1+.

28. Stateman, "Bonfire of the Inanities."

29. Samuels, "Rock Is Dead (Woodstock 1999)."

30. Barbieri, Kelly, "Sonicnet Releases Report Detailing Problems during Woodstock 1999," *Amusement Business* 112/350 (July 24, 2000), pp. 8+.

31. Sheffield, "Rage against the Latrines," pp. 52+.

32. Samuels, "Rock Is Dead (Woodstock 1999)."

33. Samuels, "Rock Is Dead (Woodstock 1999)."

34. Waddell, Ray, "Volunteering Information," *Amusement Business* 111/34 (August 23, 1999), p. 3.

35. Newman, Melinda, "Martin Is Artist of the Year . . ." *Billboard* 111–12/51–1 (December 25, 1999–January 1, 2000), pp. 18+.

36. "Darts and Laurels," *Columbia Journalism Review* 38/4 (November–December 1999), p. 18.

37. "Forever Woodstock," *National Review* 51/16 (August 30, 1999), pp. 14+.

38. Samuels, "Rock Is Dead (Woodstock 1999)."

39. *The Top 10 Differences between Woodstock 69 and Woodstock 99*, http://members.aol.com/Mary1NYS/Top10.html.

40. "Woodstock, 1999 (With Apologies to Bob Dylan)," *The Economist* 352/8130 (July 31, 1999).

41. Green Mind, *Woodstock Journal 1999*.

42. Norman, Ken, and Brenda Butterworth, "Peace, Love and Multimedia," *Video Magazine* (November 1994), p. 12.

43. Walker, David, "Pdnews," *Photo District News* 19/10 (October 1999), pp. 14+.

44. *The Music Festival Home Page*, http://www.geocities.com/~music-festival/, accessed May 13, 2003.

45. Bianco, Anthony, "Alan Gerry's Woodstock Nation," *Business Week* n3621 (March 22, 1999), pp. 66+. Reports closer to the time of the festival put the total paid attendance at closer to 55,000. See Goodman, Fred, "Performance," *Rolling Stone* n796 (October 1, 1998), p. 32.

46. Bianco, Anthony, "Alan Gerry's Woodstock Nation," *Business Week* (March 22, 1999), pp. 66+.

47. Goodman, "Performance."

48. *The Music Festival Home Page*.

49. "Look What They've Done to My Song Ma," which was written by Melanie, was a 1970 hit for the New Seekers.

50. The Bob Dylan composition "All Along the Watchtower" has long been associated with Jimi Hendrix, whose psychedelic version of the song with his band the Experience reached number 20 on the *Billboard* pop singles chart and was a well-known album track in 1968.

51. Although "The House of the Rising Sun" has been associated with The Animals as a result of their number 1 hit single version of the song of 1964. The song is actually a nineteenth-century American folk song, which, interestingly, was originally intended to be sung through the narrative voice of a female character.

An A-to-Z of the Woodstock
Music and Art Fair

ABRAHAM, MORRIS A real estate salesman by trade, Morris Abraham played a small, but absolutely crucial, role for the organizers of the Woodstock Music and Art Fair. By mid-July 1969, when it became clear that the Wallkill, New York, site would not be usable for the festival, Woodstock Ventures had only a month to go before the event was scheduled. White Lake, New York, dairy farm owner Max Yasgur was among those who saw Woodstock Ventures' advertisement soliciting property on which the festival could be held. Morris Abraham was the middle-man who introduced Michael Lang and Mel Lawrence to Max and Miriam Yasgur. The Yasgurs leased part of their farm to the concert promoters so that the festival could take place.

ABRUZZI, BILL The so-called Rock Doc, Bill Abruzzi ran medical operations for Woodstock Ventures. Dr. Abruzzi's work at Woodstock led to high regard for his medical expertise among rock musicians and promoters, hence his nickname. He would handle medical operations for other concerts and festivals following Woodstock.

ALTAMONT On December 6, 1969, The Rolling Stones held a free, one-day rock festival at California's Altamont Speedway. The original site of the event was to have been San Francisco's Golden Gate Park; however, the San Francisco City Council failed to approve the necessary permits, and the event was moved to the Altamont demolition derby track just days before it was scheduled to take place. Because of the timing of the change of venue for the festival, certain details were not fully worked out. For example, the hastily constructed stage was too low, which offered far too easy access for adventuresome audience members, and water and food were not available in sufficient supply for the size of the crowd. In addition to the Rolling Stones, performers at Altamont included Santana, The Grateful Dead, the Jefferson Airplane, Crosby, Stills, Nash, and Young, and The Flying

Burrito Brothers.[1] This concert was meant to conclude the Rolling Stones' tour of North America and looked to be a northern California—Rolling Stones version of the Woodstock Music and Art Fair of only a few months before. Unfortunately, the Hell's Angels motorcycle gang was hired to work security at the suggestion of members of The Grateful Dead. Members of the security force were involved in fights with members of the audience, knocked out the Jefferson Airplane's Marty Balin in the middle of the Airplane's set, and ended up killing one concertgoer and injuring others. The concert was the site of numerous drug overdoses and "bad trips." If Woodstock represented the high point of the hippie philosophy and lifestyle in action, then Altamont can be said to have represented the low point. ***See also* Rolling Stones, The.**

AMATUCCI, DANIEL J.   Daniel J. Amatucci was the village supervisor of Bethel, New York, at the time of the Woodstock festival. As a result of the various permits that Woodstock Ventures needed to secure for the festival, as well as due to the other various legal wranglings that preceded the festival, Amatucci played an active role in making sure that the interests of Bethel were represented in the days and weeks leading up to the Woodstock Music and Art Fair.

ART   While Woodstock is best remembered for its concerts, there was an art exhibition at the Woodstock Music and Art Fair. While the art exhibition often is overlooked, it was highly touted by Michael Lang, Artie Kornfeld, Joel Rosenman, and John Roberts when they were trying to secure clearance for the festival to take place in the Town of Wallkill. In fact, the festival organizers secured a tentative OK from the town's government for the festival by describing the event as an art show that would also include some music. Residents soon learned that the intent of Woodstock Ventures really was to focus on the music, something that played into the protests against the festival that the Concerned Citizens of Wallkill organized and that eventually drove Woodstock Ventures out of Wallkill. Peter Leeds and Howard Hirsch organized the art exhibition that was part of the Woodstock festival when it took place at the Yasgur farm in Bethel, New York. This exhibit included contemporary arts as well as Native American-influenced arts, both of which were in keeping with the hippie, Back to the Land nature of the festival. The Native American arts exhibit was coordinated in part by Billy Soza, himself a Native American artist. Probably the most visible art at the festival, however, was the various pieces that could be found around the festival site. Art students, who were working under the direction of University of Miami art professors Ron Liis and Bill Ward, with assistance from Jean Ward, produced these contemporary sculptures.

ATLANTIC CITY POP MUSIC FESTIVAL   The Atlantic City Pop Music Festival took place August 1–3, 1969, just two weeks prior to the Woodstock Music and Art Fair, at the Atlantic City Race Track, outside Atlantic City, New Jersey. The festival featured sets by a large contingent of big-name rock and jazz performers, including some who had appeared at the Newport Jazz Festival or the Newport Folk

Festival or who would appear at Woodstock. The bill included the following: Johnny Winter, Crosby, Stills, Nash, and Young, Joni Mitchell, Frank Zappa and the Mothers of Invention, Santana, the Jefferson Airplane, Creedence Clearwater Revival, the Paul Butterfield Blues Band, Janis Joplin, Canned Heat, Joe Cocker, the Buddy Rich Big Band, Chicago, Procol Harem, Booker T. and the MGs, The Sir Douglas Quintet, Little Richard, Dr. John, The Crazy World of Arthur Brown, Tim Buckley, Mother Earth, The Moody Blues, The Doors, the Buddy Miles Express, Hugh Masekela, and others. It could be argued that this roster was approximately the same strength as that of Woodstock. In contrast to Woodstock, which drew 400,000, even at conservative estimates, however, the Atlantic City Pop Music Festival, which took place in the same general region of the country and in the same month, drew approximately 110,000 fans and has since become something of a footnote in the history of 1960s and 1970s rock festivals. The contrast between the attendance at the two events and the relative historical esteem with which each is viewed today can best be attributed to location and setting (Woodstock, a bucolic dairy farm; Atlantic City, a racetrack), and the way in which Woodstock Ventures advertised their festival as a sort of underground, counterculture happening. The success of the Woodstock advertising campaign and the fact that the Music and Art Fair actually became the very sort of counterculture hippie happening it was advertised to be are especially interesting to consider in terms of the way in which it contrasted with the rather conventional pop festival that the Atlantic City event two weeks previously had been.

BABBS, KEN   At the time of the Woodstock festival Ken Babbs was a member of the Hog Farm commune. Before the festival began, promoter Michael Lang asked Babbs and fellow Hog Farm members Tom Law and Wavy Gravy to clear the site of the 50,000 early arrivals so that they would be forced to come back through the ticket gates. With their knowledge of the mind-set of the hippies, Babbs and his fellow Hog Farmers suggested to Woodstock Ventures that forcing the early arrivers out so that they would have to present tickets in order to reenter the grounds was likely to provoke outrage and possibly rioting. Ultimately, the early arrivals were allowed to stay. ***See also*** **Hog Farm, The.**

BACK TO THE LAND MOVEMENT   The Back to the Land and environmental movements were starting to capture the attention not just of the counterculture but also of the whole of U.S. society in the late 1960s. Historian David Farber credits Stewart Brand, one of author Ken Kesey's Merry Pranksters, with coordinating "an effort that produced *The Whole Earth Catalog*, a compendium of practical and theoretical information for people who wanted to set up rural communes or otherwise take part in the back-to-the-land movement."[2] The communal Back to the Land movement seemed to spring in part from disillusionment with the violence that had erupted at antiwar rallies in 1968 and in particular with the riots that marred the Democratic National Convention in Chicago. With this social movement came a new interest in country music among young people, the development of country-rock music, and an interest in returning to more natural surroundings.

Joan Baez was one of the leading protest singers in the early- to mid-1960s. Her appearance at Woodstock represented one of the few direct connections between the festival and the early 1960s Greenwich Village folk-protest movement. (Courtesy of Photofest)

The communal spirit of the Woodstock Music and Art Fair fitted right in with the Back to the Land movement. The festival also included performances of songs that reflected the spirit of the movement, most notably the Alan Wilson composition "Going up the Country," which Wilson's band, Canned Heat, performed at Woodstock. Other Woodstock performers associated with the Back to the Land movement included Joan Baez, due primarily to her bringing traditional folk and country musicians and music to the attention of hippies, and The Band, due to their country-rock style. Joni Mitchell's song "Woodstock," which chronicled the festival and was made famous by Crosby, Stills, Nash, and Young, also reflects the spirit of the Back to the Land movement in terms of the way in which she metaphorically links the concert attendees' pilgrimage to Woodstock with a return to the biblical Garden of Eden.

BAEZ, JOAN   Born January 9, 1941, in Staten Island, New York, Joan Baez became one of the most visible musical figures of the folk revival. Baez appeared frequently at antiwar rallies throughout the counterculture era, usually singing old folk songs and the songs of her contemporaries like Phil Ochs and (mostly) Bob Dylan. While other musicians may have composed the greatest anthems of the antiwar movement, Baez was highly influential in getting the music out to a wider public and in rallying like-minded protesters. Baez also encouraged older traditional country and folk musicians like Maybelle Carter and Doc Watson to perform at concerts aimed at young people. In doing so, she was in part responsible for some of the newfound popularity of these forms with new audiences, many of whom became closely aligned with the Back to the Land movement. At Woodstock, Baez mixed traditional folk songs, folk-rock songs, and topical songs, singing "Joe Hill," "Sweet Sir Galahad," "Drug Store Truck Driving Man," "Swing Low, Sweet Chariot," and "We Shall Overcome." True to her beliefs, Baez also performed a free, spontaneous solo set at the free stage at Woodstock. She was the only major star to do so. Despite her solid credentials in bringing music to the people (as she had done through her free performance at Woodstock), Baez would be one of the American folksingers who would be booed by British rock fans for having abandoned social issues in her music at the 1970 Isle of Wight Festival.

BAND, THE   This musical ensemble, which featured a unique combination of traditional folk, blues, rock, and country styles, consisted of Canadians Robbie

Robertson (acoustic bass, bass guitar, piano, vocals, and principal songwriter), Richard Manuel (keyboards, drums, vocals), Garth Hudson (keyboards, accordion, brass, woodwinds), and Rick Danko (bass, fiddle, vocals), as well as American Levon Helm (drums, vocals). The Band developed out of Canadian artist Ronnie Hawkins' backing group. By 1965, Helm and Robertson joined with keyboardist Al Kooper (a founding member and original lead vocalist of Blood, Sweat, and Tears), however, in backing Bob Dylan on his concert tour of that year. After a serious motorcycle accident put Dylan's career on hold the following year, Dylan and members of The Band moved to Woodstock, New York. Dylan and the group recorded the album that became known as *The Basement Tapes*. Dylan and The Band were central to the new rock-recording scene that was emerging in the town of Woodstock, and this scene was the impetus to Michael Lang and Artie Kornfeld's desire to build a state-of-the-art recording studio at Woodstock. Aside from their collaborations with Dylan, The Band had released the acclaimed album *Music from Big Pink* in 1968 and had made their debut at Bill Graham's venue, Winterland, in San Francisco in early 1969. Although The Band achiev-

Rock group The Band is shown during their farewell concert "The Last Waltz" at the Winterland Auditorium in San Francisco in this November 25, 1976 photo. From the left are vocalist Rick Danko, guitarist Robbie Robertson, and drummer Levon Helm. (AP/Wide World Photos)

ed its greatest success after the Woodstock festival, their work with Bob Dylan played a crucial role in the meeting of Lang, Kornfeld, Rosenman, and Roberts in their quest to organize a concert that would fund a new recording studio. At the Woodstock Music and Art Fair, The Band performed "Chest Fever," "Don't Do It," "Tears of Rage," "We Can Talk about It Now," "Long Black Veil," "Don't Ya Tell Henry," "Ain't No More Cane on the Brazos," "Wheels on Fire," "Loving You Is Sweeter than Ever," and "The Weight." Incidentally, Robbie Robertson's song "The Weight" was later a centerpiece of the counterculture film *Easy Rider*. The Band has since been enshrined in the Rock and Roll Hall of Fame.

BASTARD SONS, THE   "The Bastard Sons" was the rather self-mocking, irreverent name taken up by the members of the construction crew for the Woodstock festival. Among the major projects that had to be hastily put together by the construction crew were the stage and the large sound towers, the latter of which were routinely compromised throughout the festival by adventurous audience members who attempted to climb them.

BEATLES, THE   Arguably the biggest pop music act of the 1960s, The Beatles (John Lennon, rhythm guitar and vocals; Paul McCartney, bass guitar and vocals; George Harrison, lead guitar and vocals; and Ringo Starr, drums) performed their final concert at San Francisco's Candlestick Park three years prior to Woodstock.[3] According to the recollections of several of the principals and staff members of the Woodstock operation, there were attempts in spring 1969 to get The Beatles to appear at Woodstock. To what extent this possibility was investigated or even considered by The Beatles themselves remains somewhat unclear. The band had done a surprise forty-two-minute rooftop performance in London's posh financial district on January 30, 1969. This rooftop performance, which was done with the assistance of American keyboardist Billy Preston, took place in front of a few friends and a film crew: the event was staged for the film *Let It Be*. Rumors of possible surprise appearances by The Beatles circulated at various performance venues throughout 1969, including the Woodstock Music and Art Fair, probably fueled in part by the band's surprise rooftop performance.

BETHEL BUSINESSMAN'S ASSOCIATION   The Bethel Businessman's Association consisted of ninety business leaders in the Bethel, New York, area. In a meeting the organization held on July 28, 1969, they voted to support the Woodstock festival. In part, the association's support of the festival was probably a testament to the esteem with which Max Yasgur was held in the community. In any case, the association's vote sharply contrasted with the actions of community and business leaders in the other locations in which Woodstock Ventures had attempted to secure a festival site. *See also* **Van Loan, Ken.**

BETHEL, NEW YORK   The village of White Lake, located in the town of Bethel, Sullivan County, New York, became the site of the Woodstock Music and Art Fair after the Wallkill site fell through. Although the festival was only one month away, Max and Miriam Yasgur saw the advertisements that Woodstock Ventures had placed in several newspapers and met the festival organizers through real estate agent Morris Abraham. Although a number of citizens of the predominantly conservative community attempted to block the festival, the response to the festival was considerably more positive than the response Woodstock Ventures had received in the Town of Wallkill, New York. Judge George L. Cobb, who heard arguments pertaining to the festival, allowed the event to proceed. *See also* **Bethel Businessman's Association.**

BLOOD, SWEAT, AND TEARS   Several prominent bands that appeared at Woodstock were not represented on the multidisc recording that came out of the festival due to contractual intrigues between the various record companies involved. Such was the case with Blood, Sweat, and Tears. This jazz-rock ensemble, fronted by lead singer David Clayton-Thomas,[4] was an especially hot act at the time of the Woodstock festival: their spring 1969 singles "You've Made Me So Very Happy" and "Spinning Wheel" had both gone all the way to number 2 on the pop charts, each holding that position for several weeks. The band also appeared at the 1969 Newport Jazz Festival and would hit number 2 on the pop singles charts in late 1969 with the single "And When I Die." At Woodstock, Blood, Sweat, and Tears performed "More and More," "I Love You Baby More than You'll Ever Know," their recent hit single "Spinning Wheel," the great soul standard "I Stand Accused," and "Something Coming On." Even though Blood, Sweat, and Tears was the band that put jazz-rock on the musical map and was among the biggest commercial successes at the time of their Woodstock performance, the group's career went into

Although their popularity faded away quickly after a 1970 tour of Europe under the auspices of the U.S. State Department, Blood, Sweat, and Tears was arguably the leading jazz-rock band at the time of their appearance at Woodstock. (Courtesy of Photofest)

a hasty downhill slide. A 1970 tour of Eastern Europe that Blood, Sweat, and Tears performed under the sponsorship of the U.S. State Department put them into a bad light with many of their fans; this was the same U.S. government that was waging an increasingly unpopular war in Vietnam. The group Chicago quickly stepped in as the premier jazz-rock band in pop music and Blood, Sweat, and Tears enjoyed virtually no commercial success after 1971.

CANNED HEAT   Probably best known for their 1968 top 40 singles "Going up the Country" and "On the Road Again" (not to be confused with the Willie Nelson song with a similar title) and for the falsetto blues style of singer Bob "The Bear" Hite, Canned Heat was a Los Angeles-based "boogie" band. Their chug-along, blues-based style was popular with live audiences and can be heard to good effect in their set at Woodstock, which included "A Change Is Gonna Come/Leaving This Town," "Woodstock Boogie," "Going up the Country," "Let's Work Together," and "Too Many Drivers at the Wheel." Tragically, vocalist Hite and guitarist-songwriter Alan Wilson later died of drug-related causes.

COBB, GEORGE L.   Judge George L. Cobb of the village of Catskill, New York, heard arguments related to an action filed by the owners of four summer camps in the vicinity of the Bethel, New York, site of the Woodstock Music and Art Fair. The camp owners tried to stop the festival on the grounds that their camps would be adversely affected by being overrun by hippies. The hearing took place in late July 1969, and Woodstock Ventures attorney Paul Marshall reached an out-of-court settlement. Judge Cobb, however, also heard arguments from four co-owners of a vacation home adjacent to the Yasgur farm that sought to block the festival on similar grounds. Ultimately, the judge ruled that the festival could proceed.

A rarity in the late 1960s, English singer Joe Cocker excelled at performing songs written by others. Cocker's concert intensity is captured in this movie still from the documentary film *Woodstock: Three Days of Peace and Music.* (Courtesy of Photofest)

COCKER, JOE   Joe Cocker, born May 20, 1944, in Sheffield, England, has had a long career as a rock singer. His stage performance style is easily recognizable for the jerky, spastic motions he makes while singing. These mannerisms apparently were based on the motions of Ray Charles at the piano, and they were widely parodied when Cocker was at his popular peak in the 1970s. In one notable example, American comedian John Belushi imitated and mirrored the British singer when Cocker appeared on *Saturday Night Live.* Joe Cocker performed the following songs at Woodstock: "Delta Lady," "Something's Goin' On," "Let's Go Get Stoned" (which had been recorded by Ray Charles), "I Shall Be Released," and "With a Little Help from My Friends." Cocker was not well known in the United States at the time of his Woodstock appearance, and Woodstock Ventures had at first been reluctant to sign him. Cocker, however, would undertake the mammoth and highly publicized "Mad Dogs and Englishmen" tour of America in 1970, the year he finally reached the pop singles top 10 with his remake of the song, "The Letter." Cocker's appearance at Woodstock, his "Mad Dogs and Englishmen" tour, and the subsequent recordings that came out of it secured Cocker's place as a blues-based rock singer of major importance. He has continued to record and perform in concerts into the twenty-first century.

COHEN, RALPH   Ralph Cohen was a member of the New York Police Department who did security recruitment for the Woodstock Music and Art Fair. ***See also* New York Police Department.**

COHEN, STEVE Steve Cohen worked as a production stage manager for the Woodstock Music and Art Fair. In addition to managing the stage and the between-acts setups during the festival, Cohen's principal contribution to the festival was the actual design and construction of the stage. *See also* **Bastard Sons, The.**

CONCERNED CITIZENS COMMITTEE OF WALLKILL After it became evident that the organizers of the Woodstock Music and Art Fair were not going to be able to hold the festival in Woodstock itself (nor in Saugerties, New York, another location that fell through), they selected a site in the Town of Wallkill, New York, closer to New York City in Orange County. The Concerned Citizens Committee of Wallkill was a group of residents of the area who fought against holding the festival in their community. These citizens were concerned with what they saw as an invasion of hippies. They feared vandalism, drug use, free sex, and the ensuing corruption of the morals of the youth of the Wallkill area. Joel Rosenman's infamous "no-smoking" memo helped to galvanize the resolve of the group. Although the memo had been designed to paint festival promoters as responsible citizens who would not tolerate the use of illegal drugs, it served to raise suspicions among the citizens of Wallkill that drug-crazed hippies were actually behind the entire operation. The Concerned Citizens Committee was largely responsible for forcing representatives of Woodstock Ventures to appear before the Wallkill Town Board on June 12, 1969. By mid-July, the citizens of Wallkill had successfully driven the festival out of their community by means of legal challenges and the passage of a new local law regulating gatherings of over 5,000 people. With the festival less than a month away, there were grave concerns among the organizers that a suitable site might not be found in time and that the Concerned Citizens Committee of Wallkill may have effectively killed the festival.

COUNTRY JOE AND THE FISH Led by singer-songwriter-guitarist Joe McDonald (born 1942), Country Joe and the Fish was one of the most notorious underground groups of the counterculture era. San Francisco was fertile ground for the development of American psychedelic and protest music in the early to mid-1960s, and Country Joe and the Fish was one of the groups to come out of this environment. Unlike several of the other San Francisco bands that developed broad commercial appeal, Joe McDonald and his band developed a more underground counterculture appeal, closely tied to the Berkeley radical political movement of the time period. Country Joe and the Fish provided one of the great antiwar songs of the Vietnam conflict in their "I-Feel-Like-I'm-Fixin'-to-Die Rag," a song that was performed both by McDonald as a solo singer and by the group in separate sets at Woodstock. Joe McDonald was not scheduled to perform a solo set at the festival but agreed to do so on Friday, August 15, 1969, in order to help the festival organizers fill time while the scheduled acts arrived. McDonald performed the following songs in this solo set: "Janis," "Rocking 'round the World," "Flyin' High," "I Seen a Rocket," and "I-Feel-Like-I'm-Fixin'-to-Die Rag." The entire band appeared on Sunday, August 17, 1969, and performed "Rock and Soul

Music," "Barry's Song,"[5] "Not So Sweet Martha Lorraine," "Thing Called Love," "The Love Machine," and the aforementioned antiwar song for which they were well known. Incidentally, in live performance "I-Feel-Like-I'm-Fixin'-to-Die Rag" was usually preceded by what was known as the "FISH Cheer." McDonald would say "Give me an 'F,' " to which the crowd would shout, "F." McDonald would then continue, "Give me a 'U,' " "Give me a 'C,' " and "Give me a 'K.' " He would then ask, "What's that spell?" Since the use of the word has become considerably more commonplace in music, films, and everyday life in the early twenty-first century, the fact is sometimes lost that in the 1960s, the public use of the word was considered a strong counterculture statement uttered to defy the norms of traditional society. Incidentally, due to the relatively strong political messages of the band, Woodstock executive producer Michael Lang was hesitant to book Country Joe and the Fish. According to Bill Belmont, a concert tour organizer for the Doors who was in contact with the Woodstock Ventures office in New York City in summer 1969, Country Joe and the Fish were hired only after Jeff Beck canceled his performance, opening up a space that needed to be filled in the festival lineup.[6] Lang's reluctance to book the band is ironic in light of the fact that Country Joe and the Fish provided one truly authentic link to the counterculture, and in his public statements and appearances advertising the festival, Lang continuously played up the festival as an authentic counterculture happening. Although Country Joe and the Fish faded as a group, several members of the band remained active: Joe McDonald continued to appear in concerts (including Woodstock '94), and Barry Melton emerged in California politics and as a writer-commentator on the American counterculture.

CREEDENCE CLEARWATER REVIVAL Featuring singer-lead guitarist-songwriter John C. Fogerty, bassist Stu Cook, rhythm guitarist Tom Fogerty, and drummer Doug Clifford, Creedence Clearwater Revival was the top pop music sales leader of 1969 and 1970 in terms of record sales. Prior to the Woodstock Music and Art Fair the band had recorded three number 2 pop hits ("Proud Mary," "Bad Moon Rising," and "Green River"). After the August festival they would have six more top 10 hits into mid-1971. CCR, as they have become known, was a straight-ahead rock band that owed a debt of gratitude to blues, soul, and Louisiana swamp music. Their Woodstock set consisted of "Born on the Bayou," "Green River," "Ninety-Nine-and-a-Half (Won't Do)," "Commotion," "Bootleg," "Bad Moon Rising," "Proud Mary," "I Put a Spell on You," "Night Time Is the Right Time," "Keep on Chooglin'," and "Susie Q." Despite the fact that they were perhaps the hottest band commercially at the time of the festival, they were not represented on the *Woodstock* multidisc album due to contractual differences between the band's record label, Fantasy, and Atlantic Records, which produced the Woodstock concert disc. Tom Fogerty left the band in 1971 to pursue a solo career and died in 1990. After Creedence Clearwater Revival disbanded in the early 1970s, John Fogerty continued to write, sing, and produce chart singles as a soloist in the 1970s and 1980s, including the 1984–85 hit "The Old Man Down the Road." Cree-

One of the hottest rock bands at the time of the Woodstock Music and Art Fair, Creedence Clearwater Revival featured the talents of (left to right) Tom Fogerty, John Fogerty, Stu Cook, and Doug Clifford. (Courtesy of Photofest)

dence Clearwater Revival was inducted into the Rock and Roll Hall of Fame in 1993.

CROSBY, STILLS, NASH, AND YOUNG A "supergroup" in every sense of the term, each member of this ensemble had made important contributions to rock music before they ever performed or recorded together. David Crosby (born David Van Cortland, August 14, 1941, in Los Angeles) had been a member of the Byrds when they had recorded the hits "Mr. Tambourine Man," "Turn! Turn! Turn! (To Everything There Is a Season)," and "Eight Miles High." Stephen Stills (born January 3, 1945, in Dallas) and Neil Young (born November 12, 1945, in Toronto, Ontario, Canada) had been members of the Buffalo Springfield when that group recorded Stills' well-known commentary on the conflicts between protesters and "straight" society, "For What It's Worth." Graham Nash (born February 2, 1942, in Blackpool, Lancashire, England) had been a member of the highly commercially successful British group the Hollies ("Bus Stop," "Carrie Ann," and "Stop, Stop, Stop"). Although Crosby, Stills, and Nash had been working together for only a relatively short time when the Woodstock festival took place, and although Neil Young did not officially join the group for commercial recordings until 1970, this quartet made its debut shortly before their appearance at Woodstock. In fact, the group joked with the crowd, telling the audience that this only their second gig in front of people. Their Woodstock set consisted of "Suite: Judy Blue Eyes,"

Although David Crosby, Stephen Stills, and Graham Nash performed a trio set at Woodstock, they were joined for several songs by Neil Young. Left to right: Nash, Crosby, Young, and Stills. In addition to their performance at Woodstock, Crosby, Stills, Nash, and Young also helped to immortalize the festival through their hit recording of Joni Mitchell's composition "Woodstock." (Courtesy of Photofest)

"Blackbird," "Guinnevere," "Marrakesh Express," "4 + 20," "Mr. Soul," "Sea of Madness," "Wooden Ships," "Find the Cost of Freedom," and possibly a few other songs (*See* Appendix I for details). Most of this material was first performed by the group Crosby, Stills, Nash (and Young), although several of the songs had been associated with the Buffalo Springfield, the Hollies, and the Byrds, and one of the songs was a cover of a Beatles tune. Also central to their role with regard to the Woodstock festival was Crosby, Stills, Nash, and Young's 1970 hit recording of Joni Mitchell's composition "Woodstock," the song that captures the spirit and the story of the festival perfectly in song. Crosby, Stills, and Nash were also jointly and independently linked to the twenty-fifth- and thirtieth-anniversary festivals: as a group they appeared at Woodstock '94, and David Crosby's band CPR appeared at the 1999 edition of A Day in the Garden, which was held on the site of the 1969 Woodstock festival. Crosby, Stills, and Nash were inducted into the Rock and Roll Hall of Fame in 1997.

DIAMOND HORSESHOE, THE   This Bethel, New York, hotel was one of several establishments that provided accommodations for the Woodstock festival's staff. The Diamond Horseshoe had been a top-notch establishment during the 1930s but had fallen on disrepair by 1969. Although the facility was condemned, Woodstock staffers made use of it, right up until the hotel caught fire the night before the festival began.

DILTZ, HENRY Originally a folk-revival musician, Henry Diltz became one of the best-known rock photographers of the 1960s and 1970s. He has photographed musicians ranging from The Monkees, to Jimi Hendrix, The Doors, Joan Baez, David Crosby, and Jerry Garcia. In addition to gracing the album covers of numerous collections by pop artists, Diltz's work has appeared in countless books and magazines. Diltz was the official photographer for the Woodstock Music and Art Fair. His photographs of Janis Joplin and Jimi Hendrix performing at the festival, in particular, have been widely reproduced. Although he continued to focus on his photographic career, Diltz has made guest appearances as a banjo player on several recordings, including work with the popular early-1970s group America.

DOORS, THE The Doors (Jim Morrison, vocals; Ray Manzarek, keyboards and bass; Robbie Krieger, guitar; and John Densmore, drums) were one of the premier American rock bands of the period 1967–70. Although they appeared at the 1969 Atlantic City Pop Music Festival and were asked to appear at Woodstock, they did not sign on due to Jim Morrison's paranoia that he might be assassinated at the festival.[7] Morrison died under mysterious circumstances in Paris, France, on July 3, 1971. Eerily, Morrison's was the third death at age twenty-seven of a significant American counterculture musician in the 1970–71 period, Janis Joplin and Jimi Hendrix being the first two such deaths.

DOW, RICHARD A member of the Concerned Citizens Committee of Wallkill, New York, Richard Dow was among those who vocally and successfully lobbied to have legislation enacted in the town that made it impossible for the Woodstock festival to take place in Wallkill. ***See also* Concerned Citizens Committee of Wallkill.**

DUNBROOK, HARRISON Harrison Dunbrook was transportation director for the state of New York. As such, he was part of the decision to close down the New York State Thruway and New York Route 17 when traffic to the site of the Woodstock festival came to a standstill. ***See also* New York State Thruway.**

DYLAN, BOB Born Robert Zimmerman on May 24, 1941, in Duluth, Minnesota, Bob Dylan became the central new singer-songwriter of the folk revival-protest song movement in the early 1960s. Dylan also played a central role in the development of the folk-rock style in 1965. Although Dylan did not perform at Woodstock (despite persistent rumors before and during the festival that he would make an unscheduled appearance), he played a peripheral, albeit important, role in the festival. After a motorcycle accident in July 1966 put Dylan's career on hold, he retired to Woodstock, New York, to rehearse and record with members of the group that would eventually be known as The Band. The recordings that Dylan and The Band made were not released commercially until the mid-1970s as *The Basement Tapes* but were widely copied and circulated as bootleg recordings. The work that Dylan and The Band were doing in the town of Woodstock as well as the presence of other well-known rock musicians in the area were key factors in bringing Michael Lang, Artie Kornfeld, Joel Rosenman, and John Roberts together to try to establish a recording studio in the town. The festival itself was originally conceived as a means of financing the studio. Although Dylan did not perform at Woodstock, acts such as The Band and Joe Cocker performed his compositions, including some of the previously little-known songs from Dylan and The Band's *Basement Tapes* sessions. ***See also* Band, The.**

EAGER, SAMUEL W., JR.   Sam Eager was a well-respected lawyer in Middletown, New York, a city that is surrounded by the Town of Wallkill. When it became apparent to the Woodstock promoters that they would have to meet with the concerned citizens of the township in June 1969, they were advised that they would need to have local counsel. Stanley Goldstein, who had connections in the area, found Eager and brought him on board as the Town of Wallkill–area attorney for Woodstock Ventures. Despite Eager's high standing in the community and his best efforts on behalf of his clients, the new zoning law that town officials were drafting would make it impossible for the festival to be held on Howard Mills' property in Wallkill.

EARTHLIGHT THEATRE   A politically motivated "street theater" ensemble that performed in what Woodstock principals Joel Rosenman and John Roberts called "a pre-Festival festival."[8] Although the intent of the event was to show White Lake and Bethel residents that contemporary arts could be acceptable and need not be perceived as a threat, the guerrilla theater troupe managed to offend the assembled audience and confirm the area residents' fears of the young, long-haired hippies.

EL MONACO MOTEL, THE   This Bethel, New York, establishment was one of several hotels and resorts that provided accommodations for the festival. These out-of-the-way establishments housed many of the artists who performed at the Woodstock festival.

FABRICANT, HERBERT   Herbert Fabricant was Howard and Pat Mills' attorney and as such was involved in the negotiations between the Mills family and Woodstock Ventures when the Mills' Town of Wallkill, New York, property was the planned location for the Woodstock Music and Art Fair.

FELDMAN, BERT   The town historian for Bethel, New York, Feldman was responsible (in 1984) for having a permanent plaque placed at the site of the 1969 Woodstock festival. That Feldman was able to do so suggests the extent to which public opinion about Woodstock had generally changed in the community in the fifteen years that followed the controversial music festival.

FILIPPINI, WILLIAM   William Filippini was a chicken farmer in Bethel, New York, whose land adjourned the Yasgur farm. A pond owned by a group of farmers, including Filippini, was on the edge of the Yasgur farm and looked to be the best source of water for the festival. Negotiating on behalf of the association of owners and himself, Filippini leased the rights to pump water out of the pond to Woodstock Ventures for $5,000.

FINK, JOE   Deputy inspector with the New York City Police Department Joe Fink worked as a consultant for Woodstock Ventures to recruit off-duty police officers to work security at the festival. Fink's job was complicated by the fact that an earlier approval for off-duty NYPD officers to work at the festival was overturned by police commissioner Howard Leary just days before the event was scheduled to open. Fink was invaluable to the recruitment efforts as he was sympathetic to the festival promoters' desire to use the security force as unarmed peace officers: Fink knew how to detect prejudices against hippies among the officers who were interviewed, and he was familiar with the counterculture from his work on New York City's Lower East Side. ***See also* New York Police Department.**

FOOD FOR LOVE, INC.   The official food concessionaire for the Woodstock festival, Food for Love was formed by Charles Baxter, Lee Howard, and Jeff Joerger. This trio had experience in the food industry, but no working capital.[9] Recruited by Michael Lang's friend Peter Goodrich, Baxter, Howard, and Joerger received up-front financing from Woodstock Ventures in June 1969 to get their operation off the ground and ready for the August festival. As the final days of preparation approached, disagreements between Food for Love and Woodstock Ventures made it necessary for the concessions contract to be renegotiated. Because of the unexpectedly large size of the crowd for the festival, Food for Love ran out of food, making it necessary for concert attendees to avail themselves of macrobiotic food prepared by members of the Hog farm commune and emergency food supplies that were provided by several resorts in the surrounding area.

FOREMAN, MICHAEL   Michael Foreman produced the program books for the Woodstock festival. Due to the serious traffic problems and the roads that were closed due to abandoned cars near the festival site, the programs were late in arriving.

FREAK-OUT TENTS   Woodstock festival organizers erected several so-called freak-out tents around Max Yasgur's property. Concertgoers who were experiencing bad LSD trips came to, or were brought to, the tents in order to work through the bad trip. Medical personnel and members of the Hog Farm commune manned the tents. Although the medical staff at first wanted to treat the victims with Thorazine and other drugs, Hog Farmers, who had considerable experience with helping people through bad trips using psychological means, found the medical personnel adopting their techniques after they saw how well they worked. Techniques for talking people through their trips ranged from comforting them to confronting them in an attempt to force the trippers to break through hallucinations. Although he was loath to admit it in public since he had a "bad boy" public persona to maintain, radical political activist Abbie Hoffman also worked at the freak-out tents. *See also* **Hog Farm, The; Thorazine.**

FRIEDMAN, JANE   Jane Friedman was part of the public relations staff for Woodstock Ventures. As such, she assisted in advertising the festival and also assisted Don Ganoung, head of community relations, with selling the very idea of the Woodstock Music and Art Fair to the Town of Bethel, New York, area community. *See also* **Ganoung, Don.**

GANOUNG, DON   Based on the history of how the Woodstock Music and Art Fair came to move from Woodstock to Saugerties to Wallkill to its eventual "home" at Bethel, New York, Reverend Don Ganoung may have had the closest thing to an impossible job. Ganoung, who had been a Roman Catholic priest, served as the head of community relations for the festival. Ganoung preached sermons in area churches and youth centers and organized run-out concerts for the Boston-based band Quill. While Ganoung's preaching and the concert outreach may have helped Woodstock Ventures somewhat in their move to win acceptance from young people and the establishment in Bethel/White Lake, some of Ganoung's efforts failed. For one thing, he helped to organize baseball games involving area youth and members of Woodstock Ventures. While this may sound like a good way to demonstrate goodwill, area residents saw the ball games as rather transparent attempts to win them over, and, therefore, the plan backfired. Unfortunately, Ganoung's attempt to stage a mini-Woodstock in advance of the actual festival also failed, primarily due to the fact that one of the groups, the Earthlight Theatre, managed to offend many of the audience members and confirmed their suspicions about the long-haired hippies who were coming into their town. *See also* **Earthlight Theatre.**

GOLDMACHER, DONALD   Donald Goldmacher was a member of the Medical Committee for Human Rights and chairman of the New York City chapter of the organization. He was one of the principal members of the organization who negotiated with Woodstock Ventures to have the medical committee provide medical services at the Woodstock festival. *See also* **Medical Committee for Human Rights.**

GOLDSTEIN, STANLEY   Stanley Goldstein had worked in the recording industry at Criteria Studios in Miami. He also worked with Mel Lawrence and Michael Lang coordinating sound and recording at the Miami Pop Music Festival. He became a salaried employee of Woodstock Ventures and acted as a sort of headhunter, lining up various technical experts for the minute-to-minute running of the festival. Goldstein was at least in part responsible for bringing in members of the Hog Farm commune to assist with security and to help festival attendees live off the land for three days. *See also* **Hog Farm, The.**

Pictured at the microphone in his famed concert venue the Fillmore West, concert promoter–impresario Bill Graham played a prominent role in booking the acts that appeared at Woodstock. (Courtesy of Photofest)

GOODRICH, PETER Peter Goodrich had been a friend of Michael Lang's back in the latter's days in Florida. When it became apparent that Woodstock Ventures had completely overlooked the need for providing food concessions for festival attendees (as late as June 1969[10]), Lang contacted Goodrich, who had contacts in the food industry. Failing to find any interested parties among already established concessionaires, Goodrich arranged for Charles Baxter, Lee Howard, and Jeff Joerger and their attorney, Stephen Weingrad, to meet with Lang, Rosenman, Roberts, and their attorneys. The trio of Baxter, Howard, and Joerger was signed to handle concessions and began operating under the name Food for Love, Inc. *See also* **Food for Love, Inc.**

GRAHAM, BILL Bill Graham was one of the most important rock music promoters in the 1960s. His Fillmore Auditorium in San Francisco helped bring many of that city's acts (Janis Joplin, The Grateful Dead, the Steve Miller Band, Santana, the Jefferson Airplane) to prominence. He also operated the Fillmore East in New York City. Graham assisted with some of the artist bookings for the Woodstock festival; however, according to many who worked with him, Graham had great difficulty accepting the fact that Michael Lang, Artie Kornfeld, John Roberts, and Joel Rosenman, who had considerably less experience as concert organizers than Graham, could have pulled off something that he, Graham, never was able to do. In fact, at one point in summer 1969, Woodstock organizers feared that Graham might try to buy them out in order to stop the festival.[11] Ultimately, how-

San Francisco Bay–area favorites The Grateful Dead had to perform an extended jam while Woodstock crews repaired the sound system. The band was one of the most important hippie counterculture groups in the 1960s and 1970s. (Courtesy of Photofest)

ever, Michael Lang convinced Graham to cooperate with Woodstock Ventures. *See also* **Greenhill, Manny; Grossman, Albert.**

GRATEFUL DEAD, THE   The house band for Ken Kesey and his Merry Pranksters' LSD parties in the San Francisco Bay Area as early as 1965, The Grateful Dead[12] became one of the most significant bands of the counterculture era. Although The Grateful Dead's membership fluctuated more than that of many bands over the years, their lineup at the time of the Woodstock festival included Jerry Garcia (lead guitar), Bob Weir (rhythm guitar), Ron "Pigpen" McKaman (keyboards), Bill Kreutzmann (drums), Mickey Hart (drums), and Tom Constanten (keyboards). Their legion of hard-core fans, known as Deadheads, became a much-studied part of the hippie subculture. Just prior to their performance at Woodstock, The Dead's manager, suspecting that Woodstock Ventures was in financial trouble, demanded that the band be paid in cash. After a cashier's check was secured and it became evident that the band would be paid, the group took the stage. Unfortunately, sound system problems, which occurred off and on throughout the entire festival, plagued The Dead. The band ended up jamming onstage to fill time until the sound system could be fixed, causing some audience members who were not familiar with their music to wonder about The Grateful Dead's capabilities as musicians. Some, who were familiar with The Grateful Dead's style of jamming, might argue that this was a typical modus operandi for the band. Ray Manzarek, keyboardist of The Doors, for example, wrote of a 1967 sound check by The Dead, "They noodle, they fool around, they play out of tune, they try to tune up . . . but fail . . . and finally play a song. Vocals are out of harmony, guitars are tuned to some arcane, eccentric mode that each musician has kept as his own private secret, not telling the fellow next to him what the mode is, and the rhythm section is at cross purposes with each other, laying down what seems to be two separate and distinct rock beats that have no relation to each other. In other words, it's a typical Grateful Dead song/jam."[13] At Woodstock, however, once The Grateful Dead's equipment was in working order, the counterculture favorites proceeded to perform "St. Stephen," "Mama Tried," "Dark Star," "High Time," and "Turn on Your Lovelight." Despite the set's inauspicious beginnings, The Grateful Dead's music ultimately proved to be at least somewhat successful in the context of the overall Woodstock experience. Insiders among The Grateful Dead's camp, however, have acknowledged for years that the Woodstock performance was among the band's worst.[14] Incidentally, The Grateful Dead's set is one of the few performances of the festival that have not been released on official video or audio recordings from Woodstock, possibly due to the technical and musical problems that marred their performance. Although The Grateful Dead was not particularly successful commercially from the standpoint of top 40 recordings, their long jams were quite popular among the youth who attended their concerts. Their early advocacy of psychedelic drugs and the somewhat nomadic lifestyle of the band and its hard-core fans (Deadheads) made The Grateful Dead especially relevant within the 1960s counterculture and the Woodstock generation. The Grateful Dead continued to tour into the 1990s. After the death of lead guitarist Jerry Garcia in 1995 of a heart attack, performances by the band became sporadic. The Grateful Dead was inducted into the Rock and Roll Hall of Fame in 1994.

GREENBERG, LEON   President of the Monticello Raceway, Leon Greenberg filed suit against Woodstock Ventures when the raceway's property was overrun by hippies on their way to the Woodstock festival. Greenberg soon withdrew the suit when it became apparent that the attendant publicity he and the raceway had received would ultimately do them more good than the harm that was done by the hippies. *See also* **Monticello Raceway.**

GREENHILL, MANNY   Manny Greenhill (1916–96) was one of several artists' representatives who were involved in booking the acts for the Woodstock festival. Specifically, Greenhill was Joan Baez's manager and was deeply involved in progressive politics during the folk-revival era. Greenhill was also involved in booking traditional bluegrass musicians such as Lester Flatt and Earl Scruggs for concerts in the North when the bluegrass genre of country music was not widely known in the region. Through this kind of activity, as well as his management work with Jesse Fuller, Reverend Gary Davis, and Doc Watson, Manny Greenhill was one of the key individuals to bring traditional folk and traditional country music into the mainstream during the 1960s. *See also* **Graham, Bill; Grossman, Albert.**

GROSS, RICHARD   Richard Gross was a Bethel, New York, attorney who assisted and represented Woodstock Ventures in some of the legal wranglings that occurred as plans were being made to hold the Woodstock Music and Art Fair in the Town of Bethel. Although Woodstock Ventures had far less trouble making arrangements for the festival to take place in the Town of Bethel than they encountered with the failed Town of Wallkill site, they had to call upon Gross to assist with such legal details as the lease of a pond that was adjacent to the Yasgur farm and a lawsuit against Woodstock Ventures filed by Leon Greenberg, president of Monticello Raceway. *See also* **Filippini, William; Greenberg, Leon; Monticello Raceway.**

GROSSMAN, ALBERT   Bob Dylan's manager and the manager of other musicians during the 1960s (including Janis Joplin's band, Big Brother and the Holding Company), Albert Grossman was known as a man who could be difficult to work with. He negotiated contracts for some of the Woodstock performers and attended the festival on Saturday, August 16, 1969. According to John Morris, production coordinator for the Woodstock Music and Art Fair, Grossman looked at what was transpiring and proclaimed it "beautiful."[15] Those who knew Grossman and his hard-nosed reputation—like John Morris and the principals of Woodstock Ventures—could fully appreciate the significance of Grossman's positive assessment of the festival. *See also* **Graham, Bill; Greenhill, Manny.**

GUTHRIE, ARLO   Folksinger-songwriter-guitarist Arlo Guthrie, who was born July 10, 1947, in Coney Island, New York, is best remembered for his 18½-minute

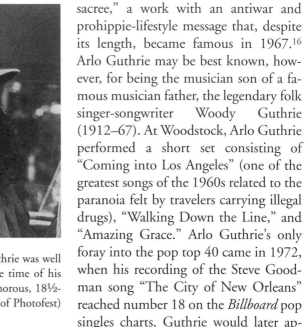

talking song "Alice's Restaurant Massacree," a work with an antiwar and prohippie-lifestyle message that, despite its length, became famous in 1967.[16] Arlo Guthrie may be best known, however, for being the musician son of a famous musician father, the legendary folk singer-songwriter Woody Guthrie (1912–67). At Woodstock, Arlo Guthrie performed a short set consisting of "Coming into Los Angeles" (one of the greatest songs of the 1960s related to the paranoia felt by travelers carrying illegal drugs), "Walking Down the Line," and "Amazing Grace." Arlo Guthrie's only foray into the pop top 40 came in 1972, when his recording of the Steve Goodman song "The City of New Orleans" reached number 18 on the *Billboard* pop singles charts. Guthrie would later appear at the 1999 A Day in the Garden Festival, a Woodstock reunion held on the site of the 1969 Woodstock Music and Art Fair.

The son of folk music legend Woody Guthrie, Arlo Guthrie was well known by members of the youth counterculture at the time of his Woodstock performance largely on the basis of his humorous, 18½-minute song "Alice's Restaurant Massacree." (Courtesy of Photofest)

HANLEY SOUND   Bill Hanley's company, Hanley Sound, provided sound amplification for the Woodstock Music and Art Fair. Although the amplification and mixing equipment Hanley used was not sophisticated by today's twenty-first-century standards, Hanley had put together amplification systems for several of the larger rock festivals of the Woodstock era. Hanley's experience in festival sound, however, went back to the Newport Jazz Festival in the 1950s. His techniques probably were better suited to a festival like Woodstock (open-air) than those of most of his competitors.

HARDIN, TIM Born December 23, 1941, singer-songwriter Tim Hardin was heavily influenced by folk and blues music. A native of Eugene, Oregon, Hardin was one of the musicians who had moved to Woodstock, New York, in the late 1960s in order to take advantage of the village's natural setting and close proximity to New York City. Hardin's only top 100 pop hit was his recording of Bobby Darin's composition "Simple Song of Freedom," which was on the *Billboard* charts at the time of the Woodstock festival. At Woodstock Hardin performed "Misty Roses," as well as his composition "If I Were a Carpenter," which had been a 1966 top 10 hit for none other than Bobby Darin. Hardin, in fact, was considerably better known and more popular as a songwriter than as a singer. In addition to the aforementioned Bobby Darin, a wide range of performers recorded Hardin's songs. The list includes such diverse musicians as Rod Stewart, Frank Sinatra, the Nice, Joan Baez, the Youngbloods, and Bob Seger. Hardin's appearance at Woodstock was filmed but was not included in Michael Wadleigh's documentary, *Woodstock: Three Days of Peace and Music*. Unfortunately, Hardin suffered from an addiction to heroin from early in his career. He ceased recording by the early 1970s and died of a drug overdose in 1980.

Tim Hardin was probably best remembered as a songwriter. His set at Woodstock included his compositions "Misty Roses" and "If I Were a Carpenter." (Courtesy of Photofest)

HAVENS, RICHIE Born January 21, 1941, in Brooklyn, New York, folk singer-guitarist Richie Havens became part of the Greenwich Village folk scene in the early 1960s. He was known for his use of an open guitar string tuning, which would enable him to play full chords using just his thumb. Before his appearance at Woodstock, Havens had just started to receive national exposure through a series of record albums that made the charts in 1968 and 1969. These included *Mixed Bag, Something Else Again, Electric Havens*, and *Richard P. Havens, 1983*. The traffic tie-ups that made it difficult for Woodstock concertgoers to get to the festival site also made it difficult for some performers to arrive in time to perform at their scheduled times. Richie Havens had made it to the concert site on Friday, August 15, 1969, as had most of his backing musicians. His bass player had not yet arrived, but Havens agreed to open the Woodstock Music and Art Fair. The Woodstock

A striking photograph of folksinger–songwriter Richie Havens from NBC-TV's *Good Vibrations '72 . . . From London.* (Courtesy of Photofest)

appearance and his appearance in the documentary film of the festival put Havens in the national spotlight and caused his career to blossom. To commemorate the fact that he opened the original festival, Havens also opened A Day in the Garden 1999. Richie Havens' set at the 1969 festival featured his own compositions, as well as his adaptations of folk standards and songs of the Beatles. He performed "Minstrel Came Down from Gault," "High Flyin' Bird," "I Had a Woman," "I Can't Make It Anymore," "With a Little Help from My Friends," "Strawberry Fields Forever," "Hey Jude," "Handsome Johnny," and "Freedom." Havens' performance of "Freedom," which happened to be largely spontaneous and improvised, was a highlight of the festival and (especially) a highlight of the subsequent *Woodstock: Three Days of Peace and Music* film and the Atlantic Records *Woodstock* multialbum set. Havens' career benefited greatly from the exposure he gained at Woodstock. The high point of his recording popularity came shortly after the festival when his recording of George Harrison's composition "Here Comes the Sun" reached the *Billboard* pop top 20 singles chart. Richie Havens has continued to record and perform in concert into the twenty-first century.

HELICOPTERS   In 1969, many young people associated helicopters with the ongoing and increasingly unpopular war in Vietnam. Interestingly, helicopters, even U.S. Army helicopters, played an important role in the Woodstock Music and Art Fair. After New York governor Nelson Rockefeller declared the site of the music festival a disaster area, military helicopters flew in emergency medical supplies. Woodstock Ventures also employed helicopters for such tasks as getting cashier's checks for The Grateful Dead and The Who to the concert site so that the musicians could be paid in advance of their scheduled performance times. *See also* **Prince, Charlie.**

HENDRIX, JIMI   A native of Seattle, Jimi Hendrix (1942–70) established himself as a, if not *the*, leading rock guitar virtuoso between 1967 and 1970. After a brief career in the military, Hendrix played guitar in several rhythm and blues and soul groups in the early to mid-1960s. He then moved to England, where he came to the attention of the former bassist with the Animals, Chas Chandler. Chandler matched the African American guitarist with British rockers Noel Redding (a lead guitarist whom Chandler turned into a bass guitarist) and Mitch Mitchell (drums). Their group, the Jimi Hendrix Experience, played a psychedelic, blues-based rock unlike anything else that was being heard in the mid-1960s. Hendrix mesmerized British audiences with his outlandish stage antics and the overt sexuality he brought to his performances. The Jimi Hendrix Experience came to the United States and released one of the most important record albums of 1967, *Are You Experienced?*, which featured a mixture of a few covers of songs by others and Hendrix's own, more important compositions. The Jimi Hendrix Experience literally burned its way into the American musical landscape when Hendrix ignited his guitar at the Monterey International Pop Music Festival. By the time of the Woodstock festival, Jimi Hendrix was widely regarded as one of a handful of the most important guitarists of the rock era. He wrote several memorable

The musical concentration of guitarist-singer Jimi Hendrix is evident in this photograph from the Woodstock Music and Art Fair. (Courtesy of Photofest)

songs, including "The Wind Cries Mary," "Voodoo Chile," "Purple Haze,"[17] and "Foxey Lady," all of which were recorded by the Experience. The Experience's recordings of the Billy Roberts composition "Hey Joe" and the Bob Dylan composition "All along the Watchtower" showed that the group could produce *the* definitive version of songs by other songwriters. The Jimi Hendrix Experience disbanded in mid-1969. At Woodstock, Hendrix appeared with an augmented band. Not only were drummer Mitch Mitchell and bass guitarist Billy Cox on hand, but guitarist-vocalist Larry Lee and percussionists Juma Sultan and Jerry Velez rounded out the ensemble. This group closed the festival by performing the following songs: "Message to Love," "Getting My Heart Back Together Again," "Spanish Castle Magic," "Red House," "Master Mind," "Here Comes Your Lover Man," "Foxey Lady," "Beginnings," "Izabella," "Gypsy Woman," "Fire," "Voodoo Chile (Slight Return)," "Stepping Stone," "Purple Haze," "Villanova Junction," and "Hey Joe." The most famous part of the Hendrix set, however, was the guitarist's solo version of "The Star-Spangled Banner." The Hendrix rendition of the national anthem of the United States of America became one of the most famous ever performed live and recorded. It played an important role in the later stages of the antiwar movement in the United States. After Woodstock, Hendrix formed a new group with Billy Cox and drummer Buddy Miles, called Band of Gypsys. By mid-1970, he was working again with Mitchell and Cox. During a stay in London in September 1970, Hendrix died from inhaling his own vomit due to barbiturate intoxication. The entire set Hendrix and his enlarged ensemble performed at Woodstock is available on a two-compact disc set released by MCA Records in 1999, *Live at Woodstock*, MCAD2-11987.

HIPPIES Young people who rebelled against commercial, straitlaced, consumer-oriented society by means of their recreational drug use, free sexuality, long hair,

Just some of the nearly half-a-million people who attended the Woodstock festival. (Courtesy of Photofest)

and communal living, hippies were in abundance at the Woodstock Music and Art Fair. Although the hippie lifestyle would not come to national attention for several years, its seeds were sown in the San Francisco Bay Area in approximately 1963 by Ken Kesey, author of the best-selling novel *One Flew Over the Cuckoo's Nest*, and his followers, who were known as the Merry Pranksters. Kesey used royalties from his 1962 book to fund what were called "acid tests," in which he and members of the Merry Pranksters took LSD (which was still legal at the time) in a partylike atmosphere. Author and music critic Barney Hoskyns documented San Francisco's Haight-Ashbury district during the 1960s in his book *Beneath the Diamond Sky*. According to Hoskyns, members of the San Francisco Beat scene in the North Beach area referred to the Merry Pranksters and other LSD-taking, long-haired, young people as "hippies," a pejorative term originally used by African American jazz musicians to describe the "white beatnik hangers-on in the jazz scene."[18] The hippies soon found a more amenable home in the Haight-Ashbury district. The hippies espoused a lifestyle of peace; turning on through either psychedelic drugs or Eastern religions and philosophy; rejecting the commercialism, materialism, and consumerism of "straight" American society; sexual freedom; long hair; and communal living. Eventually, the entire 1967 "Summer of Love" scene in San Francisco grew out of the hippie scene in Haight-Ashbury. After the "Summer of Love" the hippie scene could be found across America. Author Christopher Mele writes that by the mid-1960s "the hippies had constructed a subculture based around widespread social change,"[19] and music critic Edward Macan defined the demographics of the hippie subculture as consisting "largely of young, middle-class white people who had consciously rejected the lifestyle of their parents in favor of more experimental paths."[20] As evidenced by Weiner and Stillman's study of the demographics of the Woodstock audience,[21] and as evidenced by their generally easy adaptation to several days of communal living, free love, recreational drug use, and loud rock music, this hippie subculture made up the Woodstock audience. The success of Woodstock has been widely seen as an affirmation of the hippie lifestyle. *See also* **Yippies.**

HIRSCH, HOWARD Howard Hirsch was one of the organizers of the visual arts exhibit at the Woodstock festival. Although some books and articles on Woodstock have not even mentioned the "Art" part of the "Music and Art Fair," it is important to remember that Woodstock was not entirely about the music. Hirsch and Peter Leeds were in charge of the art exhibit at the festival, which included contemporary and Native American-influenced arts, which were in keeping with the hippie, Back to the Land nature of the Woodstock festival. *See also* **Art.**

Despite the presence of over 400,000 people at the Woodstock Music and Art Fair, the rural setting allowed for those wanting to get away from the crowd to do so. (Courtesy of Photofest)

HOFFMAN, ABBIE Abbie Hoffman (1936–89) was a figure of major importance on the political side of 1960s counterculture resistance to the government of the United States of America. He co-founded the Youth International Party (Yippies) and garnered headlines across the country with his oftentimes humorous, attention-grabbing antiestablishment exploits, such as throwing out dollar bills on the floor of the New York Stock Exchange to expose the greed of the brokers and other workers there, nominating a pig for president of the United States, and his (failed) attempt to levitate the Pentagon during an antiwar rally in Washington, D.C. Always suspicious of what he saw as corporate rip-offs, Hoffman apparently became aware of the Woodstock Music and Art Fair in June 1969, when he was in Detroit at a White Panther Party rally. Upon his return to New York, the amount of talk he heard on the street among members of the counterculture made it clear to him that the festival had the potential to become an event of major scope and importance. Naturally suspicious of anything that seemed as if it was being marketed and sold to the youth counterculture, Hoffman contacted festival promoters and charged them with trying to pull off a corporate rip-off of the counterculture and apparently threatened to disrupt the festival. The festival's organizers finally brought Hoffman on board after giving money to his political organization and making arrangements for the Yippies to be able to distribute their left-wing political literature at Woodstock.[22] In sharp contrast to his image as the bad boy of the counterculture, Abbie Hoffman played an active role in helping out in the "freak-out tent," helping young people who were having negative reactions to drugs by his talking them out of their bad trips. Hoffman also helped the festival organizers keep the crowds in check. John Morris of Woodstock Productions thanked Hoffman from the stage on Saturday. This upset Hoffman, who was very protective of his media image. Hoffman went onstage during The Who's performance and apparently attempted to take over the microphone to make a speech about the plight of White Panther Party founder John Sinclair,[23] and The Who's Pete Townshend either accidentally or intentionally (opinions vary, and the evidence is inconclusive) hit Hoffman in either the neck or the head with his guitar.

Hog Farm, The   Although they started out in California, the Hog Farm commune gained most of its fame in New Mexico. Due to their early success as a Back to the Land commune, as well as their fame within the counterculture—which was secured in part because of their association with the author Ken Kesey (*One Flew Over the Cuckoo's Nest*) and his Merry Pranksters (a group of early LSD experimenters documented in Tom Wolfe's book *The Electric Kool-Aid Acid Test*)— Woodstock Ventures flew and then bused over eighty members of the commune to the site, treating them like stars. Hog Farmers helped with festival security, planning, and construction. Perhaps their greatest contribution, however, was to set up a free kitchen and to help festival attendees, some of whom were going to have to live off the land for the first time in their lives, learn how to construct shelter and build safe fires. Members of the commune also manned the so-called freakout tents, where, by talking to concertgoers who were experiencing negative reactions to LSD, they helped them with their bad trips. *See also* **Freak-out Tents; Law, Lisa; Law, Tom; Wavy Gravy; Merry Pranksters, The.**

Holiday Inn   The Holiday Inn in Monticello, New York, was one of several hotels and resorts in the area around the Town of Bethel that lodged the crew and the performers who appeared at the Woodstock festival.

Incredible String Band, The   This Scottish group, led by Robin Williamson and Mike Heron, performed in a style that combined the influences of Scottish and Anglo-American folk music with the modal improvisations of Hindustani-inspired "raga rock" and psychedelic music. The group gained popularity at about the time of Woodstock, due in part to the growing interest in "roots" musical styles as many hippies moved back to the land. In their Saturday, August 16, 1969, set at Woodstock the Incredible String Band performed "This Moment" and "When You Find out Who You Are." Praising the band's musicianship, *Yahoo* music reviewer Jim Derogatis described the Incredible String Band as "one of the few good groups that played at Woodstock."[24] Despite the musical accomplishments of the group's members, most notably Williamson and Heron, the Incredible String Band's set was not necessarily among the best-received performances at the festival. This was due in large part to the fact that rain forced promoters to reschedule the group from the opening day, when the majority of performers performed acoustic or folk-related material, to Saturday in the midst of heavier rock bands. Incidentally, questionable programming decisions like this greatly marred the 1970 Isle of Wight Festival, an event at which concertgoers who came specifically to hear hard rock bands booed acoustic/folk-oriented musicians.

INFORMATION BOOTH During the festival, Chip Monck and other stage announcers were being barraged with messages to read to the crowd: stage announcements were the only way to get information out to concertgoers. Many of these were personal messages and quickly proved to take up too much time to read to the masses. Eventually, an information booth was set up. This area became a communications center and allowed the stage announcers to limit their talking to introducing the performers and making general announcements for the benefit of the entire crowd.

IRON BUTTERFLY, THE One of the original heavy metal bands, Iron Butterfly had their biggest hit, "In-A-Gadda-Da-Vida," in summer 1968. The seventeen-minute album version of the song featured perhaps the longest drum solo ever committed to vinyl and caused some music critics to complain about a tendency toward self-indulgent excess by the band. The Iron Butterfly was booked to perform at Woodstock but ended up placing so many last-minute transportation demands on the producers that their contract was canceled, and they were never brought to the festival site.

IT'S A BEAUTIFUL DAY A relatively little known group, It's a Beautiful Day was part of the intense negotiations that took place between Bill Graham and Woodstock Ventures. Although Graham originally made appearances of certain groups contingent upon Woodstock Ventures hiring both It's a Beautiful Day and Santana (also little known outside the San Francisco Bay Area at the time) for the Woodstock festival, It's a Beautiful Day never performed. ***See also* Graham, Bill.**

JEFF BECK GROUP, THE Led by Jeff Beck, lead guitarist with the influential British band the Yardbirds from 1965 to 1966, the Jeff Beck Group was on the *Billboard* pop top 40 right around the time of the Woodstock festival. Their curiously titled recording "Goo Goo Barabajagal" with folk-psychedelic singer Donovan would, in fact, be the band's only pop top 40 single. Beck was one of the most talented improvisers among the electric guitar virtuosos of the era, and his group had made a powerful appearance at the 1969 Newport Jazz Festival. The Jeff Beck Group was scheduled to perform at Woodstock, but their appearance was canceled.

JEFFERSON AIRPLANE, THE A mainstay of the San Francisco hippie and rock scene, the Jefferson Airplane was one of several bands that broke into the national spotlight due in part to their appearance at the Monterey International Pop Music Festival in 1967. At the time of their Woodstock appearance, the band consisted of Grace Slick (vocals), Marty Balin (guitar, vocals), Jorma Kaukonen (lead guitar), Paul Kantner (rhythm guitar, vocals), Jack Casady (bass), and Spencer Dryden (drums). The group's 1967 album *Surrealistic Pillow* was one of the most important psychedelic works of the so-called Summer of Love. The Airplane was scheduled to be the Saturday night headliner at the Woodstock festival. They actually took the stage early Sunday morning[25] because the festival perpetually ran behind schedule due to weather-related problems, problems with the sound system, and other logistical problems. The Jefferson Airplane's set included their hits "Volunteers," "Somebody to Love," and "White Rabbit," as well as "The Other Side of This Life," "Plastic Fantastic Lover," "Eskimo Blue Day," "Uncle Sam's Blues," and a medley of "Saturday Afternoon" and "Won't You Try." The Jefferson Airplane's popularity eventually faded—it was actually in something of a downturn at the time of Woodstock—although several members of the band formed the subsequent groups the Jefferson Starship and Starship. Ironically, despite the importance of the Jefferson Airplane in the psychedelic Summer of Love of 1967, the group Starship did something three times that the Jefferson Airplane never accomplished even once: had a single reach number 1 on the *Billboard* pop singles charts. The Jefferson Airplane was inducted into the Rock and Roll Hall of Fame in 1996.

JOHNSON, LARRY As sound and music editor, Larry Johnson played a prominent role in the production of Michael Wadleigh's documentary film *Woodstock: Three Days of Peace and Music.*

JOPLIN, JANIS Janis Joplin, who was born January 19, 1943, in Port Arthur, Texas, combined blues and psychedelic influences in her performances with Big Brother and the Holding Company, a mainstay of the San Francisco rock scene during the 1966–68 period. After going solo, Joplin worked with several groups, including the Full Tilt Boogie Band and the Kosmic Blues Band (the group that backed her at Woodstock). According to many who heard her performance, Joplin's set at Woodstock was disappointing. Her well-documented

Janis Joplin's set at Woodstock was not the best received performance, but this photograph captures the singer's incredible intensity. (Courtesy of Photofest)

drug and alcohol abuse had by this time in her career made her performances uneven in quality. According to those who saw her appearance at Woodstock, she
was drunk and high beyond the point at which she could give a good perform-
ance.[26] Janis Joplin performed "Raise Your Hand," "As Good as You've Been to
This World," "To Love Somebody," "Summertime," "Try (Just a Little Bit
Harder)," "Kosmic Blues," "Can't Turn You Loose," "Work Me, Lord," "Piece of
My Heart," and "Ball and Chain." Joplin died of a heroin overdose in October
1970. Her death at age twenty-seven, along with the deaths of Jimi Hendrix and
Jim Morrison at the same age, was of major importance to the counterculture.
Janis Joplin was inducted into the Rock and Roll Hall of Fame in 1995.

KEEF HARTLEY BAND, THE   Drummer Keef Hartley was born in Preston, Lancashire, England, in 1944. One of Hartley's claims to fame was that he replaced
Ringo Starr in Rory Storm and the Hurricanes when Starr left to join The Beatles in 1962. Hartley later played with John Mayall's Bluesbreakers, one of the premier British blues-rock bands of the 1960s. Hartley put together his own band in
1969 and performed at several major music festivals, including the Bath Blues Festival in England and the Woodstock Music and Art Fair. Apparently due to a hasty
decision by Hartley's then-manager Johnny Jones, the Keef Hartley Band's jazz-
blues-rock set at Woodstock was not filmed,[27] nor does it seem likely that an audio
recording exists today. Every other recording from the festival has been released
either officially or on various bootleg albums and compact discs; however, to date
nothing performed by Hartley's band has been issued in any form. The most accurate set lists from the festival come from study of the filmed and audio-recorded
performances, so no set list for the Keef Hartley Band has been published, either
in print form or electronically. There is evidence that the band performed the following tracks from their 1969 album, *Halfbreed*: "Sinning for You," "Born to Die,"
and "Leaving Trunk."[28] Miller Anderson, a former member of the band, also recalls performing "Just to Cry" at Woodstock.[29]

KORNFELD, ARTIE   The grandson of Russian immigrants, Artie Kornfeld (born
1942 in Coney Island, New York) wrote several popular hit songs in the early
1960s, the best remembered of which probably is the Jan and Dean hit "Dead
Man's Curve." As a director of artists and repertoire (A&R) for Mercury Records
in 1967, Kornfeld became acquainted with a multigenerational pop group named
The Cowsills. Kornfeld co-authored the "Summer of Love"-hippie-lifestyle-influ-
enced song "The Rain, the Park and Other Things" for the group. The song
reached number 2 on the *Billboard* pop singles charts in late 1967. Due to the
success of the recording, Kornfeld left Mercury to do independent management
and record production work with The Cowsills. In 1968, Kornfeld took a position with Capitol Records as director of East Coast contemporary product. Due
to his songwriting and A&R success, Kornfeld enjoyed an unusually high degree
of independence at Capitol. Michael Lang met with Kornfeld in November 1968
while Lang was attempting to win a recording contract for the group Train. Kornfeld and Lang apparently hit it off immediately and began a social as well as a

business relationship. Although Train failed to hit the big time, Kornfeld and Lang began plotting new forays into the music business. The two decided to try to build a recording studio in Woodstock, New York, since the Woodstock area was attracting important rock artists like Jimi Hendrix, Bob Dylan, The Band, and others. Kornfeld and Lang came to the attention of venture capitalists John Roberts and Joel Rosenman. The four became the principals behind Woodstock Ventures. Along with Lang, Roberts, and Rosenman, Kornfeld was one of the co-producers of the festival. Kornfeld's principal job was to handle festival publicity. Woodstock Ventures also relied on the contacts Kornfeld had established in the music industry.

KRAMER, EDWIN H.   Edwin Kramer was one of the recording engineers for the audio recordings made at Woodstock. Although Woodstock recordings found their way onto albums by several of the performers, the best-known vehicle for Kramer's work was the multidisc *Woodstock* album, which was released by Atlantic Records in 1970. This album has been reissued on compact disc, as has the 1971 Atlantic album *Woodstock Two*.

LANG, MICHAEL   The youngest of the principals of the Woodstock Music and Art Fair, Michael Lang was born in Brooklyn, New York, and eventually moved to Florida. While living in Florida, Lang owned a head shop and co-produced the 1968 Miami Pop Festival with Mel Lawrence. Lang then became the manager of the rock group Train upon his return to New York City. His management of Train initially brought him into contact with record executive Artie Kornfeld. Lang and Kornfeld eventually decided to try to establish a state-of-the-art recording facility in the small town of Woodstock, New York, due to the presence of musicians such as Bob Dylan, The Band, and Jimi Hendrix in the area. Their quest for venture capitalist funding for their studio then brought them into partnership with Joel Rosenman and John Roberts. Lang originally conceived of the concert festival as a means toward financing the recording studio. If Artie Kornfeld was the musical insider with industry contacts and Rosenman and Roberts were the business experts of Woodstock Ventures, then Michael Lang was the visionary. Although Rosenman's and Roberts' accounts of the history of Woodstock Ventures through the time of the festival suggest that Lang was overly extravagant and manipulative and an expert at playing people off against each other,[30] it seems likely that the festival needed a Michael Lang-type figure, someone who would dream big dreams. Michael Lang continued his connection to the Woodstock name, acting as one of the co-producers of both Woodstock '94 and Woodstock 1999.

LANGHART, CHRIS   Woodstock's technical director and designer, Chris Langhart was the head of the theatrical technical department at New York University. Due to the close proximity of the university to the famous rock concert venue the Fillmore East, Langhart was also active in the world of rock production. As Langhart described the duties for which he was hired by Woodstock Ventures, "Somehow, it fell into place that I would be dealing with all the parts of the festival that no-

Concert producer Michael Lang sits on his motorcycle as he speaks with a hippie at the free Woodstock Music and Art Fair. (CORBIS)

body else wanted to deal with—the toilets and the communications and the supply of power and the performers' pavilion."[31] Langhart's reputation as the person to whom the Fillmore East could turn to work out technical details that confounded everyone else helped to prepare him for the job.

Law, Lisa   Lisa Law was a member of the Hog Farm commune. She, along with over eighty other Hog Farmers, assisted Woodstock Ventures with the education of festival attendees in how to live off the land and with the free food distribution that the commune members carried out. Law, who was seven months pregnant at the time of the festival, also shot photographs and an hour's worth of home movies of the festival.[32] Law's perspective of the Hog Farm's role at Woodstock, in words and in photographs, has become part of an exhibition sponsored by the Smithsonian Institution.[33] *See also* **Hog Farm, The.**

Law, Tom   A member of the Hog Farm commune, Tom Law assisted with food distribution and the myriad of duties taken on by the Hog Farmers. In addition, Law led yoga exercises from the stage. These exercises, which Law touted as a nonchemical way to get high, helped to fill in time while acts arrived or had their equipment set up and played a role in keeping the 400,000 Woodstock attendees calmed. In his recollections of the Woodstock festival, Law expressed fascination with the way in which the audience members took part in these disciplined exercises as one.[34] One of more infrequently acknowledged roles played by Tom Law, however, was before the festival even began. Michael Lang approached Law and his fellow Hog Farm members Wavy Gravy and Ken Babbs and asked the three to make sure that the 50,000 early arrivals at the site were cleared so that they would have to reenter through ticket gates. According to Wavy Gravy, Law asked Lang, "Do you want a good movie or a bad movie?" referring to the documentary film the Hog Farm members knew that Woodstock Ventures had contracted with Warner Brothers to distribute. Again, according to Wavy Gravy, Lang and his associates decided within ten minutes to allow the early arrivals to stay.[35] ***See also* Hog Farm, The.**

LAWRENCE, MEL   The director of operations for Woodstock Ventures, Lawrence had co-produced the Miami Pop Festival with Michael Lang. Following the Miami festival, he produced other individual concerts, including a Jimi Hendrix concert. After Stanley Goldstein was hired as a salaried employee of Woodstock Ventures to be a sort of headhunter for people with experience in concert production, he contacted Lawrence to see if he might bring his production team to Woodstock from Florida. According to Lawrence's recollections, his "mission was to design, operate, plan for all of the functions of the festival aside from the actual show, but that included sort of a coordination of all the things that got built."[36]

LEARY, HOWARD   Howard Leary was the commissioner of the New York Police Department at the time of the Woodstock Music and Art Fair. Plans were in place for off-duty New York City Police Department officers to work security at the festival. Just days before the festival was scheduled to begin, however, Commissioner Leary issued an order forbidding the participation of the off-duty officers. Despite Commissioner Leary's order, off-duty New York police personnel who wanted to earn the extra cash arrived for interviews with Woodstock Ventures' security consultant Joe Fink. In order to disguise their identity, lest the commissioner discover that they had defied his orders, many officers applied for security under fictitious names. ***See also* New York Police Department.**

LEEDS, PETER   Peter Leeds was one of the organizers of the visual arts display that was part of the Woodstock festival. It is important to remember that, although the musical performances have garnered most of the attention, the Woodstock Music and Art Fair did include an art exhibit. Leeds and Howard Hirsch were in charge of the visual arts offerings of the festival. Leeds and Hirsch organized an exhibit that included contemporary arts, as well as Native American-influenced arts, in keeping with the hippie, Back to the Land nature of the festival. ***See also* Art.**

LIIS, RON   Ron Liis was on the Department of Art faculty of the University of Miami at the time of the Woodstock Music and Art Fair. He, his wife, Phyllis, Bill (another art instructor at the university), and Jean Ward accompanied and directed a team of University of Miami art students who produced art pieces that were placed around the site of the Woodstock festival. ***See also* Art.**

Lourie, Felix   Miles Lourie's father, Felix, had established many political connections, particularly in New York state government. Lourie arranged for John Roberts and Joel Rosenman to meet with New York state lieutenant governor Malcolm Wilson in early June 1969. At the time, sentiment in the Town of Wallkill, New York, was turning against the Woodstock festival, especially as it was becoming clearer to residents of the town that thousands of hippies would be descending on their town, possibly to indulge in drugs, nudity, and free love, as they listened to highly amplified rock music. Lourie agreed to help Woodstock Ventures try to find a political solution to their difficulties. After the meeting with Lieutenant Governor Wilson failed to produce the desired endorsement, Lourie arranged for Rosenman and Roberts to meet with one of New York state governor Nelson Rockefeller's executive secretaries to see if an endorsement could be secured from the governor's office. Although the outcome was a letter welcoming the enterprise to New York (it apparently stopped far short of actually endorsing the rock festival), it arrived too late to be produced at the June 12, 1969, meeting of the Wallkill Town Board that effectively signaled the end of the Town of Wallkill site for the festival. *See also* **Lourie, Miles.**

Lourie, Miles   Miles Lourie was the New York City attorney who was responsible for introducing Michael Lang and Artie Kornfeld to John Roberts and Joel Rosenman. Lourie would serve as one of the New York-based attorneys for Woodstock Ventures. Miles Lourie's father, Felix, would also play a role in the Woodstock saga. *See also* **Lourie, Felix.**

LSD   The common name for the drug D-lysergic acid diethylamide, first used by Albert Hofmann, a chemist with the Swiss firm Sandoz Pharmaceuticals, on August 19, 1943. The drug, also known as "acid," was used by psychiatrists to treat a variety of mental ailments into the 1960s. LSD had been the subject of experimentation by such famous early-1960s figures as author Ken Kesey and Harvard University researcher Dr. Timothy Leary. The drug became an important part of the San Francisco rock music scene, especially during the period 1965–67, and was made illegal in the United States in 1966. LSD was plentiful at the Woodstock festival, especially a powerful variety known as "Orange Sunshine." The documentary film and audio recording of the festival include stage announcements concerning some especially potent bad "acid" that was making the rounds. There were also rumors, substantiated by some eyewitnesses, that some of the water that was being distributed at Woodstock was laced with the drug. While the credibility of such reports may be suspect, the fact is that a number of festival attendees experienced bad trips. Concertgoers who experienced these bad trips were taken to one of several "freak-out" tents. These tents were manned by medical personnel, as well as by members of the Hog Farm, who had real-life experience talking people out of bad trips. Although LSD's notoriety would fade after the 1960s, the drug was very much in evidence at Woodstock '94 and at Woodstock 1999.

MARIJUANA   According to reports by Woodstock attendees and performers, marijuana use was rampant at Woodstock both among performers and among concertgoers. Marijuana use would also be very much in evidence at Woodstock '94 and at Woodstock 1999. Before the counterculture era of the 1960s and early 1970s, marijuana was not widely associated with popular music or even rock and roll, although countless jazz musicians used the drug. By 1965, however, marijuana use was becoming widespread in the rock world, both among musicians and among rock fans. At the time of the Woodstock Music and Art Fair, marijuana was seen as something of the drug of choice; it was considered more natural than alcohol or synthetic drugs like LSD.

MARSHALL, PAUL   Paul Marshall was one of Woodstock Ventures' New York City attorneys. Among the tasks he had was to represent Woodstock organizers in court in Catskill, New York, when the owners of four area summer camps filed suit to stop the festival.

MAURICE, BOB   Bob Maurice was filmmaker Michael Wadleigh's business partner. Their production company, Wadleigh-Maurice Productions, was responsible for the documentary concert film *Woodstock: Three Days of Peace and Music* (1970), which Maurice produced and Wadleigh directed. ***See also* Wadleigh, Michael;** ***Woodstock: Three Days of Peace and Music.***

McDONALD, COUNTRY JOE   Singer-guitarist Joe McDonald was born in 1942 in El Monte, California. He rose to prominence in the counterculture of the mid-1960s with his composition "I-Feel-Like-I'm-Fixin'-to-Die Rag," first recorded by his group Country Joe and the Fish in 1965. The satirical antiwar song was sung frequently at antiwar rallies for the rest of the decade. One of the challenges not adequately anticipated by the organizers of the Woodstock festival was getting performers to the concert venue. This became a major headache early on when an audience far exceeding what anyone had anticipated caused enormous traffic jams on the New York State Thruway and New York State Route 17 (the two highways were eventually closed for some time). Although he was scheduled to perform only a set with his band, Country Joe McDonald had arrived on the scene earlier than most of the performers and was prevailed upon to do a solo set to fill a gap in the program. Reports suggested that McDonald's acoustic set was not particularly well received until he did his famous "FISH" cheer ("Give me an 'F,' Give me a 'U,' Give me a 'C,' Give me a 'K.' What's that spell? *Etc.*") and sang the by-then four-year-old antiwar song "I-Feel-Like-I'm-Fixin'-to-Die Rag." Although McDonald's primary activity and influence were in the early part of the American counterculture era,[37] he has continued to compose and to perform in concerts, including an appearance at Woodstock '94. ***See also* Country Joe and the Fish.**

MEDICAL COMMITTEE FOR HUMAN RIGHTS   The Medical Committee for Human Rights was an antiwar corps of medical personnel with a chapter based in New York City. These doctors and nurses had provided medical services at numerous civil rights and antiwar rallies and did the same at the Woodstock festival. Although several doctors from the group were at the concert site at the start of the festival, more arrived from New York City (at the prompting of political activist Abbie Hoffman) when it became evident that the audience was going to be significantly larger than what any of the organizers had expected. *See also* **Goldmacher, Donald.**

MELANIE Singer-songwriter Melanie Safka (born February 3, 1947, in Queens, New York) had her greatest popular hits ("Lay Down [Candles in the Rain]," "Peace Will Come [According to Plan]," and "Brand New Key") in 1970 and 1971, after the Woodstock festival. At Woodstock, the twenty-two-year-old Melanie performed her compositions "Beautiful People" and "Birthday of the Sun." Melanie was one of the unsched-

Folksinger-songwriter Melanie made her debut at Woodstock. Her appearance at the festival propelled the young musician into the spotlight. (Courtesy of Photofest)

uled performers at Woodstock, and her appearance at the festival helped to launch her career, for although she had studied voice from an early age at the New York Academy of Fine Arts, had sung in clubs during college, and had been recording since 1967, Melanie had yet to see her performing career take hold nationally at the time of the festival. Melanie's hit song "Lay Down (Candles in the Rain)" was inspired by the sight of thousands of Woodstock concertgoers holding up matches and lighters in response to the festival's production coordinator John Morris, who had announced from the stage, "This is the largest crowd of people ever assembled for a concert in history, but it's so dark out there we can't see and you can't see each other. So when I say 'three,' I want every one of you to light a match." Melanie's composition clearly links the peace and understanding that allowed the Woodstock Music and Art Fair to succeed with the larger antiwar movement and the counterculture movement to fundamentally change capitalistic, consumer-oriented American society. She would later perform at some of the anniversary events, including the 1998 A Day in the Garden festival, which was held on the site of the former Yasgur farm.

MERRY PRANKSTERS, THE The Merry Pranksters were a loosely organized group that followed author Ken Kesey. Kesey had taken the profits from his successful first novel *One Flew Over the Cuckoo's Nest* and financed a long-standing series of "acid tests," or LSD experiences, back in the early- to mid-1960s. The group that took part in these acid tests became known as the Merry Pranksters. Kesey and the Merry Pranksters, among other things, provided an important philosophical link between the Beat poets of the 1950s and the hippies, who began to develop their own niche in the counterculture around 1965 in San Francisco. The Merry Pranksters also supported the growing rock scene in San Francisco in the mid-1960s and hired The Grateful Dead (then known as the Warlocks) as their house band for their acid parties. Although Kesey himself did not do so, the rest of the Merry Pranksters attended the Woodstock Music and Art Fair. In doing so, they connected the Beat movement, the early West Coast hippie movement, with the 1969 culmination of hippie philosophy and lifestyle that was found at the festival. Kesey's Merry Pranksters also had direct ties to the Back to the Land movement and the style of communal living espoused by members of the Hog Farm commune. *See also* **Hippies; Hog Farm, The.**

MIAMI POP FESTIVAL   A 1968 popular music festival organized and co-produced by Woodstock's executive producer Michael Lang and Woodstock's director of operations Mel Lawrence. Although the two principals had little experience in concert production, the Miami Pop Festival was an artistic success. Foreshadowing Woodstock, however, it lost a considerable sum of money, and much of the festival was marred by rain. One of the strengths of the Miami Pop Festival was the breadth of rock music that Lang and Lawrence presented, including blues master John Lee Hooker and early rock and roll pioneer Chuck Berry, as well as more modern acts like the Jimi Hendrix Experience, Blue Cheer, The Crazy World of Arthur Brown, and others.

MILLS, HOWARD, JR.   Howard Mills Jr. and his wife, Pat, owned the Town of Wallkill, New York, site intended for the festival before it was moved to Bethel. The Mills property was a huge, 600-acre tract that was set to become an industrial park. Since the industrial park had not yet been built, Mills was keen to lease 200 acres of the land for the summer of 1969 to Woodstock Ventures for their Woodstock Music and Art Fair. Legal challenges by the Concerned Citizens Committee of Wallkill that were raised in June 1969 and a July Wallkill town law regulating gatherings of more than 5,000 people (the festival was still projected to draw between 50,000 and 100,000 people over the course of three days at this point) effectively eliminated the Mills property as the site for the festival. *See also* **Concerned Citizens Committee of Wallkill.**

MINKER, JULES   Minker was the attorney for the Concerned Citizens Committee of Wallkill, the group that worked with the Town Board to have legislation passed that made it impossible for the Woodstock festival to take place in the Town of Wallkill, Orange County, New York. *See also* **Concerned Citizens Committee of Wallkill.**

MITCHELL, JONI   Singer-guitarist-songwriter Joni Mitchell was born on November 7, 1943, in Fort McLeod, Alberta, Canada. By 1967 she was living in the United States performing in clubs and coffeehouses. In that year Mitchell came to the attention of David Crosby of the Byrds and later of Crosby, Stills, Nash, and Young. Crosby encouraged Mitchell and assisted her in securing a recording contract. By 1969 Mitchell had gained fame among the folk cognoscenti and was making inroads through recordings and television appearances. Due to a commitment to appear on the *Dick Cavett Show*, Joni Mitchell was told by her manager that she would not be able to appear at Woodstock; traffic conditions would have made it impossible for her to make it from New York City to Bethel and back again in time to meet her contractual agreement to appear on the television program. As it turned out, Mitchell could have flown in by helicopter with Crosby, Stills, Nash, and Young, but by the time this possibility arose, it was too late for Mitchell to alter her plans. Perhaps inspired by being forced to sit on the proverbial sidelines, Mitchell penned the song "Woodstock." Her composition captured the mood, the spirit, and the story of the festival and became a number 11 *Billboard* pop chart hit for her friends Crosby, Stills, Nash, and Young in spring 1970. Mitchell herself would make the top 10 with "Help Me" in 1974 and would make some great jazz-based recordings. She remains best known, however, for her compositions "Big Yellow Taxi," "Both Sides Now" (a top 10 hit for singer Judy Collins in late 1968), and "Woodstock."

MONCK, CHIP   E. H. Beresford Monck, known as Chip, had been active as a stage designer and lighting designer in New York City and for various tours of folk musicians such as Josh White and Odetta. Monck worked on concert production at the important Monterey Pop Festival and by the late 1960s was one of the acknowledged experts on rock concert production. He became the lighting and technical designer for the Woodstock festival and also served as one of the masters of ceremonies. In fact, Monck is captured on the Woodstock multidisc festival recording and in Michael Wadleigh's documentary film making what would become a famous stage announcement about some bad "acid" (LSD) that was circulating around the concert grounds. Monck continued to work in concert production (including George Harrison's Concert for Bangla Desh) and more specifically in stage and lighting design after Woodstock.

MONTICELLO HOSPITAL   Located in Monticello, New York, near the site of the Woodstock festival, Monticello Hospital dealt with some of the injuries and negative drug reactions that could not be handled by the on-site Woodstock medical crew.

MONTICELLO RACEWAY   This racetrack at the intersection of New York Route 17 and New York Route 17B in Monticello, New York, was overrun by hippies looking for a place to camp as they traveled to the Bethel, New York, site of the Woodstock festival. The closure of area highways as a result of all the abandoned cars made it impossible for the raceway to operate for several days. Leon Greenberg, president of the Monticello Raceway, filed a lawsuit against Woodstock Ventures. Monticello Raceway quickly withdrew the suit when it became clear that not only would damages to the track be impossible to assess, but the attendant publicity

Monticello Raceway had achieved when the hippies moved in uninvited would end up helping the company more than hurting it.

MOODY BLUES, THE   This British band, best known for their art rock/progressive rock leanings in the late 1960s in songs like "Nights in White Satin," "Question," and "Ride My Seesaw," as well as for other hits in the 1970s and 1980s, performed at several of the major festivals of 1969 and 1970. In fact, the band was in the United States in early August 1969, when they appeared at the Atlantic City Pop festival. After their appearance in Atlantic City, New Jersey, however, they returned home to England. Woodstock Ventures contacted The Moody Blues, and the band considered performing at Woodstock. The Moody Blues declined the invitation when they were offered a performance fee that ensured that the band would have to take a huge financial loss by making the special trip back to the United States. Perhaps due in part to disappointment over The Moody Blues and other performers declining to play at Woodstock because of the relatively low fee for name bands, corporate sponsorships would be secured for Woodstock '94 and Woodstock 1999 in order that significantly more lucrative artists' contracts could be negotiated.

MORALES, HECTOR   Hector Morales was one of several booking agents who worked with the festival promoters to negotiate with, and book, artists who appeared at Woodstock.

MORRIS, JOHN   Production coordinator for the Woodstock Music and Art Fair, John Morris had considerable experience with running rock shows. Morris worked at Bill Graham's Fillmore East in New York City, where he basically ran the operation. Given his experience (greater than that of anyone else connected with Woodstock) and the fact that he had not known any of the principals (Michael Lang, Artie Kornfeld, Joel Rosenman, John Roberts) before he was contacted by Stanley Goldstein and Chip Monck to take on the job for Woodstock Ventures, Morris viewed himself as a "hired gun."[38] Part of Morris' job for Woodstock Ventures also involved booking artists. One of John Morris' biggest claims to fame during the festival, however, was his announcement from the stage, "This is the largest crowd of people ever assembled for a concert in history, but it's so dark out there we can't see and you can't see each other. So when I say 'three,' I want every one of you to light a match." Concertgoers complied with Morris' request, and the sight of tens of thousands of little lights all over the festival setting inspired Melanie to write the song "Lay Down (Candles in the Rain)."

MOUNTAIN   Led by Felix Pappalardi and guitarist Leslie West, Mountain made only a couple of forays into the pop singles charts, both times after the Woodstock festival. The power-rock band was best known for its album work and especially for its live concert work. Mountain appeared on Saturday, August 16, 1969, at Woodstock, performing "Blood of the Sun," "Stormy Monday," "Long Red," "For Yasgur's Farm," "Theme from an Imaginary Western," "Waiting to Take You Away," "Dreams of Milk and Honey," "Blind Man," "Blue Suede Shoes,"

"South Bound Train," and "Mississippi Queen."[39] Mountain guitarist Leslie West appeared at the 1999 A Day in the Garden festival and performed several of the Mountain songs he had played at Woodstock thirty years before.

NEUHOUSE, GEORGE Town supervisor for Bethel, New York, where the 1969 Woodstock Music and Art Fair took place. After the festival, Neuhouse and other members of the local government enacted legislation to make sure that a gathering like that at Max Yasgur's farm would never again occur in their town. This legislation would come into play in the late 1980s and through the 1990s, when attempts were made to organize anniversary concerts on the site of the 1969 Woodstock festival.

NEW YORK POLICE DEPARTMENT The Woodstock Music and Art Fair did not take place in New York City, but the NYPD played an important role. Festival promoters realized that it would be impossible to recruit a large, experienced, appropriate security force in the immediate White Lake/Bethel, New York, area. Arrangements were made for off-duty New York Police Department officers to work security at Woodstock; however, police commissioner Howard Leary overturned the agreement just days before the festival was to begin. Deputy inspector Joe Fink assisted Woodstock Ventures in recruiting off-duty officers, many of whom worked using fictitious names so that their decision to ignore Commissioner Leary's orders would not be discovered. Members of the NYPD who eventually assisted with security at the festival did so as unarmed peace officers.

NEW YORK STATE POLICE Members of the New York State Police were put at the disposal of festival organizers after it became clear that travel on several major routes near the site of the festival was becoming hopelessly snarled with both congested traffic and abandoned cars. The traffic problems and the lack of medical care adequate for the size of the crowd made it incumbent upon Woodstock Ventures to have the festival site declared a disaster area by the New York state government: this declaration freed up the State Police to assist festival promoters and perhaps most importantly, facilitated the rapid increase in size of the medical corps available. The New York State Police who assisted at the festival worked out of a hunting club in the White Lake, New York, area. The New York State Police would later play a prominent, but highly controversial, role in the aftermath of the riots at Woodstock 1999 when they published copyrighted photographs taken by news photographers on the Internet in an attempt to identify perpetrators.

NEW YORK STATE ROUTE 17 New York Route 17, which has now been upgraded to a limited-access freeway and renamed I-86, has been known for many years as the Southern Tier Expressway. The highway cuts across the southern part of New York, near the Pennsylvania border. At the time of the Woodstock Music and Art Fair, Route 17 was a primary highway for people traveling to the concerts. Like the New York State Thruway, Route 17 had to be shut down due to the massive traffic jams caused by festival traffic and abandoned cars.

One of the better-known movie stills from the film *Woodstock: Three Days of Peace and Music,* this photograph captures the carefree approach to public nudity taken by some members of the Woodstock audience. (Courtesy of Photofest)

NEW YORK STATE THRUWAY This toll highway, which incorporates I-90 as the primary east-west route and I-87 as the primary north-south route, played an important role in the Woodstock festival. Concert attendees from the west, south, and north used the thruway to get to Bethel. The massive traffic jams that ensued caused the closure of the highway, which was and still is an important commerce and general transportation route linking New York City to the north and west.

NEW YORK TIMES The *New York Times* covered the Woodstock Music and Art Fair as it was being organized and as it took place. The first major article that reported on the opening day of the festival detailed everything that had gone wrong and included nothing about the amazing display of brotherhood and sisterhood that was taking place. The next day, the newspaper did an abrupt about-face when confronted with accusations that the first reporter had not even been at some of the festival locations on which he had reported. Back in 1969 the *New York Times* was probably the closest thing in the United States to today's national newspapers like *USA Today.* This meant that the *Times'* coverage was one of the principal sources for information about the festival across the nation.

NUDITY As documented in Michael Wadleigh and Bob Maurice's film *Woodstock: Three Days of Peace and Music* and in photographs and other accounts from the festival, Woodstock was the scene of open nudity. The nudity seems to have been symptomatic of the free approach to sexuality in general taken by many of the Woodstock generation. This free approach to nudity and sex of the 1969 festival was seen by those who supported the free hippie lifestyle of the Woodstock generation as beautiful and by those who did not support that particular lifestyle as symbolic of a breakdown of decency and morals in American society. *See also* **Hippies.**

OSBORNE, LEE Lee Osborne was one of the recording engineers for the audio recordings made at Woodstock. Although Woodstock recordings found their way onto albums by several of the performers, the best-known vehicle for Osborne's work was the multidisc *Woodstock* album, which was released by Atlantic Records in 1970. This album has been reissued on compact disc, as has the 1971 Atlantic album *Woodstock Two.*

OWEN, JOSEPH   Attorney for the Town of Wallkill, Orange County, New York, Joseph Owen worked with the Concerned Citizens Committee and the Town Board to create legislation that ensured that the Woodstock festival would not take place in Wallkill. ***See also* Concerned Citizens Committee of Wallkill.**

PAUL BUTTERFIELD BLUES BAND, THE   While they did not produce hit singles during the 1960s and 1970s, the Paul Butterfield Blues Band was a success at live shows and was a favorite of serious rock musicians as well as of serious fans of Chicago-style electric blues. The group was led by Paul Butterfield, a Chicago harmonica player. Butterfield is credited with being the first white performer on his instrument to establish an authentic blues voice. Butterfield

Paul Butterfield in concert. (CORBIS)

is also credited with bringing electric blues to the attention of young, white American audiences in the mid-1960s. In addition to Butterfield, the band featured lead guitarist Elvin Bishop, who had been highly praised for his performance at the 1967 Monterey International Pop Music Festival. At Woodstock the Paul Butterfield Blues Band performed "Everything's Gonna Be Alright," "Driftin'," "Born under a Bad Sign," "All My Love Comin' Through to You," and "Love March." The group's performance of "Love March" was included on the two-album *Woodstock* album issued by Atlantic Records in 1970.

POMEROY, WES   Chief of security for the Woodstock festival, Wes Pomeroy had been a former special assistant to U.S. attorney general Ramsey Clark. Pomeroy's knowledge of law played an important role in Woodstock Ventures securing quick, emergency medical aid and assistance from the New York State Police. Knowing that the only way the needed resources could be assembled quickly enough was to have the festival site declared a disaster area, Pomeroy prevailed upon his contacts with the New York State Police to have New York governor Nelson Rockefeller do so. Rockefeller made the declaration, and the emergency medical personnel quickly got to Woodstock.

PRINCE, CHARLIE   Charlie Prince was the branch manager at the Sullivan County National Bank in Bethel, New York. Prince played an important role at the start of the Woodstock festival when on the first evening of the festival he went to the branch well after regular business hours to retrieve some cashier's checks at the urgent request of festival promoters. These checks made it possible for Woodstock Ventures to pay The Grateful Dead and The Who. The management of both bands, fearing that Woodstock Ventures might not be able to pay the artists (rumors to that effect were circulating backstage), demanded to be paid either by cash or cashier's check at the time of performance. The cashier's checks that Prince retrieved were flown to the concert site by helicopter.

QUILL   A rock band from Boston that was hired by Woodstock Ventures to perform at fund-raisers for social service causes in the upstate New York region in which the festival was held. In part, then, Quill was hired to serve a public relations function. Although not nearly as well known as most of the acts, Quill also appeared at the Woodstock Music and Art Fair itself. They performed the song "Waitin' for You." Interestingly, neither the Artie Kornfeld-managed Bert Sommer nor the Michael Lang-managed Quill managed to parlay their Woodstock appearances into significantly enhanced musical careers. A rare photograph (taken by Lisa Law of the Hog Farm commune) of Quill performing at Woodstock is available on the Internet at http://americanhistory.si.edu/lisalaw/7.htm, a site maintained by the Smithsonian Institution.

RAIN   If Woodstock was remembered for one natural phenomenon, it was rain. The first evening of the festival witnessed a huge rainstorm, which began during Ravi Shankar's set. The rainstorm that hit the concert site during Shankar's performance, however, would not be the last nor the heaviest of the festival. The organizers had purchased rain insurance, but it was not needed, as the festival went on despite the poor weather. The rainy conditions caused problems with amplification and other electrical equipment and caused parts of Max Yasgur's farm to become a muddy mess. Incidentally, the sight of tens and tens of thousands of young concertgoers holding up matches in the rain at the urging of Woodstock's production coordinator John Morris inspired Melanie to write the song "Lay Down (Candles in the Rain)," one of her best-known compositions.

RATNER, LOUIS   Sheriff Louis Ratner worked through Congressman Marty McKneally and New York state lieutenant governor Malcolm Wilson to arrange for army helicopters to be flown to the Woodstock festival site by pilots from Stewart Air Force Base. The helicopters flew in much-needed medical supplies after New York governor Nelson Rockefeller declared the site a disaster area.

RED TOP, THE   This Middletown, New York, establishment was one of several hotels and resorts that provided accommodations for the festival. Ironically, out-of-the-way establishments like the Red Top housed many famous musicians during the run of the Woodstock Music and Art Fair.

REYNOLDS, BILL   One of the major concerns of Woodstock Ventures was sanitation.[40] Bill Reynolds was involved in the procurement of portable toilets for the festival. ***See also* Toilets, Portable.**

REYNOLDS, CLIFF   Cliff Reynolds was a member of the Concerned Citizens Committee of Wallkill, New York. This organization managed to block Woodstock Ventures from holding the festival in their community. ***See also* Concerned Citizens Committee of Wallkill.**

ROBERTS, JOHN   One of the four principal organizers of the Woodstock Music and Art Fair, John Roberts had been born into a wealthy family in New York City in 1945. Upon the death of his mother in the early 1950s, Roberts inherited a sizable sum of money, which was held in trust. In 1961, he enrolled at the University of Pennsylvania. Upon reaching age twenty-one, he received the first $400,000 of his inheritance from the trust that had been set up for him. After college, Roberts entered the investment world, oftentimes making highly speculative investments on Wall Street funded by his inheritance. At the same time, he was taking graduate courses at Philadelphia's Annenberg School of Communications. Roberts met Joel Rosenman through Rosenman's brother Douglas, whom Roberts had known in college. Roberts and Rosenman quickly became friends and business partners as venture capitalists. The two placed an advertisement in the *Wall Street Journal* that read, "Young Men with Unlimited Capital looking for interesting and legitimate business ideas." According to conflicting accounts, the two were either trying to get ideas for possible investments or were trying to get ideas for plots for a television situation comedy about the business world they were trying to create. Roberts and Rosenman's advertisement and their work on the Media Sound recording studio were the key ingredients that brought them together with their future partners in Woodstock Ventures, Michael Lang and Artie Kornfeld. Roberts, Rosenman, and Robert Pilpel co-authored the book *Young Men with Unlimited Capital*, a fanciful account of the organization and running of the Woodstock festival. Roberts was also one of the co-producers of the Woodstock '94 festival.

ROCKELLER, NELSON   Born on July 9, 1908 in Bar Harbor, Maine, Nelson Aldrich Rockefeller was governor of New York State at the time of the Woodstock Music and Art Fair. Rockefeller played a prominent role in the festival by approving the closure of New York Route 17 and the New York State Thruway. He also declared the festival site a disaster area at the request of Woodstock Ventures so that emergency medicine and food could be flown in.

ROLLING STONES, THE   Self-proclaimed and considered by many rock critics to be "The Greatest Rock and Roll Band in the World," The Rolling Stones were scheduled to tour the United States at the same time as the Woodstock festival. As Michael Lang, Joel Rosenman, John Roberts, and the other organizers of Woodstock met to consider which bands to invite, they considered seeking out the Stones. At the time of these deliberations in 1968 and 1969, The Rolling Stones' popular hit single was "Street Fighting Man." The thought that the band's material might violate the peace, love, and understanding nature of the festival, combined with the massive security that would have been necessary had The

Rolling Stones appeared at Woodstock, not to mention the high performance fee the group routinely received, caused the festival organizers not to issue an invitation to the band. Interestingly, The Rolling Stones ended their 1969 U.S. tour with a large, festival-style concert at California's Altamont Speedway, an event meant to serve as *their* Woodstock. The Altamont concert ended as a disaster, with numerous overdoses and bad drug trips and the killing of one concertgoer by the Hell's Angels motorcycle gang that had been hired to work security. ***See also* Altamont.**

ROMNEY, BONNIE JEAN   Husband and wife Hugh and Bonnie Jean Romney were coordinators of the Hog Farm commune. While Hugh (better known as Wavy Gravy) was more visible at the festival, Bonnie Jean was an indispensable organizer of the group's many activities, from cooking organic food for concertgoers to teaching concertgoers how to live off the land.

ROMNEY, HUGH   *See* **Wavy Gravy.**

ROSENBERG'S   This Bullville, New York, establishment was one of several hotels and resorts that provided accommodations for the crew and performers of the Woodstock festival.

ROSENMAN, JOEL   Joel Rosenman grew up in Cold Spring Harbor, New York, and attended Princeton University, majoring in English literature. During his university days he did some nightclub singing, which gave him some exposure to the business side of the music industry. He then attended and graduated from Yale Law School. Rosenman was just getting his start in law when he discovered that the routine of the profession was not really as appealing as he had anticipated it might be. Rosenman's brother, Douglas, had gone to college with John Roberts. Roberts and Joel Rosenman met as a result of playing golf with Douglas in 1966. Rosenman and Roberts seemed to have hit it off immediately, soon deciding to share an apartment in New York. Roberts and Rosenman formed a business partnership with the goal of becoming venture capitalists. This partnership would allow Rosenman to make use of his legal training but to have fun in the process. As one of their ventures, Rosenman and Roberts worked on the construction of Media Sound, a New York City recording studio. The two placed an advertisement in the *Wall Street Journal* that read, "Young Men with Unlimited Capital looking for interesting and legitimate business ideas." According to conflicting accounts, Rosenman and Roberts were either trying to get ideas for possible investments or trying to get ideas for plots for a television situation comedy about the business world they were trying to create. Roberts and Rosenman's advertisement and their work on the Media Sound recording studio were the key ingredients that brought them together with their future partners in Woodstock Ventures, Michael Lang and Artie Kornfeld. Joel Rosenman would renew his association with Lang and Roberts when the three co-produced the Woodstock '94 festival.

Although they were well known in the San Francisco Bay area, it was the band's appearance at Woodstock and in the subsequent documentary film that propelled Santana into the national spotlight. (Courtesy of Photofest)

SANTANA Led by virtuoso guitarist Carlos Santana (born 1947), Santana incorporated the percussion, harmonic, and musical form-styles of Latin American music into their unique rock sound. The band was fairly well known in the San Francisco area but had not broken out nationally on the popular music charts prior to their appearance at Woodstock. Santana performed "Persuasion," "Savor," "Soul Sacrifice," and "Fried Neckbones and Some Homefries."[41] They had their greatest chart success in 1970, when both "Evil Ways" and "Black Magic Woman" made the *Billboard* pop singles top 10. Carlos Santana later emerged as an important solo artist and continues to perform into the twenty-first century.

SAUGERTIES, NEW YORK A small town in Ulster County, New York, Saugerties played a significant role in both the story of the 1969 Woodstock Music and Art Fair and the Woodstock '94 festival. Michael Lang and Artie Kornfeld had made preliminary arrangements (or at least they *thought* they had made preliminary arrangements) to negotiate a short-term lease

Dave Brown, bass player with Santana, performing at Woodstock. (Courtesy of Photofest)

of some property in Saugerties—the first Woodstock site to be proposed after the possibility of actually holding the festival in Woodstock, New York, fell through. The Saugerties site presented certain advantages, not the least of which was its close proximity to the New York State Thruway. Negotiations between John Roberts, Joel Rosenman, and the property owner's attorney in late March 1969, however, led nowhere. It became clear to Roberts and Rosenman that legal and financial restrictions that would be placed on Woodstock Ventures by the property owner would necessitate finding another location. Incidentally, the Winston farm, the site of Woodstock '94, was one of the Saugerties, New York, sites considered for the original festival. Although landowner Ralph Schaller had refused Woodstock Ventures' offer in 1969, the offer for the twenty-fifth-anniversary event was readily accepted and was seen as one way of keeping the 840-acre farm out of the hands of developers who hoped to turn it into a huge landfill. *See also* **Schaller, Ralph.**

SCHALLER, RALPH[42]   The enigmatic owner of property in Saugerties, New York, that was one of the sites considered for the Woodstock Music and Art Fair. After the original festival site in Woodstock, New York, fell out of contention, Woodstock Ventures co-founder Michael Lang thought that he had made preliminary arrangements with a "Mr. Shaler" (actually, Ralph Schaller, one of the owners on what is known as the Winston Farm) in March 1969 to lease Schaller's property in Saugerties, New York, for the festival. At a March 25, 1969, meeting in New York City with Schaller's attorney, Lang's fellow organizers Joel Rosenman and John Roberts were left with the distinct impression that Schaller must have had second thoughts. Rosenman and Roberts had noted that Schaller's initial enthusiasm had been replaced by the landowner's attorney's pointed questions about Woodstock Ventures' financial situation. The arrangements subsequently and quickly fell through.

SCHLOSSER, JACK   Supervisor Jack Schlosser led the Town of Wallkill, New York, Town Board. The board met with John Roberts, Joel Rosenman, Michael Lang, and Woodstock Ventures' legal representatives on June 12, 1969, in a hearing in which the increasingly dissonant concerns of Wallkill citizens were voiced. *See also* **Town of Wallkill, New York.**

SCHOONMAKER, THELMA   Schoonmaker worked as a film editor with Martin Scorsese on the Michael Wadleigh film *Woodstock: Three Days of Peace and Music*. She later continued her collaborations with Scorsese (later a famous movie director), doing film editing work on *Cape Fear* and *Raging Bull*. Ironically, while Martin Scorsese became famous as a movie director and Michael Wadleigh became the name most closely associated with *Woodstock: Three Days of Peace and Music*, Thelma Schoonmaker received the only Oscar nomination for the film: for Best Film Editing. *See also* **Scorsese, Martin; Wadleigh, Michael;** *Woodstock: Three Days of Peace and Music.*

SCORSESE, MARTIN Famed film director Martin Scorsese is best known for his movies *The Last Temptation of Christ*, *Taxi Driver*, *Raging Bull*, and *Gangs of New York*, among others. In 1969 and 1970, however, he served as an editor of the Michael Wadleigh film *Woodstock: Three Days of Peace and Music*. Scorsese had attended film school with Wadleigh and attended film classes with fellow film editor Thelma Schoonmaker. He also directed The Band's film *The Last Waltz*. **See also Schoonmaker, Thelma; Wadleigh, Michael; Woodstock: Three Days of Peace and Music.**

SEBASTIAN, JOHN B. John Sebastian, born March 17, 1944, in New York City, was the lead singer, principal songwriter, and rhythm guitarist of The Lovin' Spoonful, a band that made the *Billboard* top 40 pop singles charts ten times between 1965 and 1968. Sebastian's group disbanded in 1968, and he was not even originally scheduled to perform at Woodstock, but perform he did. Sebastian's "walk-on" solo set featured the songs "How Have You Been?" "Rainbows All Over Your Blues," "I Had a Dream," "Darlin' Be Home Soon," and "Younger Generation." Many who saw him live at the festival or in the film *Woodstock* suggest that Sebastian's performance was quite possibly under the influence of psychedelic drugs: he was unable to remember the words to some of his own compositions at times. This was possibly also due in part to the fact that he was performing some new songs and was just in the

Known in the early- and mid-1960s as the voice and principal songwriter of The Lovin' Spoonful, John Sebastian made his first major appearance as a solo artist at Woodstock. Ironically, Sebastian was not scheduled to perform, but did so to help the festival's producers fill an open slot on the first day of the festival. (Courtesy of Photofest)

process of putting together a band at the time of his walk-on performance at Woodstock. John Sebastian was a major star, and his impromptu performance lent Woodstock the feeling of a real happening. As Robert Spitz wrote in his book on Woodstock, "Something magical transformed the stage when John Sebastian ambled out, waving at his fans, and it was at that moment that, [John] Morris [production coordinator for Woodstock Ventures] thought, that the Woodstock Music and Art Fair truly became a festival."[43] Although Sebastian's solo career never reached the heights of popularity his work of 1965–68 with the Lovin' Spoonful had done, Sebastian managed to score a number 1 pop hit with his 1976 song "Welcome Back," which also served as the theme song for the popular television comedy *Welcome Back Kotter*.

Seen here in a photograph from the 1970s, Sha-Na-Na brought 1950s- and early 1960s-style rock and roll to the Woodstock festival. (Courtesy of Photofest)

SHA-NA-NA Although the Woodstock festival took place just after the days of acid rock and psychedelia and at a time in which hard rock was emerging in popularity and importance, the festival provided a link to rock and roll's 1950s past in the form of the new group Sha-Na-Na. The group's members dressed like 1950s "greasers" and performed a distinctly retro, 1950s repertoire—all of this despite the fact that the group's members were all young students from New York City's Columbia University. At Woodstock, this second-generation, early rock-style group performed songs that had been hits for Danny and the Juniors, the Coasters, Elvis Presley, and other stars of the late 1950s and early 1960s. Their set consisted of the following songs: "Na Na Theme," "Yakety Yak," "Teen Angel," "Jailhouse Rock," "Wipe Out," "The Book of Love," "Duke of Earl," and "At the Hop." Although the group had been formed in 1969 on a whim, and although some members of the Woodstock audience initially thought that Sha-Na-Na's performance was a joke, members of the vocal group were serious in their desire to pay tribute to the early, lighthearted days of rock and roll. Sha-Na-Na later had a television variety show, which featured their blend of humor and 1950s and early 1960s music. The group boasted one member, Henry Gross, who enjoyed success as a solo performer in the mid-1970s.

SHANKAR, RAVI The famous Indian classical musician Ravi Shankar (born April 7, 1920) has been acknowledged as an important master of the sitar since the 1950s. He was well known in India before he gained notoriety in the West in the mid-1960s as a performer and as the sitar teacher of George Harrison of The Beatles. Shankar was one of the principal exponents of Indian music at a time when many young people were developing an interest in the music, religion, and philosophy of the Indian subcontinent. Shankar appeared at several important pop music festivals as a result, including the 1967 Monterey Pop Festival, Woodstock, and George Harrison's 1971 Concert for Bangla Desh. At Woodstock, Shankar and his ensemble performed the classical Indian compositions "Raga Puriya-Dhanashri/ Gat In Sawarital," "Tabla Solo In Jhaptal," "Raga Manj Kmahaj," "Alap Jor," "Dhun In Kaharwa Tal," and "Medium

The great Indian sitarist Ravi Shankar greatly enhanced the eclecticism of the Woodstock festival with his group's performance of Hindustani music. (Courtesy of Photofest)

and Fast Gat In Teental." Unfortunately, Shankar's performance was cut short by the rain that became such an important part of the Woodstock story.

SIA, JOSEPH J. Photographer Joseph J. Sia attended and photographed the major summer 1969 U.S. popular music festivals: the Newport Jazz Festival, the Newport Folk Festival, the Atlantic City Pop Music Festival, and the Woodstock Music and Art Fair. Sia's photographs, many of which were published in the book *Woodstock '69, Summer Pop Festivals: A Photo Review*, are illuminating in what they show about the similarities and the differences between the performers and audiences for these four festivals. Sia's book, which was marketed by Scholastic to junior high school students, brought the famous 1969 rock-heavy music festivals to the attention of a generation too young to have attended the events.

SINCLAIR, JOHN During the mid-1960s, John Sinclair founded the radical White Panther Party and managed the left-wing, politically motivated Detroit band the MC5. Sinclair was arrested on what some members of the leftist counterculture saw as trumped-up marijuana possession charges and was in prison at the time of the Woodstock Music and Art Fair. As a way of protesting Sinclair's imprisonment, Abbie Hoffman took the stage during the Woodstock performance by The Who. Accounts vary as to exactly what then transpired, but it appears that in the middle of a stage announcement dealing with the plight of John Sinclair on what Hoffman described as political grounds, Who guitarist Pete Townshend either accidentally or on purpose hit Hoffman with his guitar. After his release from prison, Sinclair became a radio commentator and writer on jazz and the relationships between music and politics, as well as a poet. ***See also* Hoffman, Abbie.**

SKOLNICK, ARNOLD   Arnold Skolnick was the artist who designed the famous dove and guitar logo used by Woodstock Ventures in their advertisements for the Woodstock Music and Art Fair. Although his name might not be included in some of the "who's who" of Woodstock lists one might find, Arnold Skolnick played an important role in advertising the festival. In addition to highlighting the peaceful counterculture-happening nature of the festival, Skolnick's design became one of the most famous advertising icons of the late 1960s.

Sylvester Stewart, better known as Sly Stone, at the Woodstock festival. (Courtesy of Photofest)

SLY AND THE FAMILY STONE   Led by keyboardist-singer-songwriter Sylvester "Sly Stone" Stewart (born 1944), this multiracial and multigendered band had already had several top 10 pop hits by the time of the Woodstock festival ("Dance to the Music," "Everyday People," and "Hot Fun in the Summertime"). At Woodstock they performed "Love City," "Dance to the Music," "Music Lover," and "I Want to Take You Higher." Stewart and his band would make important musical contributions to the growing Black Consciousness movement in 1970 and 1971 and are credited with defining a funk-based musical style that would heavily influence early disco music in the 1970s. Due to the nearly all-out riot that Sly and the Family Stone had generated at the 1969 Newport Jazz Festival and other difficulties that various promoters were having with the group, Woodstock organizers were reluctant to book them. Because of this reluctance, Sly and the Family Stone was signed rather late in the booking cycle for the Woodstock festival. Although Sly Stone's influence continued to be felt in funk and disco through the 1970s, Sly and the Family Stone's own hit-making appeal had pretty much run its course by 1972. The band was inducted into the Rock and Roll Hall of Fame in 1993.

SOMMER, BERT   One of the lesser-known musicians to play Woodstock, Bert Sommer (1948–90) performed the songs "Jennifer" and "America." Before the festival, Sommer had recorded with Michael Brown of The Left Banke.[44] After Woodstock, he recorded two albums that were produced by Artie Kornfeld. Interestingly, neither the Michael Lang-managed group Quill nor the Kornfeld-managed Bert Sommer parlayed their Woodstock appearances into significantly enhanced careers in the music industry.

STAGE ANNOUNCEMENTS   As one might expect, some of the announcements made by the masters of ceremonies (MCs) of the Woodstock Music and Art Fair were introductions of the performers. At the start of the Woodstock festival, however, the only way to communicate over the distance of the Yasgur farm site was by means of stage announcements. Announcers like Chip Monck, John Morris, and others (including Hog Farm stalwart Wavy Gravy) were forced to make introductions and both important announcements that were necessary for the entire crowd to hear (such as those concerning reports of bad LSD making the rounds of the festival site and requests for audience members to cease climbing the sound towers) and personal announcements. The personal announcements eventually could be dispensed with once a communications center and information booth had been set up. Stage announcements concerning safety continued to be made throughout the festival. Woodstock Ventures principals also made sure that the concertgoers heard that news reporters and some politicians were suggesting that the festival could spill over into violence. These announcements were meant to help the crowd maintain control in order to prove critics wrong. They worked. ***See also* Information Booth.**

SWAMI SATCHADINANDA   By the late 1960s Transcendental Meditation and other Hindu-related religious and philosophical movements had become popular with young people. The Indian guru Swami Satchadinanda was at the site of the Woodstock Music and Art Fair on the opening day, Friday, August 15, 1969. The guru's entourage showed up at production coordinator John Morris' office and asked if the swami could speak to the crowd. Since acts were having considerable difficulty reaching the site and there was time to kill, Morris agreed. Swami Satchadinanda spoke to the audience about peace and love, themes he frequently addressed.

SWEETWATER   The relatively unknown band Sweetwater might have opened the Woodstock festival had their equipment truck not been stuck in traffic trying to make it to the festival site. The group, which combined the sounds of traditional rock band instruments with flute and cello, consisted of Nansi

The 1969 Woodstock festival featured a great diversity of musical styles. Sweetwater, with its combination of folk, rock, and classical instruments, was one of the most diverse groups to grace the stage. (Courtesy of Photofest)

Nevins, August Burns, Elpidio Cobain, Alex Del Zoppo, Fred Herrera, Albert Moore, and Harvey Gerst. At Woodstock Sweetwater performed "Motherless Child," "Look Out," "For Pete's Sake," "Day Song," "What's Wrong," "Crystal Spider," "Two Worlds," and "Why, Oh Why?" Unfortunately, the group's lead singer, Nansi Nevins, was seriously injured in an automobile accident just a few months after the Woodstock festival. Although the group continued on for a time after Nevins' accident, Sweetwater disbanded in 1971. They have reunited from time to time in more recent years and were the subject of a VH-1 documentary.

TAPOOZ, ALEXANDER   Alexander Tapooz owned the land in Woodstock, New York, where the festival was originally proposed to take place; however, the Woodstock site quickly fell out of contention. The property was purchased by Woodstock Ventures and eventually fell under Michael Lang's ownership when Woodstock Ventures was dissolved in 1972.

TEN YEARS AFTER   Ten Years After, the band that boasted the man who was described as the world's fastest rock guitar player, performed one of more exciting sets at the Woodstock Music and Art Fair. Led by guitarist-vocalist Alvin Lee, this British blues-based band was best known for its albums (their singles did not fare well in the United States) and especially for its high-energy live performances. The other members of the group were bass guitarist Leo Lyons, keyboardist Chick Churchill, and drummer Ric Lee. At Woodstock, Ten Years After performed "Good Morning Little Schoolgirl," "I Can't Keep from Crying Sometimes," "I May Be Wrong, but I Won't Be Wrong Always," and "I'm Going Home." The last song was also included on the multidisc recording of highlights from the Woodstock festival and a listening to the track shows why Alvin Lee was not considered just a technical virtuoso (he was often called the world's fastest rock guitar player), but a high-caliber musician as well.

THORAZINE   Thorazine, the trade name for SmithKline Beecham's version of the drug chlorpromazine, has been used to treat psychotic disorders for many years. An advertisement for the drug when its maker was known as Smith Kline & French Laboratories states, " 'Thorazine' is especially effective when the psychotic episode is triggered by delusions or hallucinations. At the outset of treatment, Thorazine's combination of antipsychotic and sedative effects provides both emotional and physical calming. Assaultive or destructive behavior is rapidly controlled."[45] Thorazine was the drug of choice within the medical establishment for dealing with bad LSD trips at the time of the Woodstock festival. According to members of the drug counterculture, however, the fact that Thorazine prevented the tripper from concluding his or her trip did more harm than good. Members of the Hog Farm commune persuaded doctors in the freak-out tents not to use Thorazine to treat overdose cases at Woodstock but to talk the victims out of their troubles instead.

TIEBER, ELLIOTT   Elliott Tieber was the owner of El Monaco Motel in Bethel, New York. Tieber made the motel available to many of the Woodstock Music and Art Fair's performers. *See also* **El Monaco Motel.**

TOILETS, PORTABLE   Sanitation was one of the major concerns for Woodstock Ventures, given that the festival took place on a farm and not at a completely outfitted public concert venue. Chris Langhart and Bill Reynolds made the arrangements to have portable toilets at the festival site. Because the size of the audience far exceeded what any of the organizers anticipated, the sanitation facilities proved to be less than adequate. Unfortunately, the portable toilets played a role in one of the few true catastrophes of the festival. The driver of a wagon that was used to extract sewage from the portable toilets backed over a young concert attendee, killing him. Interestingly, problems with portable toilets would also plague Woodstock '94 and Woodstock 1999, despite the fact that the anniversary festivals had more portable toilets to serve the needs of smaller crowds than the 1969 festival.

TOWN OF WALLKILL, NEW YORK   Not to be confused with the at-the-time unincorporated hamlet of Wallkill located in Ulster County, New York, the Town of Wallkill, located in Orange County, New York, was one of the proposed sites for the Woodstock Music and Art Fair. John Roberts and Joel Rosenman decided (apparently independently from Michael Lang and Artie Kornfeld) in late March 1969 that the search for a suitable site for the Woodstock festival in or near Woodstock, New York, had been proceeding too slowly. Financial concerns expressed by the attorney for the landowner of the Saugerties, New York, site originally proposed for the festival at a March 25, 1969, meeting with Roberts and Rosenman had made it clear that a new site would need to be found. As Roberts put it, "As was our custom, we decided to act boldly, i.e., without proper thought."[46] On March 30, 1969, the two promoters met with Howard Mills, the owner of a 600-acre tract in the Town of Wallkill. Mills was interested in leasing the land, which was scheduled to be turned into an industrial park. Roberts and Rosenman met with the Wallkill Zoning Board of Appeals on April 18, 1969, and secured an OK for the festival. Through May, the Mills property still looked to be the site for the concert. Some Wallkill residents, however, began to fear an invasion of hippies. Their suspicions were heightened when they learned of a no-marijuana-smoking memorandum that Joel Rosenman circulated among the employees of Woodstock Ventures. The memo was designed primarily to show the banking and accounting companies with which Woodstock Ventures was working, as well as the citizens of Wallkill, that the Woodstock promoters were responsible, law-abiding citizens who would not tolerate experimentation with drugs. The memo backfired. Town of Wallkill citizens now not only feared the festival attendees but also suspected that counterculture hippies were running the entire operation. Rosenman, Roberts, Lang, and their attorneys met with the Wallkill Town Board on June 12, 1969, but failed to convince citizens of the value of the festival. By July 1969, the Wallkill, New York, town board had enacted a new local law regulating gatherings of over 5,000 people, effectively putting an end to the Woodstock festival's presence in the community.

TRAFFIC JAMS   Travel by hundreds of thousands of Woodstock concertgoers to the site of Max Yasgur's farm created an enormous traffic jam on the New York State Thruway and on New York Route 17. Not only was traffic backed up because of cars moving toward White Lake, New York, but many cars simply were abandoned, which compounded the traffic problems. The traffic jams forced New York State Police to close the thruway and Route 17, two of the primary highways in the region.

TRAIN   This obscure acid rock/heavy metal band (not to be confused with the late-twentieth-century/early-twenty-first-century group of the same name) included Garland Jeffries, Bob Lenox, Don Tyler, and Abbie Rader[47] and was managed by Michael Lang. Although they did not appear at Woodstock, Lang's management of the group was the catalyst for Lang, Artie Kornfeld, Joel Rosenman, and John Roberts eventually forming a team to build a recording studio in Woodstock, New York, to be funded by the Woodstock music festival. The reader may occasionally see this band referred to as "Diesel" as a result of the use of that name in the 1974 Rosenman, Roberts, and Robert Pilpel book *Young Men with Unlimited Capital.*[48]

TRI-COUNTRY CITIZENS BAND RADIO CLUB   Coordination of the festival relied on communications over a fairly wide area of land, with the festival organizers and producers always on the move. Citizens Band (CB) radios provided by the Tri-Country Citizens Band Radio Club helped to make these communications possible.

UP AGAINST THE WALL MOTHERFUCKERS   A radical, Maoist group from New York City's Lower East Side. When this group learned that Woodstock Ventures had made arrangements for off-duty New York police officers to work security at the festival, Up against the Wall Motherfuckers circulated the information among members of the radical underground. The group suggested that if the radicals wanted to be able to take on and do bodily harm to unarmed police officers, Woodstock would provide an opportunity to do so. As it turned out, the peace officers and audience members generally got along well together, and radicals like the Up against the Wall Motherfuckers did not significantly affect the festival.

VAN LOAN, KEN   Ken Van Loan was a member of, and spokesperson for, the Bethel Businessman's Association, an organization that voted in late July 1969 to support the Woodstock festival on the site of Max Yasgur's dairy farm. Van Loan owned Bethel, New York's, Ken's Garage. Woodstock Ventures hired Van Loan just days before the start of the festival to tow ticket booths into place. He moved only a few before the size of the crowd and the traffic jams created by cars, both slowly moving and abandoned, made it impossible for him to bring in any more. Due in part to the unexpectedly large crowd, the lack of ticket booths, and the fact that the fences were being taken down by early arriving concertgoers as quickly as they could be put up, the Woodstock Music and Art Fair became a free event. *See also* **Bethel Businessman's Association.**

WADLEIGH, MICHAEL Born in Ohio and making rather obscure films from an East Coast base, Michael Wadleigh was the director of the documentary film *Woodstock: Three Days of Peace and Music* (1970). His company, Wadleigh-Maurice Productions, had negotiated a deal with John Roberts and Joel Rosenman in August 1969 to film the festival at its own expense and then try to place the finished film with a distributor. Woodstock Ventures was to receive 50 percent of the producer's royalty (minus the distributor's cut), with Wadleigh-Maurice Productions receiving 30 percent of that. Soon after the deal had been finalized, Wadleigh and his business partner Bob Maurice tried to get Woodstock Ventures to renegotiate the deal. Under the proposed arrangement, Woodstock Ventures would put up the approximately $100,000 that it would take to shoot and produce the film and would reap a significantly larger share of the profits. John Roberts nixed the deal, fearing that the festival still might not take place. Wadleigh's film eventually became a huge financial success, and Roberts' refusal to renegotiate the deal cost Woodstock Ventures a great deal of money. In addition to a sizable film crew, Wadleigh selected several young filmmaker-editors to help with the project. Of these, editor Martin Scorsese, a friend of Wadleigh's from film school, would later find considerable fame as a movie director, and editor Thelma Schoonmaker would receive *Woodstock: Three Days of Peace and Music*'s sole Oscar nomination: for Best Film Editing. Michael Wadleigh would later write and direct the 1981 film *Wolfen*. *See also* **Maurice, Bob; Schoonmaker, Thelma; Scorsese, Martin;** *Woodstock: Three Days of Peace and Music.*

WARD, BILL Bill Ward was a professor of sculpture at the University of Miami. He, his wife, Jean, Ron (another art instructor at the university), and Phyllis Liis accompanied and directed a team of University of Miami art students who produced art pieces that were placed around the site of the Woodstock festival. *See also* **Art.**

WAVY GRAVY Born Hugh Romney, Wavy Gravy was a former stand-up

Wavy Gravy speaks onstage at the free Woodstock Music and Art Fair. (CORBIS)

comic and an organizer of the Hog Farm, one of the early communes of the counterculture era. He and over eighty members of his commune worked for Woodstock Ventures to maintain a peaceful atmosphere at the Woodstock festival and to help the festival attendees (some of whom possibly had never even experienced camping in an organized campgrounds) have a positive experience living off the land. In addition to the work he did along with other members of his commune, he made stage announcements at the Woodstock festival. Wavy Gravy would later try to enter politics and would attend and contribute stage announcements at Woodstock '94 and Woodstock 1999. ***See also* Hog Farm, The.**

WHITE LAKE, NEW YORK   Max Yasgur's farm was located in this village, which was part of the Town of Bethel in Sullivan County.

WHO, THE   Consisting of vocalist Roger Daltry, guitarist Pete Townshend, bassist John Entwistle, and drummer Keith Moon, The Who was one of the premier British rock bands of the 1960s. Townshend's composition "My Generation" captured the spirit of the youth movement and generation gap of the entire counterculture era. By the time of their Woodstock appearance, The Who had created the "rock opera" *Tommy*, which was largely composed by Townshend. With the exception of "Heaven and Hell," "I Can't Explain," "Summertime Blues," "Shakin' All Over," "My Generation," and "The Naked Eye," The Who's lengthy set at Woodstock featured songs from *Tommy*. Although audience members and those associated with Woodstock Ventures had been disappointed with Janis Joplin's performance on Saturday, August 16, 1969, reports of some of the principals involved, including festival organizer Michael Lang and official photographer Henry Diltz, suggest that The Who's high-energy performance more than made up for Joplin's difficulties.[49]

The Who in live performance around the time of the Woodstock festival. (Courtesy of Photofest)

WILSHEIM, INGRID VON   Ingrid von Wilsheim was one of the behind-the-scenes people without whom the Woodstock Music and Art Fair could not have taken place. She handled purchasing for Woodstock Ventures.

WILSON, MALCOLM   New York state lieutenant governor Malcolm Wilson met with Joel Rosenman, John Roberts, and Felix Lourie at Lourie's urging in June 1969. At this point, just prior to the meeting of the Wallkill Town Board that effectively sealed the fate of the Wallkill site for the Woodstock Music and Art Fair, Woodstock Ventures was in desperate need of help from the New York state political establishment. Roberts and Rosenman prevailed upon the lieutenant governor to support the festival. The meeting did not produce an endorsement of the event, but eventually Roberts and Rosenman, with Felix Lourie's help, secured a letter from Governor Nelson Rockefeller's office welcoming the festival to New York state. The letter arrived too late to be produced at the June 12, 1969, meeting of the Wallkill Town Board that effectively shut out Woodstock Ventures from the Wallkill area.

WINTER, JOHNNY   Blues-rock guitarist Johnny Winter (born 1944) created a sensation in 1969, when, even though he was virtually unknown, Columbia Records offered him a lucrative recording contract. The record company heavily publicized the guitarist as the next important guitar virtuoso (presumably after Jimi Hendrix, Eric Clapton, Jeff Beck, and Jimmy Page, all of whom had already made an impact in the rock world). Although Winter's later career did not fulfill the promise of Columbia's early publicity, he was attracting considerable fan and media attention at the time of his appearance at Woodstock. Many of the early Woodstock set lists included only "Mean Town Blues" as Winter's sole contribution to Woodstock. There is evidence, however, that Winter and his band also performed the following songs at the festival: "Talk to Your Daughter," "Six Feet in the Ground," "Tell the Truth," "Johnny B. Goode," "Mean Mistreater," "I Can't Stand It," and "Tobacco Road." Winter's keyboardist brother Edgar, who would later gain fame with his song "Frankenstein," made a guest appearance with the band.[50]

WOODSTOCK MUSIC AND ART FAIR   The Woodstock Music and Art Fair, held August 15–17, 1969, on Max Yasgur's farm in Bethel, New York. Woodstock was organized by an executive staff consisting of Michael Lang, John Roberts, Joel Rosenman, and Artie Kornfield. The festival attracted some 400,000 and featured performances by Richie Havens; Jimi Hendrix; Crosby, Stills, Nash, and Young; The Who; Country Joe and the Fish; Creedence Clearwater Revival; John Sebastian; the Incredible String Band; Sweetwater; Ravi Shankar; Melanie; Arlo Guthrie; Joan Baez; Santana; Canned Heat; Mountain; Sly and the Family Stone; Jefferson Airplane; Joe Cocker; Ten Years After; Sha-Na-Na; Blood, Sweat, and Tears; the Paul Butterfield Blues Band; Janis Joplin; and The Grateful Dead. The demographics of the festival's attendees are detailed in Weiner and Stillman (1979). Woodstock is considered by many historians to represent the high point of the counterculture movement, at least the high point of how the philosophy of "peace, love, and understanding" could effectively work in a real-life situation. Due to the size of the crowd and inadequate sanitation and food, audience members had to live a communal life of sharing and cooperation for four days; by and large they succeeded. The film synopsis of the festival, entitled *Woodstock: Three Days of Peace and Music*, brought this sociological phenomenon to the entire world. ***See also Woodstock: Three Days of Peace and Music.***

WOODSTOCK: THREE DAYS OF PEACE AND MUSIC   The documentary film (1970) about the Woodstock Music and Art Fair, which was produced by Bob Maurice and directed by Michael Wadleigh. Maurice and Wadleigh, whose previous experience was largely in experimental films, negotiated with Woodstock Ventures to produce a documentary of the festival. The deal that was struck ended up benefiting Woodstock Ventures far less than might have been the case due to the reluctance of John Roberts to buy the full rights to the film from Wadleigh-Maurice Productions.[51] In addition to Wadleigh and Maurice, the film crew included film editors Martin Scorsese (who would later become a famous film director) and Thelma Schoonmaker (who would receive an Oscar nomination for Best Film Editing for the *Woodstock* film), location coordinator John Binder, cameramen David Myers and Dick Pierce, camera assistant Jeanne Field, and others. Warner Brothers was the distributor for the film. *Woodstock: Three Days of Peace and Music* has been deemed "culturally significant" by the U.S. Library of Congress and has been preserved in the National Film Registry.

WOODSTOCK VENTURES   Michael Lang, Artie Kornfeld, Joel Rosenman, and John Roberts formed this corporation in March 1969. Each of the principals had a 25 percent share in the company. The purpose of Woodstock Ventures was to put together the music and art festival as a means of raising money for a recording studio to be built in Woodstock, New York. Working primarily with friends and past business partners, they managed to produce the Woodstock Music and Art Fair in August 1969. Although Woodstock Ventures was disbanded as a corporation in 1972, Lang, Rosenman, and Roberts would later reestablish the name and produce Woodstock '94 and Woodstock 1999, in conjunction with associates from PolyGram and Metropolitan Entertainment.

WOODSTOCK, NEW YORK   The Woodstock Music and Art Fair was originally to have taken place not in Bethel, New York, but in the unincorporated Village of Woodstock. Rock band manager Michael Lang, Capitol Records executive Artie Kornfeld, and venture capitalists John Roberts and Joel Rosenman had planned to open a recording studio in Woodstock; the music festival was designed to draw attention to the studio as well as to provide funding for the studio's construction. Woodstock residents fought the festival, fearing an invasion by hordes of hippies. Although the venue was changed, the Woodstock name was retained. Part of the initial attraction of Woodstock, New York, was the growing presence of rock musicians who were moving into the area. Some of these included Jimi Hendrix, Tim

This movie still from the Michael Wadleigh–Bob Maurice film *Woodstock: Three Days of Peace and Music* shows some of the festival's audience, film crew, musicians, and stage hands. (Courtesy of Photofest)

Hardin, Janis Joplin, The Band, Van Morrison, and Bob Dylan. These musicians were attracted by Woodstock's combination of a nearly idyllic nature setting and proximity to the New York State Thruway, making for an easy drive to New York City. Woodstock, New York, has also boasted a flourishing visual arts community for generations. This thriving visual arts community combined with the presence of so many significant musicians gave Woodstock a cultural significance far exceeding the village's small population, which was 1,073 according to the 1970 U.S. census.

YASGUR, MAX   Yasgur and his wife, Miriam, owned the farm in Bethel, New York, on which the famed Woodstock Music and Art Fair took place. As documented in the film of the music festival, Yasgur and festival attendees seemed to develop a mutual respect, if not admiration, despite their generational differences. Yasgur's farm supplied dairy products to larger hotels and some retail stores. He was especially known for his chocolate milk, cream, and sour cream. Once Yasgur agreed to lease his land to Woodstock Ventures in July 1969, he became an important supporter of the festival. The Hasidic community in White Lake was especially vocal against the festival, as members of that community feared an invasion of hippies. Yasgur was well respected and well liked by the entire White Lake community and helped to calm the fears of residents. Yasgur died in February 1973.

Max Yasgur poses at his farm near Bethel, New York, on March 23, 1970. Yasgur, who rented his farms for the Woodstock festival in 1969, received over 3,000 letters from young people who came to the weekend festival, some letters addressed to "the groovy farmer at the festival." (AP/Wide World Photos)

YASGUR, MIRIAM   Husband and wife Max and Miriam Yasgur owned the farm in Bethel, New York, where the Woodstock festival eventually took place. After Max's death, Miriam became a primary source for insight into how festival organizers worked with the Yasgurs. Miriam Yasgur's recollections of the organization of the festival and the events of the festival itself are quoted in several sources, most notably Joel Makower's book *Woodstock: The Oral History*. By the time Makower conducted his interviews, Max Yasgur was dead; therefore, Miriam Yasgur's recollections were invaluable.

YASGUR'S FARM   Max and Miriam Yasgur's dairy farm in Bethel, New York, was the site of the Woodstock Music and Art Fair. After Max Yasgur's death in 1973, ownership of the farm became the subject of prolonged contention. Eventually, June Gelish took over ownership of the site until her death at age sixty-seven on April 15, 1997.[52] Cable television entrepreneur Alan Gerry purchased the land on which the music festival took place after Gelish's death. Gerry planned to open a music-related theme park, despite the opposition of area residents and those who felt that his plans for a commercial enterprise contradicted the original intent of the festival.[53]

YIPPIES   The Yippies of the late 1960s and early 1970s were members of Jerry Rubin, Paul Krassner, Ed Sanders, and Abbie Hoffman's Young People's International Party. Although their outward appearances might have made these young people virtually indistinguishable from the hippies of the era, the Yippies were active participants in left-wing radical politics and its associated demonstrations, leftist street theater, pamphleteering, and other forms of active rebellion against the U.S. government and the mores of conventional, straitlaced American society. After Yippie leader Abbie Hoffman learned of the plans for the Woodstock festival in June 1969, he became suspicious that the festival was something that corporate America was marketing to the youth counterculture. Hoffman contacted the festival promoters and charged them with trying to pull of a corporate rip-off of the counterculture and threatened to disrupt the festival. After Hoffman was promised a sum of money that would be used by the Young People's International Party and was assured that Yippies would be permitted to distribute political literature at what was otherwise carefully calculated not to be an overtly political event, Hoffman supported the Woodstock festival. *See also* **Hippies; Hoffman, Abbie.**

YOGA EXERCISES   Tom Law, one of the important members of the Hog Farm commune who assisted at the Woodstock festival, led morning yoga exercises for crowds approaching half a million people. Law touted yoga as a drug-free method for the concert attendees to gain self-awareness and to "get high." In his later recollections, Law expressed fascination with the way in which thousands of young people took part in these exercises as one.[54] One of the reasons that the principals of Woodstock Ventures wanted Law to lead concertgoers in yoga was to help maintain a calm mood at the festival. All accounts agree that the yoga experience was a success in that regard. *See also* **Law, Tom.**

NOTES

1. Although not perhaps as well remembered today as some of the other bands that performed at Altamont, The Flying Burrito Brothers was a group that was led by Gram Parsons, a onetime and short-term member of The Byrds. Both the Parsons version of The Byrds and The Flying Burrito Brothers were important influences on the new country-rock genre that was emerging in the late 1960s.

2. Farber, David, "The Intoxicated State/Illegal Nation: Drugs in the Sixties Counterculture," in Braunstein, Peter, and Michael William Doyle, eds., *Imagine Nation: The American Counterculture of the 1960s and '70s* (New York: Routledge, 2002), p. 36.

3. The famed British group did perform an impromptu rooftop concert in London in January 1969 for their film *Let It Be.*

4. Blood, Sweat, and Tears had been founded in 1967 by keyboardist-singer Al Kooper. Kooper left the band in 1968, and Clayton-Thomas was signed on as the group's vocalist.

5. Sometimes called "Barry's Caviar Dream."

6. Belmont, Bill, quoted in Makower, Joel, *Woodstock: The Oral History* (New York: Doubleday Press, 1989), p. 129.

7. Makower, *Woodstock*, p. 129.

8. Rosenman, Joel, John Roberts, and Robert Pilpel, *Young Men with Unlimited Capital* (New York: Harcourt Brace Jovanovich, 1974), p. 109.

9. The Food for Love principals had, in fact, done the food concession work for the Miami Pop Festival, the event that Michael Lang and Mel Lawrence had co-produced the year before the Woodstock Music and Art Fair.

10. Rosenman, Roberts, and Pilpel, *Young Men with Unlimited Capital*, p. 64.

11. Spitz, Robert Stephen, *Barefoot in Babylon: The Creation of the Woodstock Music Festival, 1969* (New York: Viking Press, 1979), pp. 180–81.

12. The band was known as The Warlocks at the time of their association with Ken Kesey and the Merry Pranksters.

13. Manzarek, Ray, *Light My Fire: My Life with The Doors* (New York: G. P. Putnam's Sons, 1998), p. 236.

14. *Grateful Dead: The Illustrated Trip* (New York: DK, 2003), p. 101.

15. Makower, *Woodstock*, p. 224.

16. The 1969 movie based on the song (*Alice's Restaurant*) brought Guthrie further exposure and a broader fame.

17. At the close of the twentieth century, Hendrix's "Purple Haze" was included on several lists of the most important American compositions of the century, along with works like George Gershwin's *Rhapsody in Blue* and Aaron Copland's *Fanfare for the Common Man.*

18. Hoskyns, Barney, "The Birth of Hippie Culture," in Kaleen, Stuart A., ed., *Sixties Counterculture,* (San Diego: Greenhaven Press, 2001), p. 109.

19. Mele, Christopher, *Selling the Lower East Side: Culture, Real Estate, and Resistance in New York City* (Minneapolis: University of Minnesota Press, 2000), p. 159.

20. Macan, Edward, *Rocking the Classics: English Progressive Rock and the Counterculture* (New York: Oxford University Press, 1996), pp. 15–16.

21. Weiner, Rex, and Deanne Stillman, *Woodstock Census: The Nationwide Survey of the Sixties Generation* (New York: Viking, 1979).

22. Rosenman, Roberts, and Pilpel, *Young Men with Unlimited Capital.*

23. Sinclair, who also had managed the political rock band the MC5, had been jailed on what many members of the counterculture felt was a trumped-up drug charge.

24. Derogatis, Jim, "Incredible String Band," *Yahoo! LAUNCH,* http://launch.yahoo.com, accessed January 13, 2004.

25. Jefferson Airplane member Paul Kantner recalls that their set did not begin until approximately 7:00 A.M. on Sunday, quoted in Makower, *Woodstock*, p. 239.

26. Makower, *Woodstock*, p. 234.

27. The Keef Hartley Band's lead vocalist Miller Anderson is quoted as saying, "I remember being back stage, waiting to go on, when a fella approaches me with a clipboard. Turns out he's with the people filming the show, and he starts asking me what numbers we're doing, where the solos will be, etc. Up walks Johnny [Johnny Jones was the Keef Hartley Band's manager], asks what's going on, then says something like, 'Sorry, you're not filming my boys without a written contract.'" *A Brief History of Keef,* http://www.ammoniterecords.demon.co.uk/KeefHartley/keith_hist.html. A personal e-mail to the author from Ian Southworth, a representative of Hartley's current record company, however, suggests that the set was filmed but that the footage of the Keith Hartley Band simply has never been released.

28. Personal e-mail to the author from Ian Southworth, a representative of Hartley's current (spring 2004) record company, Kashmir Records.

29. Personal e-mail to the author from Ian Southworth, a representative of Hartley's current (spring 2004) record company, Kashmir Records.

30. Rosenman, Roberts, and Pilpel, *Young Men with Unlimited Capital* and Makower, *Woodstock* contains numerous examples of the tension between the four principals, at which Michael Lang was often at the center.

31. Quoted in Makower, *Woodstock*.

32. Lisa Law, "Organizing Woodstock," http://americanhistory.si.edu/lisalaw/7.htm.

33. Some of Law's insights into the festival (especially the Hog Farm's role), as well as some of her photographs from Woodstock, are available on the Internet at http://american history.si.edu/lisalaw, a Web page produced by the Smithsonian Institution.

34. Makower, *Woodstock*, pp. 244–45.

35. Samuels, David, "Rock Is Dead (Woodstock 1999)," *Harper's Magazine* (November 1999).

36. Makower, *Woodstock*, p. 45.

37. The counterculture era is generally defined as 1960–75.

38. Makower, *Woodstock*, p. 48.

39. "Mississippi Queen" would be the group's sole top 40 hit, hitting number 21 on the *Billboard* pop singles charts in spring 1970.

40. Both Makower, *Woodstock* and Rosenman, Roberts, and Pilpel, *Young Men with Unlimited Capital* detail to humorous effect the issue of the principals of Woodstock Ventures calculating the number of toilets that would be needed for the festival.

41. The first three of these songs were included on Santana's self-titled debut album.

42. Curiously, none of the published books on the Woodstock festival include his first name.

43. Spitz, *Barefoot in Babylon*, p. 416.

44. The Left Banke was best known for their 1966 hit "Walk Away Renee," which reached number 5 on the *Billboard* pop singles charts. The band experienced business-related problems subsequently and keyboardist Mike Brown recorded with various musicians, including vocalist Bert Sommer, using the moniker The Left Banke.

45. Smith Kline & French Laboratories, Thorazine advertisement, reproduced at http://www.biopsychiatry.com/chlorpromazine/thorazine.jpg, accessed January 28, 2004.

46. Rosenman, Roberts, and Pilpel, *Young Men with Unlimited Capital*, p. 36.

47. Makower, *Woodstock*, pp. 34–35.

48. Rosenman, Roberts, and Pilpel, *Young Men with Unlimited Capital*, pp. 23–25. The changing of Train's name to Diesel is one of several curious changes in the Woodstock story made by the authors, possibly to avoid legal entanglements. The most telling other "discrepancy" between the recollections of Roberts and Rosenman in *Young Men with Unlimited Capital* and their recollections in Joel Makower's *Woodstock* is the constant reference to what was obviously marijuana and hashish as "tobacco" in their earlier book.

49. Makower, *Woodstock*, pp. 234–35.

50. Schmid, Thomas, and Kees de Lange, "1969 Woodstock Performers Song List," *Woodstock '69.* http://www.woodstock69.com/Woodstock_songs.htm, accessed June 29, 2003.

51. Roberts, John, quoted in Makower, *Woodstock*, p. 306.

52. Apparently, there were competing claims to ownership from Jeryl Abramson and Roy Howard in 1996.

53. As the reader will see in the chapter about the Woodstock Music and Art Fair, the

event was designed to be a commercially successful, moneymaking event from the start. Woodstock Ventures carefully avoided emphasizing this aspect of the operation, however, fearing that it would alienate members of the counterculture, the people who were potential attendees. When the festival became a free event when the crowds far exceeded the capacity of the ticket booths and fences and with the spirit of peaceful cooperation that helped over 400,000 people make it through the festival, Woodstock came to be seen as a great counterculture coming together without commerciality. The truth is that Woodstock was really more of a commercial venture that failed in its original intent.

54. Makower, *Woodstock*, pp. 244–45.

Appendix J: Woodstock Set Lists

Like virtually everything else surrounding the Woodstock Music and Art Fair, compiling a completely documented, accurate set list for the acts presents problems. Some acts (e.g., Joe McDonald's solo set on August 15, 1969, and John Sebastian's walk-on performance) were not even scheduled to appear but did so. It has been an oft-repeated contention that at least one act, the Keef Hartley Band, was not filmed and presumably was not audio-recorded, and their performance set list seems not to have ever been published anywhere. A partial set list with Hartley's current record company, though confirmed, is possibly incomplete. Recollections of audience members and some performers were sometimes in disagreement, perhaps due to the passage of time and/or the enjoyment of some of the illicit drugs that were so easy to come by at Woodstock. Adding to the confusion, some performances that were scheduled for a particular evening actually took place the following morning—in fact, the "Three Days of Peace and Music" turned into four days, at least unofficially. The following list uses published sources and notes songs about which there is the greatest amount of disagreement. The festival is split up into four days due to the fact that the Paul Butterfield Blues Band, Sha-Na-Na, and Jimi Hendrix performances took place during the daylight hours of Monday, August 18, 1969. In the following list, songwriters' names are in parentheses.

DAY ONE (FRIDAY, AUGUST 15, 1969)

Richie Havens

"Minstrel Came down from Gault" (Richie Havens, Mark Roth)[1]

Medley: "High Flyin' Bird" (Billy Wheeler)/"I Had a Woman" (Joe Josea, B. B. King)[2]

"I Can't Make It Anymore" (Gordon Lightfoot)

"With a Little Help from My Friends" (John Lennon, Paul McCartney)

"Strawberry Fields Forever" (John Lennon, Paul McCartney)

"Hey Jude" (John Lennon, Paul McCartney)[3]

"Handsome Johnny" (Richie Havens, Louis Gossett Jr.)

"Freedom" (traditional, adapted by Richie Havens)

Country Joe McDonald[4]

"Janis"[5] (Joe McDonald)

"Rocking All Around the World" (Joe McDonald)

"Flying High All Over the World" (Joe McDonald)

"I Seen a Rocket"[6] (Joe McDonald)

"The 'FISH' Cheer"/"I-Feel-Like-I'm-Fixin'-to-Die Rag" (Joe McDonald)

John B. Sebastian[7]

"How Have You Been?" (John B. Sebastian)

"Rainbows All Over Your Blues" (John B. Sebastian)

"I Had a Dream" (John B. Sebastian)

"Darling Be Home Soon" (John B. Sebastian)

"The Younger Generation" (John B. Sebastian)

Sweetwater

"Motherless Child" (traditional)

"Look Out" (Nansi Nevins)

"For Pete's Sake" (Alex Del Zoppo)

"Day Song" (Nansi Nevins)

"What's Wrong" (Alex Del Zoppo)

"My Crystal Spider" (Alex Del Zoppo)

"Two Worlds" (Nansi Nevins)

"Why, Oh Why?" (Albert B. Moore)

Bert Sommer

"Jennifer" (Bert Sommer)

"America" (Paul Simon)

Tim Hardin

"Misty Roses" (Tim Hardin)[8]

"If I Were a Carpenter" (Tim Hardin)

Ravi Shankar[9]

Raga Puriya-Dhanashri/Gat In Sawarital

Tabla Solo In Jhaptal

Raga Manj Kmahaj

    "Alap Jor"

    "Dhun In Kaharwa Tal"

    "Medium and Fast Gat In Teental"

Melanie

"Beautiful People" (Melanie Safka)

"Birthday of the Sun" (Melanie Safka)

Arlo Guthrie

"Coming into Los Angeles" (Arlo Gurthrie)

"Walking Down the Line" (Bob Dylan)

"Amazing Grace" (traditional)

Joan Baez

"Joe Hill" (Earl Robinson, Alfred Hayes)

"Sweet Sir Galahad" (Joan Baez)

"Drug Store Truck Driving Man" (Roger McGuinn, Gram Parsons)

"We Shall Overcome" (traditional)

"Swing Low, Sweet Chariot" (traditional)

DAY TWO (SATURDAY, AUGUST 16, 1969)

Quill

"Waiting for You" (unknown)[10]

The Keef Hartley Band[11]

"Sinning for You" (Peter Dines, Fred Finnegan, Keef Hartley, Steve Hewitson)

"Born to Die" (Peter Dines, Keef Hartley, Steve Hewitson, Gary Thain)

"Leaving Trunk" (Sleepy John Estes)

"Just to Cry" (Fred Finnegan, Lowther)

Santana

"Persuasion" (Carlos Santana, Gregg Rolie, José Areas, Mike Carabello, David Brown, Michael Schrieve)

"Savor" (Carlos Santana, Gregg Rolie, José Areas, Mike Carabello, David Brown, Michael Schrieve)

"Soul Sacrifice" (Carlos Santana, Gregg Rolie, José Areas, Mike Carabello, David Brown, Michael Schrieve)

"Fried Neckbones and Some Homefries" (Willie Bobo, Melvin Lastie)

The Incredible String Band[12]

"Sleepers Awaken" (Mike Heron)[13]

"Catty Come" (unknown)[14]

"This Moment Is Different" (Mike Heron)

"When You Find out Who You Are" (Robin Williamson)

Canned Heat

Medley: "A Change Is Gonna Come" (Sam Cooke)/"Leaving this Town" (Adolfo De La Parra, Harvey Mandel, Samuel Lawrence Taylor)

"Woodstock Boogie" (Canned Heat)

"Going up the Country" (Alan Wilson)

"Let's Work Together" (Wilbert Harrison)

"Too Many Drivers at the Wheel" (Big Bill Broonzy)

Mountain[15]

"Blood of the Sun" (Gail Collins, Felix Pappalardi, Leslie West)

"Stormy Monday" (T-Bone Walker)

"Long Red" (Leslie West, Felix Pappalardi, John Ventura, Norman Landsberg)

"For Yasgur's Farm"[16] (Gail V. Collins, George Gardos, Laurence Gordon Laing, Felix Pappalardi, David Rea, Gary Ship)

"Theme from an Imaginary Western" (Peter Brown, Jack Bruce)

"Waiting to Take You Away" (Leslie West)

"Dreams of Milk and Honey" (Norman Landsberg, Felix Pappalardi, John Ventura, Leslie West)

"Blind Man" (Gail V. Collins, Felix Pappalardi, John Ventura, Leslie West)

"Blue Suede Shoes" (Carl Perkins)

"South Bound Train" (Norman Landsberg, John Ventura, Leslie West)

"Mississippi Queen" (Laurence Gordon Laing, Felix Pappalardi, David Rea, Leslie West)[17]

Creedence Clearwater Revival

"Born on the Bayou" (John C. Fogerty)

"Green River" (John C. Fogerty)

"Ninty-Nine-and-a-Half (Won't Do)" (Wilson Pickett, Steve Cropper, Eddie Floyd)

"Commotion" (John C. Fogerty)

"Bootleg" (John C. Fogerty)

"Bad Moon Rising" (John C. Fogerty)

"Proud Mary" (John C. Fogerty)

"I Put a Spell on You" (Jay Hawkins)

"Night Time Is the Right Time" (Lew Herman)

"Keep on Chooglin'" (John C. Fogerty)

"Susie Q"[18] (Dale Hawkins, Stanley Lewis)

The Grateful Dead

"St. Stephen" (Jerry Garcia, Robert Hunter, Phil Lesh)

"Mama Tried" (Merle Haggard)

Medley: "Dark Star" (Jerry Garcia, Mickey Hart, Bill Kreutzmann, Phil Lesh, Ron McKernan, Bob Weir)/"High Time" (Jerry Garcia, Robert Hunter)

"Turn on Your Lovelight" (Don Robey, Joseph Scott)

Janis Joplin

"Raise Your Hand" (Steve Cropper, Eddie Floyd, Alvertis Isbell)

"As Good As You've Been to This World" (Nick Gravenites)

"To Love Somebody" (Barry Gibb, Robin Gibb)

"Summertime" (Dubois Heywood, George Gershwin)

"Try (Just a Little Bit Harder)" (Jerry Ragovoy, Chip Taylor)

"Kozmic Blues" (Janis Joplin, Gabriel Meckler)

"I Can't Turn You Loose" (Otis Redding)

"Work Me Lord" (Nick Gravenites)

"Piece of My Heart" (Jerry Ragovoy, B. Berns)

"Ball and Chain" (Willie Mae Thornton)

Sly and the Family Stone[19]

"M'Lady" (Sylvester Stewart)

"Sing a Simple Song" (Sylvester Stewart)

"You Can Make It if You Try" (Sylvester Stewart)

"Stand!" (Sylvester Stewart)

"Love City" (Sylvester Stewart)

Medley: "Dance to the Music" (Sylvester Stewart)/"Music Lover" (Sylvester Stewart)/"I Want to Take You Higher" (Sylvester Stewart)

The Who

"Heaven and Hell" (John Entwistle)

"I Can't Explain" (Pete Townshend)

"It's a Boy" (Pete Townshend)

"1921" (Pete Townshend)

"Amazing Journey" (Pete Townshend)

"Sparks" (Pete Townshend)

"Eyesight to the Blind" (Sonny Boy Williamson)

"Christmas" (Pete Townshend)

"Tommy, Can You Hear Me" (Pete Townshend)

"Acid Queen" (Pete Townshend)

"Pinball Wizard" (Pete Townshend)

"Do You Think It's Alright?" (Pete Townshend)

"Fiddle About" (John Entwistle)

"There's a Doctor I've Found" (Pete Townshend)

"Go to the Mirror, Boy" (Pete Townshend)

"Smash the Mirror" (Pete Townshend)

"I'm Free" (Pete Townshend)

"Tommy's Holiday Camp" (Keith Moon)

"We're Not Gonna Take It" (Pete Townshend)

"See Me, Feel Me" (Pete Townshend)

"Summertime Blues" (Jerry Capehart, Eddie Cochran)

"Shakin' All Over" (Daniel Racicot)

"My Generation" (Pete Townshend)

"The Naked Eye" (Pete Townshend)

DAY THREE (SUNDAY, AUGUST 17, 1969)

The Jefferson Airplane[20]

"The Other Side of This Life" (Fred Neil)

"Plastic Fantastic Lover" (Marty Balin)

"Volunteers" (Paul Kantner, Marty Balin)

"Saturday Afternoon" (Paul Kantner)

"Won't You Try" (Paul Kantner)

"Eskimo Blue Day" (Paul Kantner, Grace Slick)

"Uncle Sam Blues" (traditional, arranged by Paul Kantner, Jack Casady, Jorma Kaukonen)

"Somebody to Love" (Darby Slick)

"White Rabbit" (Grace Slick)

Joe Cocker

"Delta Lady" (Leon Russell)

"Something's Comin' On" (Joe Cocker, Christopher Stainton)[21]

"Just Like a Woman" (Bob Dylan)[22]

"Dear Landlord" (Bob Dylan)[23]

"Let's Go Get Stoned" (Jo Armstead, Nickolas Ashford, Valerie Simpson)

"I Shall Be Released" (Bob Dylan)

"With a Little Help from My Friends" (John Lennon, Paul McCartney)

Country Joe and the Fish

"Barry's Song" (Barry Melton)[24]

"Not So Sweet Martha Lorraine" (Joe McDonald)

"Rock and Soul Music" (Joe McDonald, Barry Melton, Chicken Hirsch, Bruce Barthol, David Cohen)

"Thing Called Love" (Bruce Barthol, Barry Melton, Joe McDonald, Chicken Hirsch, David Cohen)

"Love Machine" (Barry Melton)

"The 'FISH' Cheer"/"I-Feel-Like-I'm-Fixin'-to-Die Rag" (Joe McDonald)

Ten Years After

"Good Morning Little Schoolgirl" (Sonny Boy Williamson)

"I Can't Keep from Crying Sometimes" (Al Kooper)

"I May Be Wrong, but I Won't Be Wrong Always" (Chick Churchill, Alvin Lee, Ric Lee, Leo Lyons)

"I'm Going Home" (Alvin Lee)

The Band

"Chest Fever" (J. R. Robertson)

"Baby Don't You Do It" (Brian Holland, Lamont Dozier, Eddie Holland Jr.)

"Tears of Rage" (Bob Dylan, Richard Manuel)

"We Can Talk" (Richard Manuel)

"Long Black Veil" (Danny Dill, Marijohn Wilkin)

"Don't You Tell Henry" (Bob Dylan)

"Ain't No More Cane" (traditional)

"Wheels on Fire" (Bob Dylan)

"Loving You (Is Sweeter than Ever)" (Ivy George Hunter, Stevie Wonder)

"The Weight" (J. R. Robertson)

"I Shall Be Released" (Bob Dylan)[25]

Blood, Sweat, and Tears

"All in a Day" (unknown)[26]

"More and More" (Pea Vee, Don Juan)

"I Love You Baby More than You'll Ever Know" (Al Kooper)

"Spinning Wheel" (David Clayton-Thomas)

"I Stand Accused" (T. Colton, R. Smith)

"Something's Comin' On" (Joe Cocker, Christopher Stainton)

Johnny Winter[27]

Medley: "Talk to Your Daughter" (Alex Atkins, J. B. Lenoir)/"Six Feet in the Ground" (St. Louis Jimmy Oden?)[28]

"Tell the Truth" (Lowman Pauling?)[29]

"Johnny B. Goode" (Chuck Berry)

"Rock Me Baby" (Arthur Crudup)

"Mean Mistreater" (James Gordon)

"I Can't Stand It" (unknown)

"Tobacco Road" (John D. Loudermilk)[30]

"Mean Town Blues" (Johnny Winter)

Crosby, Stills, Nash, and Young

"Suite: Judy Blue Eyes" (Stephen Stills)

"Blackbird" (John Lennon, Paul McCartney)

"Guinnevere" (David Crosby)

"Marrakesh Express" (Graham Nash)

"4 + 20" (Stephen Stills)

"Mr. Soul" (Neil Young)

"Sea of Madness" (Neil Young)

"Wooden Ships" (David Crosby, Stephen Stills)

"Find the Cost of Freedom" (Stephen Stills)

DAY FOUR (MONDAY, AUGUST 18, 1969)

The Paul Butterfield Blues Band[31]

"Everything's Gonna Be Alright" (Little Walter)

"Driftin' " (unknown)

"Born under a Bad Sign" (William Bell, Booker T. Jones Jr.)

"All My Love Comin' through to You" (unknown)

"Love March" (Gene Dinwiddie, Philip Wilson)

Sha-Na-Na

"Na Na Theme" (unknown)

"Yakety Yak" (Jerry Leiber, Mike Stoller)

"Teen Angel" (Dion Di Mucci, Frederick Patrick, Murray Singer)

"Jail House Rock" (Jerry Leiber, Mike Stoller)

"Wipe Out" (Robert Berryhill, Patrick Connolly, James Fuller, Ronald Wilson)

"The Book of Love" (Warren Davis, George Malone, Charles Patrick)

"Duke of Earl" (Eugene Dixon, Earl G. Edwards Sr., Bernice Williams)

"At the Hop" (A. Singer, J. Medora, P. White)

"Na Na Theme" (unknown)

Jimi Hendrix

"Message to Love" (Jimi Hendrix)

"Getting My Heart Back Together Again" (Jimi Hendrix)

"Spanish Castle Magic" (Jimi Hendrix)

"Red House" (Jimi Hendrix)

"Master Mind" (Jimi Hendrix and band)[32]

"Here He Comes (Your Lover Man)" (Jimi Hendrix)

"Foxey Lady" (Jimi Hendrix)

"Beginnings" (Jimi Hendrix)

"Izabella" (Jimi Hendrix)

"Gypsy Woman" (Jimi Hendrix)

"Fire" (Jimi Hendrix)

Medley: "Voodoo Chile (Slight Return)"/"Stepping Stone" (Jimi Hendrix)

Medley: "The Star-Spangled Banner" (traditional, arranged by Jimi Hendrix)/"Purple Haze" (Jimi Hendrix)

Improvised Segue to "Villanova Junction" (Jimi Hendrix)

"Villanova Junction" (Jimi Hendrix)

"Hey Joe" (Billy Roberts)

NOTES

1. Schmid, Thomas, and Kees de Lange, "1969 Woodstock Performers Song List," *Woodstock '69* [World Wide Web Resource], http://www.woodstock69.com/Woodstock_songs.htm, accessed June 29, 2003. Schmid and de Lange cite the source of this inclusion as e-mail from "Woodstock Alumni."

2. As far as I can determine, Havens never commercially recorded a song entitled "I Had a Woman," nor is the song included in any of the official releases of Woodstock material on audio recordings or film. A search of the American Society of Composers, Authors and Publishers (ASCAP) and Broadcast Music Incorporated (BMI) song title databases suggests that the Joe Josea and B. B. King blues composition of this title may have been the piece performed by Havens at the festival.

3. In addition to the Beatles songs "With a Little Help from My Friends," "Strawberry Fields Forever," and "Hey Jude," some set lists have also suggested that Richie Havens performed George Harrison's "Something." Since the earliest public appearance of the song came with the United Kingdom release of the Beatles' *Abbey Road* album on September 26, 1969 (the album and the 45-rpm single of "Something" were both released in the United States on October 1, 1969), it seems highly unlikely that Havens performed the song at Woodstock.

4. Makower, Joel, *Woodstock: The Oral History* (New York: Doubleday Press, 1989), p. 191. Other sources, most notably Schmid and de Lange and Internet sources based on

Schmid and de Lange, list McDonald's as a performer on Saturday, August 16, 1969. It should be noted that McDonald was not scheduled to do a solo set; he performed as a soloist to help the organizers fill time since some of the acts were having difficulty getting to the concert site.

5. The title is sometimes given as "I Find Myself Missing You."

6. Every set list I have seen incorrectly lists this title as "Seen a Rocket."

7. Makower, *Woodstock*, pp. 192–193. Schmid and de Lange list Sebastian as a performer on Saturday, August 16, 1969. It should be noted that Sebastian was not scheduled to perform; he did a walk-on performance to help fill time.

8. Schmid and de Lange. The source of this is listed as an e-mail from "Woodstock Alumni."

9. The pieces performed by sitarist Ravi Shankar and his ensemble were improvised in the Hindustani tradition. These improvised works, which use traditional *raga* (scale patterns), frequently do not carry composer credit.

10. Since Quill apparently never recorded a song with this title, but the Incredible String Band did, the song may have been performed by the latter group or may have been a Quill cover of the Incredible String Band piece.

11. Exactly what songs were performed by the Keef Hartley Band has long been a mystery. Set lists for other groups have largely been based on film and audio recordings of the festival. As discussed elsewhere, due to an apparent oversight on the part of Hartley's manager, the group's set was not audio-recorded. Information in this set list comes from a personal e-mail from Ian Southworth at Keef Hartley's current record company.

12. Http://www.robotwisdom.com/jorn/isb.html also lists "Sleepers Awaken" as part of the Incredible String Band's set. There seems to be no other independent verification of the group's performance of this song.

13. This song is not included in some of the set lists that have been published on the Internet.

14. This song is not included in some of the set lists that have been published on the Internet.

15. There has been some confusion about when Mountain performed at Woodstock. Schmid and de Lange place their performance immediately following Country Joe and the Fish on Sunday, August 17, 1969. *Woodstock Festival 1969: Set Lists*, http://geocities.com/Beatlefreak1/page3.html cites film and photographic evidence to suggest that the band followed Canned Heat on Saturday, August 16, 1969.

16. It appears that this song was as yet untitled at the time of Mountain's performance. Subsequently, it was issued under the title, "For Yasgur's Farm."

17. *Woodstock Festival 1969: Set Lists*, http://geocities.com/Beatlefreak1/page3.html. Some of the other published set lists for Mountain's performance at the festival do not include "Mississippi Queen." Since it was one of Mountain's best-known and most commercially successful songs at the time, it seems likely that they did indeed perform it.

18. This title sometimes is given as "Suzie Q." The legal title for copyright registration is "Susie Q."

19. Schmid and de Lange cite e-mails from "Woodstock Alumni" as the source for the inclusion of "M'Lady," "Sing a Simple Song," "You Can Make It if You Try," and "Stand!" Previous Woodstock set lists did not include these songs.

20. Jefferson Airplane was scheduled to be the headlining Saturday night act at Woodstock. Since the festival ran considerably behind schedule due to weather problems, longer-than-anticipated sets, the difficulty some artists found in getting to the site, and the

insertion of unscheduled performers into the festival, the Airplane actually began their performance around dawn on Sunday morning.

21. Many of the set lists that are circulating on the Internet give this title as "Something's Goin' On"; however, I can find no evidence that Cocker ever recorded or performed a song of this title.

22. *Woodstock Festival 1969: Set Lists*, http://geocities.com/Beatlefreak1/page3.html. Some published set lists do not include this Bob Dylan song, despite the fact that the Woodstock documentary film shows Cocker adding it to his set list. *Woodstock Master Tapes for Sale*, http://www.digibuilders.com/jobs/woodstock/index.html confirms Cocker's performance of "Just Like a Woman" at Woodstock.

23. *Woodstock Festival 1969: Set Lists*, http://geocities.com/Beatlefreak1/page3.html. Some set lists do not include this Bob Dylan song; however, the author(s) of the *Woodstock Festival 1969: Set Lists* page cite film evidence of Cocker's performance. *Woodstock Master Tapes for Sale*, http://www.digibuilders.com/jobs/woodstock/index.html confirms Cocker's performance of "Dear Landlord" at Woodstock.

24. Many of the set lists that are circulating on the Internet give this title as "Barry's Caviar Dream." Search of performing rights databases and the catalog of titles recorded by Country Joe and the Fish, however, suggest that "Barry's Song" is the official title of the piece the group actually performed.

25. Schmid and de Lange cite *Woodstock Master Tapes for Sale* as the source for this listing.

26. Schmid and de Lange cite *Woodstock Master Tapes for Sale* as the source for this listing. Other previously published set lists do not include the song.

27. Winter's performance of "Mean Town Blues" has been confirmed by several verified releases of recorded material from the Woodstock festival. The apparent original source for information on the remainder of Winter's set is the Web site *Woodstock Master Tapes for Sale*. To the extent that these tapes are authentic, they represent confirmation of Winter's entire Woodstock set.

28. Johnny Winter never officially released a recording of a song with this title. I speculate that his performance at Woodstock was of the old St. Louis Jimmy Oden blues song "Six Feet in the Ground."

29. Johnny Winter never officially released a recording of a song with this title. I speculate that his performance at Woodstock was of the Lowman Pauling song "Tell the Truth," a song recorded by several blues and soul musicians.

30. Schmid and de Lange suggest that Edgar Winter made a guest appearance with his brother Johnny's band for the performance of this song.

31. Although the Paul Butterfield group and the performers that followed them were scheduled for Saturday, August 17, 1969, they actually took the stage early Monday morning, August 18, 1969.

32. "Master Mind" was a blues jam. The ASCAP list of titles credited to Hendrix does not include "Master Mind," as the song spontaneously improvised at Woodstock. It might be noted that throughout 1969 Hendrix turned increasingly to improvisatory instrumental music. In 1980, Hendrix's record label, Reprise Records, issued an album of instrumental jams Hendrix had recorded in the studio between March 25, 1969, and June 25, 1969. Many of the pieces on the album *Nine to the Universe* are blues-based and suggest a fusion of rock, blues, and jazz.

Appendix II:
Recordings and Films

THE AUDIO RECORDING AND DOCUMENTARY FILM (1969)

Michael Wadleigh directed the film documentary of the Woodstock Music and Art Fair, *Woodstock: Three Days of Peace and Music*. Wadleigh and his partner, Bob Maurice, had negotiated with Woodstock Ventures to produce the film and had originally asked Woodstock Ventures to fund the project in return for additional future revenue once the film was released theatrically. Had the deal been finalized as proposed, Woodstock Ventures would have received a far greater share of the box office receipts. Concerned with the up-front costs and having no way of knowing that the film eventually would make a huge profit and be successfully issued on video and DVD, Woodstock Ventures agreed to have Wadleigh-Maurice Productions make the film but would not contribute the up-front cash for the project. In writings and interviews reproduced in numerous places, Joel Rosenman and John Roberts have long lamented over their decision.

Although Michael Wadleigh directed *Woodstock: Three Days of Peace and Music* and Bob Maurice produced the film, work on the documentary certainly was not a two-person operation. Two of the film's editors, Thelma Schoonmaker and Martin Scorsese, in fact, would make the transition to Hollywood blockbusters. Scorsese became a famed film director and is best known for his movies *The Last Temptation of Christ, Taxi Driver, Raging Bull*, and *Gangs of New York*. The Algerian-born Schoonmaker later continued her collaborations with Scorsese and worked as a film editor on movies like *Raging Bull* and *Cape Fear*. Incidentally, *Woodstock: Three Days of Peace and Music* received one Oscar nomination: for Best Film Editing, with Thelma Schoonmaker receiving the nomination from the Academy of Motion Picture Arts and Sciences.

The film opened up the world of late 1960s hippies to the entire world. Its significance as a chronicle of the youth counterculture of the era is perhaps best summed up in the title of editor Dale Bell's 1999 book *Woodstock: An Inside Look at the Movie That Shook up the World and Defined a Generation.*[1] Even after its theatrical run, *Woodstock: Three Days of Peace and Music* continued to be a favorite film on college and university campuses for years.

The *Woodstock: Three Days of Peace and Music* film also has been reissued on videocassette, videodisc, and DVD. The 1997 director's cut edition included over thirty minutes of extra performances not included in the original theatrical release. The following performers are featured in the currently widest-available cut of the film: Joan Baez, Joe Cocker, Country Joe and the Fish, Crosby, Stills, and Nash, Arlo Guthrie, Richie Havens, Jimi Hendrix, the Jefferson Airplane, Janis Joplin, Santana, John Sebastian, Sha-Na-Na, Sly and the Family Stone, Ten Years After, and The Who.

The two-album set was released by Atlantic Records in 1970 and was marketed as a sound track from the Wadleigh-Maurice film. As such, it included stage announcements and crowd chants in addition to music from the festival. One of the things that have plagued live festival recordings from the jazz age through the rock era is the need for the various record companies with which the artists are affiliated to agree to have their artists appear on a festival album that some other company—a competitor—releases. In some cases, artists who appeared on the soundtrack album did not appear in the film, due to contractual, artistic, and technical problems. Despite this difficulty, the Woodstock album represented the diverse styles of the festival well. In the compact disc age, the album has undergone several reissues, both in single-CD and two-CD form. The currently most widely available compact disc reissue, Atlantic 7567-80593-2 (2001), includes the following tracks:

Disc 1

1.	John B. Sebastian	"I Had a Dream"
2.	Canned Heat	"Going up the Country"
3.	Richie Havens	"Freedom"
4.	Country Joe and the Fish	"Rock & Soul Music"
5.	Arlo Guthrie	"Coming into Los Angeles"
6.	Sha-Na-Na	"At the Hop"
7.	Country Joe and the Fish	The "FISH" Cheer and "I-Feel-Like-I'm-Fixin'-to-Die Rag"
8.	Joan Baez[2]	"Drug Store Truck Drivin' Man"
9.	Joan Baez	"Joe Hill"
10.	Crosby, Stills, and Nash	"Suite: Judy Blue Eyes"
11.	Crosby, Stills, Nash, and Young	"Sea of Madness"

12. Crosby, Stills, Nash, and Young   "Wooden Ships"

13. The Who   "We're Not Gonna Take It" from *Tommy*

14. Joe Cocker   "With a Little Help from My Friends"

Disc 2

1. Crowd Rain Chant

2. Santana   "Soul Sacrifice"

3. Ten Years After   "I'm Going Home"

4. The Jefferson Airplane   "Volunteers"

5. Sly and the Family Stone: Medley: "Dance to the Music," "Music Lover," "I Want to Take You Higher"

6. John B. Sebastian   "Rainbows All over Your Blues"

7. The Paul Butterfield Blues Band   "Love March"[3]

8. Jimi Hendrix   Medley: "The Star-Spangled Banner," "Purple Haze," Instrumental Solo

In addition to these tracks, the Woodstock sound-track recording includes several of the stage announcements by Chip Monck, John Morris, Wavy Gravy, and Hog Farm member Muskrat, as well as Max Yasgur's famous brief talk to the crowd praising them for being so well behaved.

A 1971 two-album set, *Woodstock Two*, also issued by Atlantic Records, included the following tracks:

1. Jimi Hendrix   "Jam Back at the House"

2. Jimi Hendrix   "Izabella"

3. Jimi Hendrix   "Get My Heart Back Together"

4. The Jefferson Airplane   "Saturday Afternoon"

5. The Jefferson Airplane   "Won't You Try"

6. The Jefferson Airplane   "Eskimo Blue Day"

7. Paul Butterfield Blues Band   "Everything's Gonna Be Alright"

8. Joan Baez   "Sweet Sir Galahad"

9. Crosby, Stills, Nash, and Young   "Guinnevere"

10. Crosby, Stills, Nash, and Young   "4 + 20"

11. Crosby, Stills, Nash, and Young	"Marrakesh Express"
12. Melanie	"My Beautiful People"
13. Melanie	"Birthday of the Sun"
14. Mountain	"Blood of the Sun"
15. Mountain	"Theme from an Imaginary Western"
16. Canned Heat	"Woodstock Boogie"
17. Audience	"Let the Sunshine In" from *Hair*

The *Woodstock Two* album has also been reissued as a two-compact disc set, most recently in 1995 as Atlantic 7567-80594-2. Atlantic Records also issued a four-disc set that included tracks from the *Woodstock* and *Woodstock Two* sets, as well as a few additional tracks, in 1995 (Atlantic 82634) to commemorate the twenty-fifth anniversary of the Woodstock Music and Art Fair. Most importantly, the four-disc set included performances by Creedence Clearwater Revival, Tim Hardin, The Band, and Johnny Winter, none of which appeared on either *Woodstock* or *Woodstock Two*.

AUDIO RECORDING (1994)

One way in which Woodstock '94 did not succeed particularly well was as a business venture. There were some successes in this particular area, as well as some failures. Certainly, having at least 50,000 and perhaps as many as 150,000 people attend the festival for free after the security fences were torn down ate into gate receipts seriously. The double-CD *Woodstock '94* album earned profits for A&M Records, making it to number 50 on the *Billboard* top 200 album charts. In relationship to the success of the sound recording release from the 1969 festival, however, this chart ranking was less than stellar. Nonetheless, the *Woodstock '94* box set brought together a wide variety of artists and styles. The track listing of the two compact discs is as follows:

Disc 1

1. Live	"Selling the Drama"
2. Blues Traveler	"But Anyway"
3. Melissa Etheridge	"I'm the Only One"
4. Joe Cocker	"Feelin' Alright"
5. Stage Announcements	
6. The Cranberries	"Dreams"

  7. Blind Melon   "Soup"

  8. Green Day   "When I Come Around"

  9. Salt-N-Pepa   "Shoop"

10. Stage Announcements

11. The Red Hot Chili Peppers   "Blood Sugar Sex Magik"

12. Porno for Pyros   "Porno for Pyros"

13. Primus   "Those Damned Blue-Collar Tweek-ers"

14. Jackyl   "Headed for Destruction"

15. Aerosmith   "Draw the Line/F.I.N.E."

16. Stage Announcements

17. Nine Inch Nails   "Happiness in Slavery"

Disc 2

  1. Metallica   "For Whom the Bell Tolls"

  2. Paul Rodgers   "The Hunter"

  3. The Neville Brothers   "Come Together"

  4. Sheryl Crow   "Run, Baby, Run"

  5. Crosby, Stills, and Nash   "Déjà Vu"

  6. The Violent Femmes   "Kiss Off"

  7. Collective Soul   "Shine"

  8. The Candlebox   "Arrow"

  9. Cypress Hill   "How I Could Just Kill a Man"

10. The Rollins Band   "Right Here Too Much"

11. Bob Dylan   "Highway 61"

12. Traffic   "Pearly Queen"

13. Peter Gabriel   "Biko"

AUDIO RECORDING AND DOCUMENTARY FILM (1999)

As had been the case with the 1969 Woodstock Music and Art Fair and Wood-stock '94, an audio recording and film/video of Woodstock 1999 entered the marketplace soon after the festival. The Sony double-compact disc compilation was somewhat more commercially successful than its 1994 counterpart. *Woodstock 1999* reached number 32 on the *Billboard* top 200 album charts, besting the *Woodstock '94* set by eighteen positions. Contrary to what had been done in compiling the 1969 and 1994 sets, Sony decided to segregate artists stylistically on *Woodstock 1999*. Disc 1 contained the funk, rap, metal, and punk-oriented acts, while Disc 2 featured more mainstream rock acts and styles. The track listings for the discs are as follows:

Disc 1

1. Korn   "Blind"
2. The Offspring   "The Kids Aren't Alright"
3. Lit   "For"
4. Buckcherry   "Lit Up"
5. Kid Rock   "Bawitdaba"
6. Limp Bizkit   "Show Me What You Got"
7. Rage against the Machine   "Bulls on Parade"
8. Metallica   "Creeping Death"
9. Creed (with Robbie Krieger)   "Roadhouse Blues"
10. Sevendust   "Bitch"
11. DMX   "Stop Being Greedy"
12. Godsmack   "Keep Away"
13. Megadeth   "Secret Place"
14. Bush   "Everything Zen"
15. Live   "I Alone"
16. The Red Hot Chili Peppers   "Fire"

Disc 2

1. The Dave Matthews Band   "Tripping Billies"
2. The Brian Setzer Orchestra   "Rock This Town"
3. Sheryl Crow   "If It Makes You Happy"
4. Everlast   "Ends"
5. Everclear   "Santa Monica"

6.	Jewel	"Down So Long"
7.	Elvis Costello	"Alison"
8.	Alanis Morissette	"So Pure"
9.	Jamiroquai	"Black Capricorn Day"
10.	G. Love and Special Sauce	"Cold Beverage"
11.	The Chemical Brothers	"Block Rockin' Beats"
12.	The Roots	"Adrenaline!"
13.	Guster	"Airport Song"
14.	Our Lady Peace	"Superman's Dead"
15.	Rusted Root	"Ecstasy"
16.	Bruce Hornsby	"Resting Place"

The Internet store Amazon.com includes listener reviews of the compact discs the company sells, and study of music fans' reactions to the Woodstock 1999 two-disk set makes for particularly interesting reading. Although at least one review complains about the stylistic segregation of the discs violating the rock-music-transcends-generational-boundaries philosophy of Woodstock, the vast majority of the reviews are sharply divided about the merits of the two discs: reviewers who enjoyed Disc 1 (The Red Disc) generally found little to like about Disc 2 and vice versa.[4]

NOTES

1. Bell, Dale, ed., *Woodstock: An Inside Look at the Movie That Shook up the World and Defined a Generation* (Studio City, California: Michael Wiese Productions, 1999).

2. Baez's performance featured Jeffrey Shurtleff, as is noted in the track listing for this song.

3. This recording was not included in the theatrical release of the *Woodstock: Three Days of Peace and Music* film.

4. See the ever-evolving reviews of *Woodstock 1999* at http://amazon.com.

Annotated Bibliography

Adams, Rebecca G., and Robert Sardiello, eds. *Deadhead Social Science: You Ain't Gonna Learn What You Don't Want to Know*. Walnut Creek, California: AltaMira Press, 2000. An important study of sociology of the Deadheads.

Adato, Allison. "The Big Picture." *Life* 17/10 (October 1994): 12+. This special collection of photographs includes images from the Woodstock '94 festival.

"Again, Police Use Photos in Post-Riot Hunt." *News Photographer* 54/8 (August 1999): 22+. This lengthy article is a report on the New York State Police's posting of photographs of rioters at the Woodstock 1999 festival on the World Wide Web in an attempt to try to identify perpetrators of the arson and riots. This unauthorized use of photos created controversy—perhaps not as much as the riots themselves, but controversy nonetheless.

"The Age of Aquarius: Woodstock Music and Art Fair." *Newsweek* 74 (August 25, 1969): 88. A brief report on the event.

"All Nature Is but Art." *Vogue* 154 (December 1969): 194–201. A report on the social significance of the Woodstock Music and Art Fair.

Anderson, Terry H. *The Movement and the Sixties*. New York: Oxford University Press, 1995. Contains references to the 1969 Woodstock Festival and the 1960s counterculture.

Angel, Johnny. "Music: Why Woodstock '94 Was Born to Fail." *The San Francisco Bay Guardian* 28/45 (August 10, 1994): 37. A report on the commercialism of Woodstock '94.

Angier, J. "Live Aid vs. Woodstock." *Nation* 241-7 (1985). A comparison of the two festivals.

Ankeny, Jason. "Godsmack." *All Music Guide*. http://allmusic.com. Accessed March 30, 2004. Contains a biography and critical commentary on the group.

Ankeny, Jason. "Violent Femmes." *All Music Guide*. http://allmusic.com. Accessed March 22, 2004. Contains a biography and critical commentary on the group.

Applefeld, Catherine. "Music PPV Proves Disappointing." *Billboard* 107/42 (October 21, 1995): 16+. Among the music-related cable television pay-per-view events that disappointed the cable industry was the Woodstock '94 festival. This was due in part to free cable coverage by MTV.

Applefeld, Catherine. "Video Previews: Music." *Billboard* 106/50 (December 10, 1994):
    83. The author gives the *Woodstock '94* video a positive review.

Applefeld, Catherine. "Video Previews: Music." *Billboard* 107/15 (April 15, 1995): 52.
    This article includes a review of the video *Woodstock 1969*, the documentary on
    the organizing of the Woodstock Music and Art Fair.

"Arborcidal Maniacs." *New York* 27/35 (September 5, 1994): 14. This is a brief report on
    the demand by Dutchess County, New York, officials that Woodstock Ventures
    pay damages for the environmental damage suffered by the county as a result of
    the Woodstock '94 festival, which took place near the border of Dutchess and Ul-
    ster Counties.

Aron, Marlene. *Woodstock, NY*. Youngstown, Ohio: Youngstown State University, 1994.
    This is a sixteen-page transcript of a taped interview conducted by Christopher L.
    Helm as part of the Department of History's Oral History Program.

Ashare, Matt. "Music." *Boston Phoenix* 23/33 (August 19, 1994): 12. This article contains
    information on the live and pay-per-view broadcasts of the Woodstock '94 festival.

Ashare, Matt. "Out There." *Boston Phoenix* 23/30 (July 29, 1994): 3. As part of the *Boston
    Phoenix*'s special "Woodstock vs. Lollapalooza" issue, Ashare deals with the ques-
    tion, "Woodstock or Lollapalozza: where would you rather be?"

Ashare, Matt, and Brett Milano. Review of the *Woodstock II CD*. *Boston Phoenix* 23/47
    (November 25, 1994): 12. A brief review of the recordings from Woodstock '94.

"At Deadline." *MediaWeek* 9/29 (July 19, 1999). According to this brief report, pre-event,
    pay-per-view sales for the cable television broadcast of Woodstock 1999 are slug-
    gish.

Azerrad, M. "Now They Spell It 'Wood$tock.' " *Rolling Stone* n549 (April 6, 1989): 17.
    This is a brief report on the commercial ventures surrounding plans to mark the
    twentieth anniversary of the Woodstock Music and Art Fair.

"Backside: Hated Woodstock '94? Hey, It Could Be Worse!" *Musician* n191 (September
    1994): 98. This article attempts to put the commercialism and mild violence of
    the festival into perspective.

"Back to the Garden." *Maclean's* 107/34 (August 22, 1994): 20. This article is a brief re-
    port on Woodstock '94.

Baez, Joan. *And a Voice to Sing With*. New York: New American Library, 1987. Baez's au-
    tobiography contains her reactions to the Woodstock Music and Art Fair.

"Bands and Fans Feel the Heat at Woodstock Reunion." *Christian Science Monitor* July
    26, 1999: 5. A brief report on Woodstock 1999.

Barbieri, Kelly. "Sonicnet.com Releases Report Detailing Problems during Woodstock
    1999." *Amusement Business* 112/30 (July 24, 2000). This article deals with the find-
    ings of Sonicnet.com, which investigated the problems of the Woodstock 1999
    festival and found considerable fault with the festival's producers; Rome, New
    York, city officials; and the hired security guards, blaming most of the troubles
    squarely on them.

Barron, J. "Woodstock 1989: Wallowing Again in Mud and Nostalgia." *New York Times*
    August 14, 1989: A1+. This is a cover story on the twentieth anniversary of Wood-
    stock and the media event that is developing around the historic anniversary—all
    of this in spite of the fact that the concerts planned for the festival have failed to
    materialize.

Barry, Thomas. "Why There Can't Be Another Woodstock." *Look* 34 (August 25, 1970):
    28+. On the one-year anniversary of the Woodstock Festival, this article reflects
    on Woodstock as a sociological phenomenon.

Barth, J. "Rock and Roll Tourism." *Rolling Stone* n504–5 (July 16–30, 1987): 104+. This article deals with rock music-related tourist highlights and includes the site of the 1969 Woodstock festival.

Bell, Dale, ed. *Woodstock: An Inside Look at the Movie That Shook up the World and Defined a Generation.* Studio City, California: Michael Wiese Productions, 1999. This book documents the making of Michael Wadleigh's *Woodstock: Three Days of Peace and Music* film.

Belz, Carl. *The Story of Rock*, 2nd ed. New York: Oxford University Press, 1972. This book contains information on the Woodstock Music and Art Fair.

Benezra, Karen. "Woodstock: Onetime Defining Moment Mines Equity of Its Name." *Brandweek* 35/34 (September 5, 1994): 32. This article deals with officially sanctioned Woodstock '94 merchandise as well the planned opening of the first Woodstock Café in New York's SoHo district.

Berger, Joseph. "The Commercial and the Utopian: Can They Reconcile for a Woodstock Theme Park?" *New York Times* April 25, 1997: B4. This article reports on cable television entrepreneur Alan Gerry's plans for the site of the original Woodstock Music and Art Fair, a piece of land he had recently purchased.

Berger, Joseph. "Peace, Music, Profit." *New York Times* April 27, 1997: D2. This article deals with Alan Gerry's purchase of the site of the original Woodstock Music and Art Fair and his plans for the site.

Berger, Joseph. "Town Is Weighing a Shrine to the '60s at Woodstock Site." *New York Times* January 26, 1997: 1. This article deals with Sullivan County, New York's, attempts to erect a monument at the site of the 1969 Woodstock festival. Continuing litigation and controversy surrounding June Gelish's ownership of the former Yasgur farm are complicating the county's plans.

"Best and Worst of 1994 Special Achievement Awards." *Hispanic* 7/11 (December 1994): 34. *Hispanic* magazine gave its Longevity Award to Carlos Santana, for performing at both the 1969 Woodstock Music and Art Fair and Woodstock '94.

Bianco, Anthony. "Alan Gerry's Woodstock Nation." *Business Week* n3621 (March 22, 1999). This article is a report on Alan Gerry's plans to turn the site of the Woodstock Music and Art Fair in to a music-related tourist attraction.

Bindas, Kenneth J., and Craig Houston. " 'Takin' Care of Business' ": Rock Music, Vietnam and the Protest Myth." *Historian* 52 (November 1989): 1–23.

Binelli, Mark. "Kid Rock on a Roll." *Rolling Stone* n820 (September 2, 1999): 67+. This profile of singer Kid Rock describes the set he performed at Woodstock 1999.

Biskind, Peter. *Easy Riders, Raging Bulls: How the Sex-Drugs-and-Rock'n'Roll Generation Saved Hollywood.* New York: Simon and Schuster, 1998.

Blair, Jayson. "New York City Cancels a Music Event, and Some See a Link to Woodstock." *New York Times* July 31, 1999: B5. This article reports on the cancellation of a music festival scheduled to take place in Brooklyn in the wake of the rapes and riots that took place at Woodstock 1999.

Bloom, Alexander, and Wini Breines, eds. *Takin' It to the Streets: A Sixties Reader.* New York: Oxford University Press, 1995.

Blum, David. "The Woodstock War." *New York Times* September 5, 1993: Section 9, 1. This article is an account of the ongoing battles between Woodstock Ventures, planners of the Woodstock '94 festival, and the Multiple Sclerosis Society, planners of the competing A Day in the Garden festival.

Boehlert, Eric. "Global Woodstock Takes Shape." *Rolling Stone* n808 (March 18, 1999): 32. This article reports on the artists, dates, and venue for Woodstock 1999.

Boehlert, Eric. "Rock and Roll." *Rolling Stone* n727 (February 8, 1996): 17+. Boehlert reports on the release of the *Woodstock '94* multi-compact disc set. He describes it as a relative failure compared with the multialbum recording from the original Woodstock festival.

Boehlert, Eric, and Matt Hendrickson. "Rock and Roll." *Rolling Stone* n804 (January 21, 1999). This article contains a very preliminary report on plans for the Woodstock 1999 festival.

Borzillo, Carrie. "Nets Going All out for Woodstock '94." *Billboard* 106/29 (July 16, 1994): 82+. This is a report on network and syndicated radio and television coverage that was planned for Woodstock '94.

"Bouquets to the Flower Cops: Woodstock Music and Art Fair." *Christian Century* 86 (September 3, 1969): 1130.

Bowermaster, J. "20 Years, and 50 Miles, Down the Road." *New York Times Magazine* 138/4783 (July 2, 1989): 22+. This is a report on plans that were under way at the time for celebrations of the twentieth anniversary of the Woodstock Music and Art Fair.

Braham, Hugh. *Woodstock, 1969.* Youngstown, Ohio: Youngstown State University, 1994. This is a sixteen-page transcript of a taped interview conducted by Christopher L. Helm as part of the Department of History's Oral History Program.

Braham, Jeannette. *Woodstock, 1969.* Youngstown, Ohio: Youngstown State University, 1994. This is a seventeen-page transcript of a taped interview conducted by Christopher L. Helm as part of the Department of History's Oral History Program.

Brand, Stewart. "We Owe It All to the Hippies." *Time* 145/12 (Spring 1995, Special Issue): 54+. According to the author, who was one of the leaders of the communal Back to the Land movement in the late 1960s, the antiwar movement and Woodstock were not the most important legacy of the 1960s: the computer revolution was.

Braungart, Richard G. Review of *Woodstock Census: The Nationwide Survey of the Sixties Generation* by Rex Weiner and Deanne Stillman. *Journal of Political and Military Sociology* 8/1 (Spring 1980): 149.

Braunstein, Peter, and Michael William Doyle, eds. *Imagine Nation: The American Counterculture of the 1960s and '70s.* New York: Routledge, 2002. This book contains references to the sociology of the Woodstock generation.

Brief History of Keef, A. http://www.ammoniterecords.demon.co.uk/KeefHartley/keith_hist.html. Accessed June 30, 2003.

"Briefs." *TVB Europe* 8/9 (September 1999): 3+. This article contains a technical report on some of the special effects that were done for the cable television coverage of the Woodstock 1999 festival.

Brill, E. H. "Muddy Grooving at White Lake." *Christian Century* 86 (September 17, 1969): 1206–8. This article recaps the Woodstock Music and Art Fair.

Brooks, Tim, and Earle Marsh. *The Complete Directory to Prime Time Network and Cable TV Shows,* 6th ed. New York: Ballantine Books, 1995.

Brown, Ethan. "Third Time's the Charm." *New York* 32/28 (July 26, 1999): 82+. Published before the riots that seriously marred Woodstock 1999, this article compares Woodstock II (1994) and the 1999 event. Brown highlights the problems that occurred at the 1994 event.

Buckley, Christopher. "Peace, Love and Profits." *New York Times* May 1, 1997: A27. This article reports and comments on Alan Gerry's plans for a theme park at the site of the original Woodstock Music and Art Fair.

Budds, Michael J., and Marian M. Ohman, eds. *Rock Recall: Annotated Readings in American Popular Music from the Emergence of Rock and Roll to the Demise of the Woodstock Nation.* Needham Heights, Massachusetts: Ginn Press, 1993.

Burke, Kate. *Woodstock, NY.* Youngstown, Ohio: Youngstown State University, 1994. This is a nine-page transcript of a taped interview conducted by Christopher L. Helm as part of the Department of History's Oral History Program.

Burks, John. "In the Aftermath of Altamont." *Rolling Stone* n51 (February 7, 1970): 7–8. Excerpted in Budds, Michael J., and Marian M. Ohman, eds., *Rock Recall: Annotated Readings in American Popular Music from the Emergence of Rock and Roll to the Demise of the Woodstock Nation*, 320. Needham Heights, Massachusetts: Ginn Press, 1993.

Bush, John. "Rusted Root." *All Music Guide.* http://allmusic.com. Accessed April 2, 2004. Contains a biography and critical commentary on the group Rusted Root.

Byfield, Link. "Why Doesn't Someone Do Us a Favour and Drop a Bomb on Woodstock '94?" *Alberta Report* 21/34 (August 8, 1994): 2. This is a negative report on plans for Woodstock '94, in which the festival is compared and contrasted with the original Woodstock Music and Art Fair.

Caldwell, Christopher. "When in Rome. The Horrid Spirit of Woodstock." *National Review* 51/16 (August 30, 1999): 29. This article concerns the riots and rapes and other problems at the Woodstock 1999 festival.

"CD-ROM Titles." *CD-ROM News Extra: The Bimonthly News Supplement to CD-ROM Professional Magazine* 2/5 (October 1994): 13. This article contains a review of the *Woodstock Twenty-fifth Anniversary CD-ROM.*

Cerio, Gregory, and Lucy Howard. "Dog Days Edition." *Newsweek* 124/8 (August 22, 1994): 6. This contains a very brief reference-joke concerning the overtly commercial nature of the Woodstock '94 festival.

"CFA Represented at Woodstock." *Free Inquiry* 19/4 (Fall 1999): 70. This is a brief report that the Center for Inquiry Institute collected signatures for a "Bill of Rights for Nonbelievers" at the Woodstock 1999 festival.

Christgau, Robert. *Any Old Way You Choose It.* Baltimore: Penguin Books, 1973.

Christgau, Robert. "A Weekend in Paradise." *The Village Voice* 39/35 (August 30, 1994): 28. This article is a report on the Woodstock twenty-fifth-anniversary festival of 1994. The author points out that despite the differences between the 1969 event and the anniversary festival, rock music brought both crowds together.

Chung, L. A. "Opinion: Woodstock of a Different Color." *The San Francisco Bay Guardian* 28/45 (August 10, 1994): 6. Compares and contrasts the 1969 and 1994 Woodstock festivals.

Clauson, Arabella, and MacKenzie Wilson. "Guster." *All Music Guide.* http://allmusic.com. Accessed March 30, 2004. Contains a biography and critical commentary on the group Guster.

"Coast to Coast: Woodstock II Feed Masses Music and Munchies." 1994. *Nation's Restaurant News* 28/32 (August 15, 1994): 11. A report on the food vendors of Woodstock '94.

Cohn, Nik. *Rock from the Beginning.* New York: Pocket Books, 1969.

Coker, Wilson. *Music and Meaning.* New York: Free Press, 1971.

"Collectibles." *Billboard* 106/40 (October 1, 1994): 57. This article includes a brief report on memorabilia from the 1969 Woodstock Music and Art Fair that are being displayed at the HMV's music store on New York's Upper East Side.

Collins, Gail. "Oh, to Be Young and at the Wrong Woodstock." *New York Times* July 28, 1999: A18. This article is a comparison of the 1969 Woodstock Music and Art Fair and Woodstock 1999, with a focus on the many problems that took place at the 1999 event.

Cooper, B. Lee, and Wayne S. Haney. *Rock Music in American Popular Culture II: More Rock 'n' Roll Resources.* New York: Harrington Park Press, 1997. Contains references and citations related to the 1969 Woodstock Music and Art Fair.

Cortese, Amy. "Three Days of Peace, Love and E-Mail." *Business Week* n3380 (July 11, 1994): 142g. A report on the use of computer technology at Woodstock '94.

"Cover: The Undoing of Hip." *Time* 144/6 (August 8, 1994): 48. Virtually on the eve of the Woodstock '94 festival, *Time*'s cover story deals with the extent to which counterculture "hipness" has become a part of mass popular culture.

Crespi, A. Review of *Woodstock: 25th Anniversary Director's Cut. Cineforum* 34/9 (September 1994).

Crouch, Stanley. *The Sixties: The Decade Remembered Now by the People Who Lived Then.* New York: Rolling Stone Press, 1977. Contains references to the 1969 Woodstock festival and to the sociology of the hippies of the late 1960s.

"Cue." *New York* 27/45 (November 14, 1994): 93. This article contains a review of the *Woodstock* CD-ROM.

Cultural Politics and Social Movements, ed. Marcy Darnovsky, Barbara Epstein, and Richard Flacks. Philadelphia: Temple University Press, 1995. Contains references to the hippie counterculture of the late 1960s.

Curry, Jack. *Woodstock: The Summer of Our Lives.* New York: Weidenfeld and Nicolson, 1989. Curry's book contains the stories of a number of people who attended the 1969 Woodstock Music and Art Fair either as performers, producers, or audience members.

Curtley, Bob. "Woodstock's Drug Message." *Alcoholism and Drug Abuse Weekly* 6/32 (August 22, 1994): 5. This article focuses on the seemingly all-pervasive use of marijuana at the Woodstock '94 festival and the failure of U.S. drug enforcement and control policies.

Daly, Steven. "Rock and Roll." *Rolling Stone* n798 (October 29, 1998): 17+. This profile of Joni Mitchell comes on the heels of her appearance at the 1998 A Day in the Garden festival in front of 25,000 music fans. Mitchell's career is documented as well as the craftsmanship of her musical compositions. Although she made her debut in 1968, Mitchell gained considerable fame as a result of her song "Woodstock," which documented the original 1969 festival, an event that Mitchell was unable to attend due to a television commitment she had in New York City.

Darlington, Sandy. "Country Joe and the Fish: 1965–68." In Marcus, Greil, ed., *Rock and Roll Will Stand*, 150–69. Boston: Beacon Press, 1969. Contains biographical material on the group.

"Darts and Laurels." *Columbia Journalism Review* 38/4 (November-December 1999): 18–19. Contains negative references to the violence of Woodstock 1999.

Dean, Maury. *The Rock Revolution.* Detroit: Edmore Books, 1966.

Decter, Midge. "Rome Burns." *Wall Street Journal* (Eastern Edition) July 30, 1999: W15. In addition to reporting on the riots and rapes that marred Woodstock 1999, this article contrasts the festival with the 1969 Woodstock Music and Art Fair.

Deedy, John. "Knocking Rock-Land: Rock Festival." *Commonweal* 91 (November 14, 1969): 196. Contains critical commentary on the Woodstock Music and Art Fair.

Denisoff, R. Serge. Review of *Barefoot in Babylon: The Creation of the Woodstock Music Festival* by Robert Stephen Spitz. *Popular Music and Society* 7/3 (1980).

Denisoff, R. Serge, and Richard A. Peterson, eds. *The Sounds of Social Change: Studies in Popular Culture.* Chicago: Rand McNally, 1972.

DeNitto, Emily. "Make Peace, Make Love, Make Money." *Advertising Age* 65/33 (August 8, 1994): 13+. The author contrasts the financial arrangements for Woodstock '94 with those of the original Woodstock Music and Art Fair and the failed twenty-fifth-anniversary concert at Bethel, New York.

DeNitto, Emily. "Pepsi, Haagen-Dazs Find Harmony at Woodstock '94." *Advertising Age* 65/35 (August 22, 1994): 13. This is a brief report on some of the corporate sponsorships at the Woodstock '94 festival.

DeNitto, Emily. "Promoters Hoping the Sun Shines in." *Advertising Age* 65/33 (August 8, 1994): 2. This is a report on the financial hopes of Woodstock '94 promoters.

DeNitto, Emily. "You Can't Go Home Again, but You Can Go to Woodstock." *Advertising Age* 65/33 (August 8, 1994): 13+. Contains references to the corporate sponsorships of the Woodstock '94 festival.

Derogatis, Jim. "Incredible String Band." *Yahoo! LAUNCH.* http://launch.yahoo.com. Accessed January 13, 2004. Contains a biography and critical commentary on the group.

DeRoos, F. J., J. Perrone, W. J. Meggs, R. S. Hoffman, and B. Quanne. "Epidemiology of Substance Abuse at the 1994 Woodstock Music Festival." *Journal of Toxicology—Clinical Toxicology* 33/5 (1995): 503. This is an abstract of a paper the writers presented at the 1995 North American Congress of Clinical Toxicology annual meeting.

DeRoos, F. J., J. Perrone, W. J. Meggs, R. S. Hoffman, and B. Quanne. "Laboratory Confirmation of Suspected Substance Abuse at the 1994 Woodstock Music Festival." *Journal of Toxicology—Clinical Toxicology* 33/5 (1995): 502. This is an abstract of a paper the writers presented at the 1995 North American Congress of Clinical Toxicology annual meeting.

"Despite Hard Rain and Muddled Organization—or Perhaps Because of Them—Woodstock '94 Served up Three Days of Good Vibes, Music and Mud." *People Weekly* 42/9 (August 29, 1994): 102. An overview of Woodstock '94.

Dessner, Lawrence J. " 'Woodstock,' A Nation at War." In Huebel, Harry Russell, ed., *Things in the Driver's Seat: Readings in Popular Culture,* 245–51. Chicago: Rand McNally, 1972. This essay deals with political conflict in the United States at the time of the Woodstock festival.

de Yampert, Rick. "Suffering from Entertainment Writers' Guilt No More." *Editor and Publisher* 127/40 (October 1, 1994): 48+. This article deals with the reporter's negative experiences covering Woodstock '94. Like several other reports from the site, this places the number of attendees at 350,000. The author also mentions that 1,800 journalists covered the festival.

"Dig This!" *Seventeen* 54/1 (January 1995): 54. This article contains a review of the Woodstock '94 festival CD.

DiLucchio, Patrizia. "Glower Power." *Entertainment Weekly* n498 (August 13, 1999): 83. This article deals with the live broadcasts from Woodstock 1999 on the World Wide Web.

Dominis, John, and B. Eppridge. "Big Woodstock Rock Trip." *Life* 67 (August 29, 1969): 14B-23.

Donohue, Steve. "No Love for TV at Woodstock." *Electronic Media* 18/31 (August 2, 1999): 35+. This article concerns the violence against members of the media at Woodstock 1999 and television networks' plans to broadcast this activity.

Dotter, Daniel. "Growing Up Is Hard to Do: Rock and Roll Performers as Cultural Heroes." *Sociological Spectrum* 7 (1987): 25–44.

Dowling, Claudia Glenn. "Woodstock." *Life* 12/8 (August 1989): 20+. This is a feature retrospective on the twentieth anniversary of the Woodstock Music and Art Fair.

Dowling, Claudia Glenn, and Harriet Barovick. "*Life* Goes to a Party." *Life* 17/11 (November 1994): 75+. This photo-essay includes shots from the Woodstock '94 festival.

Drozdowski, Ted. "Music." *The Boston Phoenix* 23/30 (July 29, 1994): 12. This article deals in part with the politics of Jimi Hendrix at the original Woodstock festival.

Dunn, Jancee. "Soul Asylum." *Rolling Stone* n695 (November 17, 1994): 55+. In this interview with Soul Asylum's Dave Pirner, the musician discusses the spontaneous A Day in the Garden festival that took place opposite the Woodstock '94 festival.

Echols, Alice. *Scars of Sweet Paradise: The Life and Times of Janis Joplin*. New York: Metropolitan Books, 1999.

Echols, Alice. *Shaky Ground: The Sixties and Its Aftershocks*. New York: Columbia University Press, 2002. Echols' book contains references to the sociology of the Woodstock generation.

"Editors Object to Police Use of Photos from Woodstock." *New York Times* August 6, 1999: B8. This article deals with reaction to the New York State Police's use of copyrighted photographs to identify the perpetrators of violence at Woodstock 1999.

Elmer-DeWitt, Philip, and Christopher John Farley. "Winners and Losers." *Time* 144/7 (August 15, 1994): 10+. According to this article, among the week's losers is the Woodstock '94 festival, on the "strength" of sluggish ticket sales.

Epstein, Jonathon S., ed. *Adolescents and Their Music: If It's Too Loud, You're Too Old*. New York: Garland, 1994.

Erlewine, Stephen Thomas. "Salt-N-Pepa." *All Music Guide*. http://allmusic.com. Accessed March 22, 2004. Contains a biography and critical analysis of the popular rap group.

Erlewine, Stephen Thomas, and Greg Prato. "Primus." *All Music Guide*. http://allmusic. com. Accessed April 12, 2004. Contains a biography and critical commentary of the group.

Espen, Hal. "The Woodstock Wars." *The New Yorker* 70/25 (August 15, 1994): 70+. This article presents a comparison of the anticommercial spirit of the 1969 Woodstock festival with the commercial spirit of Woodstock '94.

Farber, David. *The Age of Great Dreams: America in the 1960s*. New York: Hill and Wang, 1994. Contains references to the Woodstock Music and Art Fair and the sociology of the hippie counterculture.

Farber, David. "The Intoxicated State/Illegal Nation: Drugs in the Sixties Counterculture." In Braunstein, Peter, and Michael William Doyle, eds., *Imagine Nation: The American Counterculture of the 1960s and '70s*, 17–40. New York: Routledge, 2002.

Farley, Christopher John, and David E. Thigpen. "Woodstock Suburb." *Time* 144/8 (August 22, 1994): 78+. This article deals with the "clean-cut" nature of many of the mainly white and middle-class Woodstock '94 fans.

Farrell, Barry. "Second Reading: Bad Vibrations from Woodstock." *Life* 67 (September 5, 1969): 4. A brief report on some of the negative aspects of the Woodstock Music and Art Fair.

Fawcett, Adrienne Ward. "Michael Lang." *Advertising Age* 66/26 (June 26, 1995): S33+. This profile of Michael Lang and Woodstock Ventures, Ltd. focuses on the ways in which the Woodstock '94 festival was promoted and on the use of corporate sponsors for the event.

"Features—Crowded Venues—EMS Insiders on What Really Happened at Woodstock '99." *JEMS: A Journal of Emergency Medical Services* 24/11 (1999): 68–71.

Feehan, Paul G. Review of *Barefoot in Babylon: The Creation of the Woodstock Music Festival, 1969* by Robert Stephen Spitz. *Library Journal* 104/22 (December 15, 1979): 2651. According to this review, *Barefoot in Babylon* "is a vital slice of recent social history which should stand as the definitive document of the Woodstock event."

Feinberg, Andrew. "Wired Promoter." *Forbes* 155/5 (February 27, 1995): 26+. This is a profile of Joel Rosenman, with a focus on his use of technology.

"FiberWatch." *Wire Journal International* 27/10 (October 1994): 47. This article deals with the use of fiber optics at the Woodstock '94 festival.

"First Impressions." *CD-ROM World* 9/9 (October 1994): 26. This article contains a review of the *Woodstock* CD-ROM.

Flick, Larry, Carla Hay, and Robyn Lewis. "Post-Woodstock Activity on Track." *Billboard* 111/32 (August 7, 1999): 8+. This article reports on plans for audio and video releases from the Woodstock 1999 festival.

Fliger, Jerry E. *An Analogical Comparison of Woodstock 1969 and 1994: Rhetorical Events as Cultural Indices*. Thesis: Miami University, 1995.

Foege, Alec. "Billie Joe of Green Day." *Rolling Stone* n695 (November 17, 1994): 24+. Among the topics discussed by the member of the rock band Green Day is the Woodstock '94 festival.

"Forever Woodstock." *National Review* 51/16 (August 30, 1999): 14+. A recap of the Woodstock 1999 festival.

Francese, Carl. *From Tupelo to Woodstock: Youth, Race, and Rock-and-Roll in America, 1954–1969*. Dubuque, Iowa: Kendall/Hunt, 2001.

Fricke, D. "Woodstock Remembered: The Artists." *Rolling Stone* n559 (August 24, 1989): 65+. On the twentieth anniversary of the Woodstock Music and Art Fair, this article details the artists who appeared at the festival and presents some of their recollections of the event.

Fricke, D. "Woodstock Remembered: Minor Epiphanies and Momentary Bummers." *Rolling Stone* n559 (August 24, 1989): 61+. The author of this article attended the 1969 Woodstock festival. He recounts his experiences and discusses the various performers, as well as the social impact of the event.

Friedman, Wayne. "Woodstock Revisited Finds Few Sponsors." *Advertising Age* 70/27 (June 28, 1999): 4. This article concerns the low number of corporate sponsors and dollars for Woodstock 1999, as compared with the massive sponsorship of Woodstock '94 by PepsiCo.

Frith, Simon. *Sound Effects: Youth, Leisure, and the Politics of Rock 'N' Roll*. New York: Pantheon Books, 1981. Frith deals with the sociology of the 1960s Woodstock generation.

Fuchs, John M. Review of *Woodstock Census: The Nationwide Survey of the Sixties Generation* by Rex Weiner and Deanne Stillman. *Library Journal* 104/21 (December 1, 1979): 2556+.

Garfield, Bob. "A Multimedia Bad Trip." *Civilization* 2/1 (January-February 1995): 80+. The author describes a multimedia upgrade to his computer that was necessitated by his attempt to use the new *Woodstock* CD-ROM.

Garlock, Frank. *The Big Beat: A Rock Blast.* Greenville, South Carolina: Bob Jones University Press, 1971. This ultraconservative book represents a very different view of the Woodstock generation from the view commonly described in the popular media. The author's contention is that rock music has led to wholesale breakdown in American societal institutions.

Gates, David. "Twenty-Five Years Later, We're Living in Woodstock Nation." *Newsweek* 124/6 (August 8, 1994): 38+. As the title of this article suggests, the author details many of the ways in which the spirit of the late 1960s is still extant in 1994. Interestingly, many of the images Gates evokes are negatives. Several Woodstock attendees make brief reflections on the festival.

Gates, David. "Woodstock." *Newsweek* 114/1 (July 3, 1989): 50+. This is a retrospective on the 1969 Woodstock festival.

Gehr, Richard. "Wired." *The Village Voice* 39/33 (August 10, 1994): 38. This article contains Gehr's review of the *Woodstock 25th-Anniversary CD-ROM.*

"Gelish, June—Death." *New York Times* April 19, 1997: 48. According to this obituary, at the time of her death on April 15, 1997, June Gelish was the owner of the site of the Woodstock Music and Art Fair. This was a point of some contention in the legal community, however.

"Gibson at Woodstock II." *Music Trades* 142/10 (November 1994): 34. This article details the use of Gibson guitars at the Woodstock twenty-fifth-anniversary festival.

Gillers, Stephen, Bruce Sanford, and Bruce Brown. "Arguments." *The American Lawyer* 21/9 (October 1, 1999): 37. The authors argue various legal and ethical points related to the New York State Police's unauthorized World Wide Web posting of copyrighted photographs of rioters at the Woodstock 1999 festival in an effort to identify the perpetrators.

Gitlin, Todd. *The Sixties: Years of Hope, Days of Rage.* New York: Bantam Books, 1987. This book details the 1960s counterculture and the beliefs of the Woodstock generation.

Giuliano, Geoffrey. *Dark Horse: The Private Life of George Harrison.* New York: Dutton, 1990. Contains information pertaining to the organization of the Concert for Bangla Desh.

Gogola, Tom. "Muckstock." *Nation* 259/7 (September 5–12, 1994): 221+. The author focuses on the mud that was in abundance at Woodstock '94, as well as some of the other curiosities of the festival.

Goldman, Albert Harry. *Freakshow: The Rocksoulbluesjazzsickjewblackhumor-sexpoppsych Gig and Other Scenes from the Counter-Culture.* New York: Atheneum, 1971. Republished as *Freakshow: Misadventures in the Counterculture, 1959–1971.* New York: Cooper Square Press, 2001. Includes the author's recollections of important 1960s rock and folk performers.

Goldstein, Richard. "Woodstock: Grand Slam Rush." *Vogue* 154 (October 1, 1969): 158. A favorable report on Woodstock.

Goodman, Fred. "Back to the Garden." *Rolling Stone* n683 (June 2, 1994): 16. This brief report indicates that the Woodstock '94 promoters had the two necessary permits to hold the twenty-fifth-anniversary festival approved by the town of Saugerties, New York, on March 31, 1994. The report mentions that the performers will be

primarily current artists rather than musicians who appeared at the 1969 festival
and that the festival will include technology installations.

Goodman, Fred. "No Encore for Woodstock." *Rolling Stone* n558 (August 10, 1989): 26.
This is a report on the failure of the organizers of a twentieth-anniversary festival
at the site of the 1969 Woodstock festival to secure the rights to use the Woodstock name, their failure to reach agreement with Warner Brothers, and the general state of malaise of the organizers' plans.

Goodman, Fred. "Performance." *Rolling Stone* n796 (October 1, 1998): 32. Goodman
documents the August 14–16, 1998, A Day in the Garden festival, which was
held in Bethel, New York, on the site of the original Woodstock Music and Art
Fair.

Goodman, Fred. "Summer Tours." *Rolling Stone* n683 (June 2, 1994): 15. This article
deals in part with the upcoming Woodstock '94 festival.

Gordinier, Jeff, and Nisid Hajari. "Music." *Entertainment Weekly* n237–38 (August 26,
1994): 108. This article contains a report on the Woodstock '94 festival, as well
as reflections from various individuals on the original Woodstock festival.

Gordon, Jim. "The Woodstock Landfill?" *E Magazine: The Environmental Magazine* 6/1
(January–February 1995): 13. This is a report on Woodstock Ventures Michael
Lang's plan to develop a permanent performance venue on the site of the Winston farm and the Ulster County Resource Recovery Agency's competing plan to
turn the area into a landfill.

Gould, K. L. "Peace, Love, and Meier: Pavilion Designed for Woodstock Site."
Architectural Record 189/8 (August 2001): 34.

"Graduate Students Head for Woodstock '94." *The Chronicle of Higher Education* 40/50
(August 17, 1994): A27. In light of the fact that the original Woodstock Music
and Art Fair received relatively little sociological study at the time it took place,
graduate students of sociology are planning on attending the twenty-fifth-
anniversary festival in order to give the event serious academic study.

Graham, Jennifer. "All She Wants to Do." *TV Guide* 47/29 (July 17, 1999): 24. This article, which features musician Sheryl Crow, also contains a list of performers scheduled for Woodstock 1999.

Grateful Dead: The Illustrated Trip. New York: DK, 2003.

Graves, Tom. "Peace, Love, Music: From the Peace-Jubilee of 1869 to Woodstock."
American History 30/6 (January–February 1996): 47+. This article describes the
Woodstock festival in the context of the historically similar Peace-Jubilee of 1869.

Gray, J. "Tangerine Dreams." *Maclean's* 102/35 (August 28, 1989): 50+. This article is by
a Canadian writer who looks at the 1969 Woodstock festival from the viewpoint
of a Canadian who attended.

Green Mind. *Woodstock Journal 1999.* http://www.geocities.com/TheTropics/Bay/ 9641/
wjournal.html. Accessed January 29, 2004. This purported Woodstock 1999 attendee provides a diary of his experiences at the festival.

Greenfield, Robert. *Dark Star: An Oral Biography of Jerry Garcia.* New York: William Morrow, 1996.

Grossberger, Lewis. "Woodshocked." *MediaWeek* 4/32 (August 8, 1994): 30. This article
deals with the massive amounts of media attention garnered by the approaching
Woodstock '94 festival.

Grotticelli, Michael. "Woodstock (Digitally) Revisited." *Videography* 19/11 (November
1994): 72. This article concerns the use of Macintosh computers to create daily
news shows at Woodstock '94.

Hamilton, Neil A. *The ABC-CLIO Companion to the 1960s Counterculture in America*. Santa Barbara, California: ABC-CLIO, 1997.

Hammersmith, James P. Review of *Barefoot in Babylon: The Creation of the Woodstock Music Festival, 1969* by Robert Stephen Spitz. *Southern Humanities Review* 15/3 (1981): 257+.

Hanan, Stephen Mo. "Passing a Doubtful Torch: D-Day in the Eyes of the Woodstock Generation." *Tikkun* 9/5 (September–October 1994): 62+. This article deals in part with the significance of the celebration of the twenty-fifth anniversary of the Woodstock festival.

Handy, Bruce. "Remembrance of Things Past." *New York* 27/32 (August 15, 1994): 28. This article deals in part with the anniversary of Woodstock, Altamont, and the Manson murders.

Hansen, Gary N. "Transportation Planning for a Large Special Event: The Woodstock '94 Experience." *ITE Journal* 66/4 (1996): 34+.

Harrington, Joe S. *Sonic Cool: The Life and Death of Rock 'n' Roll*. New York: Hal Leonard Corporation, 2002.

Harris, R. R. Review of *Woodstock: The Oral History* by Joel Makower. *New York Times Book Review* 138/4786 (July 23, 1989): 7.

Harrison, Hank. *The Dead Book*. New York: Links Books, 1973. This book on The Grateful Dead contains information pertaining to their appearance at the Woodstock Music and Art Fair.

Havens, Richie, with Steve Davidowitz. *They Can't Hide Us Anymore*. New York: Spike, 1999. An autobiographical book by the performer who led off the Woodstock Music and Art Fair.

Helander, Brock. *The Rock Who's Who*, 2nd ed. New York: Schirmer Books, 1996. This general-purpose reference book contains biographies of several of the prominent Woodstock performers.

Helligar, Jeremy. "*Woodstock '94*." *People* 42/21 (November 21, 1994): 25+. This is a mixed review of the *Woodstock '94* live album.

Henderson, David. "Jimi Hendrix Deep within the Blues and Alive Onstage at Woodstock—25 Years after Death." *African American Review* 29/2 (1995): 213+. Henderson discusses, among other things, the release of the *Jimi Hendrix: Woodstock* compact disc.

Henderson, David. *Jimi Hendrix: Voodoo Child of the Aquarian Age*. Garden City, New York: Doubleday, 1978.

Henderson, David. *'Scuse Me While I Kiss the Sky: The Life of Jimi Hendrix*. New York: Bantam Books, 1983. Republished 1996. This book is condensed and revised from Henderson's 1978 book *Jimi Hendrix: Voodoo Child of the Aquarian Age*.

Hernandez, Debra Gersh. "No Nudes Is Good Nudes." *Editor and Publisher* 128/6 (February 11, 1995): 9+. This is a report on *Washington Times* photographer Kenneth Lambert's photograph of a long-haired nude male at the Woodstock '94 being looked at cynically by a female festival attendee. Although the photograph was never published in a newspaper in its original, uncensored form, Lambert entered it in a news photography contest. The photographer said that he wanted to show how different Woodstock '94 was from the 1969 festival.

Herndon, David. "No Peace in the Valley." *Rolling Stone* n667 (October 14, 1993): 36. This is a report on the rival plans of Woodstock Ventures and the National Multiple Sclerosis Society for a Woodstock twenty-fifth-anniversary festival.

Herszenhorn, David M. "Flower Power in the High-Tech 90's." *New York Times* August 16, 1998: 36. This article is a profile of the 1998 A Day in the Garden festival, which was held on the site of the 1969 Woodstock Music and Art Fair.

Hertzberg, Hendrik. "The Magic of Woodstock: You Had to Be There." *New Republic* 201/9 (August 28, 1989): 13+. The author of this article attended the 1969 Woodstock festival, and he recounts his experiences at the event.

Hiltbrand, David. Review of *Woodstock: Lost Performances*. *People* 42/7 (August 15, 1994): 13. This is a review of the Showtime cable television network's program *Woodstock: Lost Performances*. The special, which featured previously unreleased footage of Joe Cocker, Janis Joplin, Mountain, Canned Heat, and Johnny Winter, was given an "A–."

Hirshey, Gerri. "The '60s. The Beatles, Motown, Woodstock: It Was the Best of Times." *Life* 15/13 (December 1, 1992): 60. This 1960s retrospective includes Woodstock-related material.

Hodenfield, Chris. *Rock '70*. New York: Pyramid Books, 1970. Contains references to the importance of Woodstock.

Hoffman, Abbie. *Woodstock Nation*. New York: Vintage Books, Random House, 1969. Hoffman deals with the importance of Woodstock and the 1960s counterculture.

"Hollywood Meets Woodstock." *Newsweek* 121/3 (January 11, 1993): 23.

Hopkins, Jerry. *The Rock Story*. New York: New American Library, 1970.

Horak, Terri. "PolyGram Offers *Woodstock* Book in an Effort to Diversify." *Billboard* 106/50 (December 10, 1994): 73.

Hoskyns, Barney. *Beneath the Diamond Sky: Haight-Ashbury, 1965–1970*. New York: Simon and Schuster, 1997. This book deals with the development of the 1960s hippie movement.

Hoskyns, Barney. "The Birth of Hippie Culture." In Kallen, Stuart A., ed., *Sixties Counterculture*. San Diego: Greenhaven Press, 2001: 107+. This article is excerpted from Hoskyns 1997.

Hudis, Mark. "Wease Whacks Woodstock." *MediaWeek* 4/33 (August 22, 1994): 33. This article reports on Woodstock master of ceremonies, radio DJ Brother Wease and his negative views of the festival.

Huey, Steve. "Sheryl Crow." *All Music Guide*. http://allmusic.com. Accessed March 30, 2004. Contains a biography and critical commentary on Sheryl Crow.

Huey, Steve. "Wyclef Jean." *All Music Guide*. http://allmusic.com. Accessed March 30, 2004. Contains a biography and critical commentary on Wyclef Jean.

"In Business This Week." *Business Week* n3387 (August 29, 1994): 40. This article contains, among other things, a report on the Woodstock '94 festival.

Isserman, Maurice. "Woodstock '99." *Christian Science Monitor* July 23, 1999: 11. This article concerns the author's observations about the differences between Woodstock 1999 and the 1969 Woodstock festival, as well as differences between the generations involved in the two music festivals.

Ives, Sandor. *Woodstock, 1969*. Youngstown, Ohio: Youngstown State University, 1995. This is an eighteen-page transcript of a taped interview conducted by Christopher L. Helm as part of the Department of History's Oral History Program.

Jacobs, Lewis. *The Documentary Tradition: From Nanook to Woodstock*. New York: Hopkinson and Blake, 1971. This book includes discussion of the *Woodstock: Three Days of Peace and Music* film within the context of the history of documentary films.

Jasper, Tony. *Understanding Pop*. London: SCM Press, 1972.

Jonnes, Jill. *Hep-Cats, Narcs, and Pipe Dreams: A History of America's Romance with Illegal Drugs*. New York: Scribner, 1996.

Joseph, Peter. *Good Times: An Oral History of America in the Nineteen Sixties*. New York: Charterhouse, 1973. Contains references to the importance of the Woodstock Music and Art Fair.

"July. Lollapalooza Updates Woodstock; Axl Rose Meets St. Louis; and Ice Cube Joins Boyz 'n the Hood." *Rolling Stone* n619–20 (December 1991): 59–63. I have included this article as an illustration of the extent to which major concert festivals were still being compared with Woodstock over twenty years after the August 1969 event.

"Just One More." *Life* 22/9 (August 1, 1999): 92. A photographic retrospective of the 1969 Woodstock festival.

Kallen, Stuart A., ed. *Sixties Counterculture*. San Diego: Greenhaven Press, 2001.

Kauffman, Stanley. "Woodstock." *New Republic* 162/18 (May 2, 1970): 20. This is a review of the film *Woodstock: Three Days of Peace and Music*.

Kaufman, M. T. "This Time a Personal Woodstock." *New York Times* August 16, 1989: B1. This is a report on the hundreds of people who have been returning to the site of the Woodstock Music and Art Fair on the twentieth anniversary of the opening of the festival.

Keil, Beth Landman. "All You Need Is Love, and Lawyers." *New York* 32/9 (March 8, 1999): 15+. This is a report on bass guitarist Rob Wasserman's lawsuit against the producers of the Woodstock 25th Anniversary Festival for injuries he suffered at the site.

Keil, Beth Landman. "Have Film, Need Money." *New York* 32/28 (July 26, 1999): 10. This is a report on filmmaker Barbara Kopple's difficulties getting funding for a film on the Woodstock festivals.

Keil, Beth Landman. "Woodstock Rocks on for Al Roker." *New York* 31/19 (May 18, 1998): 10. This article follows up on the author's March 8, 1998, article in New York dealing with injured bass player Rob Wasserman's lawsuit against the producers of Woodstock '94. Well-known television personality Al Roker was being photographed backstage at the time of Wasserman's fall over a tent cable.

Kelly, Linda. *Deadheads: Stories from Fellow Artists, Friends, and Followers of the Grateful Dead*. Secaucus, New Jersey: Carol, 1995.

Kenny, Glenn, and Ty Burr. "Video." *Entertainment Weekly* n252 (December 9, 1994): 92. This article contains a review of the Woodstock '94 audio CD.

Kiester, Edwin, Jr. "Woodstock and Beyond, Why?" *Today's Health* 48 (July 1970): 20+.

Kimball, Roger. "Charles Reich and America's Cultural Revolution." *New Criterion* 13/1 (September 1994): 12+. In this article, Kimball suggests that Charles Reich (author of *The Greening of America*) and other writers of the late 1960s and early 1970s were in part responsible for the common misconception that the 1969 Woodstock Music and Art Fair was a spontaneous, antimaterialistic happening that represented a revolution in American life. The article is largely critical of Reich's seminal book.

Kopkind, A. "The New Culture of Opposition." *Current* 111 (October 1969): 56–59.

Lacayo, Richard. "If Everyone Is Hip . . . Is Anyone Hip?" *Time* 144/6 (August 8, 1994): 48+. This article on what it means to be "hip" includes comparisons of the Woodstock nation with the Woodstock '94 generation.

Laing, David. *The Sounds of Our Time*. Chicago: Quadrangle Books, 1970.

Lamb, Gregory M. "Downloading Woodstock '99." *Christian Science Monitor* July 23, 1999: 13. The author contrasts the United States of 1969 with the nation at the time of Woodstock 1999.

Landau, Jon. *It's Too Late to Stop Now*. San Francisco: Straight Arrow Books, 1972.

Landy, Elliott. *Woodstock 1969: The First Festival. Three Days of Peace & Music: A Photo Commemorative*. Santa Rosa, California: Squarebooks, 1994.

Landy, Elliott. *Woodstock Vision: The Spirit of a Generation*. New York: Continuum, 1994.

Lanker, Brian, and Jim Calio. "A Session with Grace Slick." *Life* 15/13 (December 1, 1992): 70+. The former lead singer of the Jefferson Airplane shares her recollections of both Woodstock and Altamont in this article.

Lapresta, Timothy. *Woodstock, NY*. Youngstown, Ohio: Youngstown State University, 1995. This is a fourteen-page transcript of a taped interview conducted by Christopher L. Helm as part of the Department of History's Oral History Program.

Latham, Aaron. "Zucchero." *All Music Guide*. http://allmusic.com. Accessed April 12, 2004. Contains a biography and critical commentary on the singer Zucchero.

Law, Lisa. "Organizing Woodstock." http://americanhistory.si.edu/lisalaw. Accessed October 23, 2003. Law, who helped organize the 1969 Woodstock festival, includes her perspective and photographs of the event.

"Legacy." *Westchester County Business Journal* 33/34 (August 22, 1994): 14A. This article credits Max Yasgur with making the original Woodstock festival possible and details the ways in which Max and Miriam Yasgur's son, Sam, and grandchildren are keeping the family's legacy alive.

Lerman, Leo. "Part of the Whole Thing: Name It Woodstock, Name It Bethel." *Mademoiselle* 70 (November 1969): 160–61.

Levin, Bob. "An Overdose of Nostalgia." *Maclean's* 112/31 (August 2, 1999): 48. This article includes thoughts on the thirtieth anniversary of the Woodstock festival.

Lewisohn, Mark. *The Beatles Recording Sessions: The Official Abbey Road Studio Session Notes, 1962–1970*. New York: Harmony Books, 1988.

Lewisohn, Mark. *The Beatles Live!: The Ultimate Reference Book*. New York: Henry Holt, 1986.

Lhamon, W. T., Jr. "Woodstock Again." *New Republic* 171/23 (December 7, 1974): 28+. Lhamon reviews Joel Rosenman, John Roberts, and Robert Pilpel's book *Young Men with Unlimited Capital* in this article.

Lichtman, Irv. "Added Day at Woodstock." *Billboard* 106/30 (July 23, 1994): 137.

Lichtman, Irv. "Bethel '94: Is the Show on?" *Billboard* 106/33 (August 13, 1994): 102. This is a chronicle of the organizational difficulties Sid Bernstein is encountering with getting financial backing for the planned twenty-fifth Woodstock reunion festival in Bethel, New York. According to the report, Bernstein has decided to limit the attendance to less than 10,000 in order to avoid having to obtain the town's mass-gathering permit.

Liesse, Julie. "Haagen-Dazs Spoons up a Revival." *Advertising Age* 65/35 (August 22, 1994): 38. A report on Haagen-Dazs' sponsorship of the Woodstock '94 festival.

"Life Special." *Life* 17/8 (August 1994): 32. This is a report on the A Day in the Garden festival and an anniversary photo album by Gregory Heisler.

Lipski, Alexander, and Suzenna Martin. "Bangla Desh." In liner notes to *The Concert for Bangla Desh*. Three 33-1/3 rpm phonodiscs. Apple Records STGX 3385, 1971.

"Live Aid vs. Woodstock." *Nation* 241/8 (September 14, 1985): 194. This letter to the editor ponders the differences between Woodstock and the Live Aid festival.

Loder, Kurt. "Joan Baez." *Rolling Stone* n641 (October 15, 1992): 105+. This is a reprint of an interview with Baez that originally appeared in issue 393 of *Rolling Stone*.

Loder, Kurt. "Tales from Satan's Playground." *Rolling Stone* n820 (September 2, 1999): 56+. This article is a report on the riots and other misbehavior at the Woodstock 1999 festival.

Long Time Gone: Sixties America Then and Now, ed. Alexander Bloom. Oxford: Oxford University Press, 2001.

Lukas, P. "Marketing—That Fresh Woodstock Feeling." *Fortune* 139/9 (May 10, 1999): 2.

Lyons, D. "Woodstock and the Web." Forbes 164/4 (August 23, 1999): 1.

Macan, Edward. *Rocking the Classics: English Progressive Rock and the Counterculture.* New York: Oxford University Press, 1996.

MacIntosh, Jeanne. "Stock Portfolio." *DNR* 24/131 (July 11, 1994): 8. This is a report on corporate sponsorship of Woodstock '94.

Maglitta, Joseph E. "Woodstock '99: Think E-Commerce, Dude." *Computerworld* 33/33 (August 16, 1999): 42+. This article deals with the marketing of the Woodstock 1999 festival on the Internet, as well as the relatively small amount of e-mailing that was being done from the festival site (at least in relationship to the amount of marijuana that audience members were smoking).

Maglitta, Joseph E. "Woodstock 2.0: Techno-tainment Born. Joe Maglitta Discovers That There Are Information Technology Lessons to Be Learned from Woodstock." *Computerworld* 28/35 (August 29, 1994): 37. This article deals with the use of computer technology at Woodstock '94 as well as the relationships between hippies and the world of computers.

Makower, Joel. *Woodstock: The Oral History.* New York: Doubleday Press, 1989. Makower's book is one of the principal sources of participants' insights into the 1969 Woodstock Music and Art Fair.

Mallory, Kenneth. *Woodstock, 1969.* Youngstown, Ohio: Youngstown State University, 1995. This is an eleven-page transcript of a taped interview conducted by Christopher L. Helm as part of the Department of History's Oral History Program.

"Man Accused of Sex Attack at Woodstock." *New York Times* August 1, 1999: 35. This article concerns Timothy A. Weeden, a New York prison guard, who was charged with sexual assault at the Woodstock 1999 festival.

Manzarek, Ray. *Light My Fire: My Life with the Doors.* New York: G. P. Putnam's Sons, 1998.

Marcus, Greil. "A New Awakening." In Denisoff, R. Serge, and Richard A. Peterson, eds., *Sounds of Social Change*, 127–36. Chicago: Rand McNally, 1972.

Marcus, Greil. "Real Life. Greil Marcus' Top Ten." *Artform International* 33/4 (December 1994): 14+. The famed rock music critic names the newly issued Jimi Hendrix recording *Live at Woodstock* among the top 10 rock music recordings.

Marcus, Greil. "A Singer and a Rock and Roll Band." In Marcus, Greil, ed., *Rock and Roll Will Stand*, 90–105. Boston: Beacon Press, 1969.

Marcus, Greil, ed. *Rock and Roll Will Stand.* Boston: Beacon Books, 1970.

Marcus, Greil. "So What Was It about Woodstock '69 That Made It Historic?" *Interview* 24/7 (July 1994): 56+. Marcus compares the commercialism of Woodstock '94 to the communal nature of the 1969 festival.

May, Rollo. "Opinion: On Bethel and After." *Mademoiselle* 70 (November 1969): 28+.

Mayfield, Geoff. "Between the Bullets." *Billboard* 106/36 (September 3, 1994): 125. This article looks at the upsurge in sales of albums for artists who appeared at Woodstock '94, like Melissa Etheridge and Sheryl Crow.

Mayfield, Geoff. "Between the Bullets." *Billboard* 106/43 (October 22, 1994): 111. Mayfield discusses the positive impact Trent Reznor's Nine Inch Nails had on the artist's latest recording.

Mayfield, Geoff. "Between the Bullets." *Billboard* 111/32 (August 7, 1999): 80. This article deals with trends in chart activity as related to various artists' appearances at the Woodstock 1999 festival.

"Mayhem at Woodstock Festival Has Led to 39 Arrests So Far." *New York Times* August 5, 1999: B7. A report on the rapes and riots that took place at Woodstock 1999.

McCormick, Moria. "Kidstock Adds New Angle to Woodstock '99." *Billboard* 111/31 (July 31, 1999): 78+. This article is a report on the Kidstock festival of children's music that was part of the Woodstock 1999 festival.

McGowan, Chris. "Woodstock Revisited." *Billboard* 106/47 (November 19, 1994): 69. This is a positive review of the laser-disc edition of *Woodstock: Three Days of Peace and Music.*

McHugh, Catherine. "Mind over Mud." *Lighting Dimensions* 18/8 (November 1994): 62. This article deals with Woodstock '94 lighting designer Allen Branton and his use of cutting-edge technology.

Mead, Margaret. "Woodstock in Retrospect." *Redbook* 134 (January 1970): 30.

Mehta, Stephanie N. "Local Businesses Worry Woodstock '94 Won't Pay Off." *Wall Street Journal* (Eastern Edition) August 8, 1994: B1.

"Melanie." *People* 45/24 (June 17, 1996): 136+. This profile of singer-songwriter Melanie Schekeryk (formerly Melanie Safka) describes her set at the 1969 Woodstock festival as "career-making."

Mele, Christopher. *Selling the Lower East Side: Culture, Real Estate, and Resistance in New York City.* Minneapolis: University of Minnesota Press, 2000. In dealing with counterculture activity in New York City, this book helps to put figures like Abbie Hoffman into context.

Melton, Barry. "Everything Seemed Beautiful: A Life in the Counterculture." In Bloom, Alexander, ed., *Long Time Gone: Sixties American Then and Now*, 145–57. New York: Oxford University Press, 2001. The one-time member of Country Joe and the Fish reflects on the 1960s.

"Memories of Woodstock." *Society* 27/1 (November–December 1989): 2+. This article reports that according to a Gallup poll, Jimi Hendrix, Janis Joplin, and Joan Baez are the performers most Woodstock attendees remember twenty years after the festival.

"The Message of History's Biggest Happening." *Time* 94 (August 29, 1969): 32–33. Reprinted without lyrics quotations in Budds, Michael J., and Marian M. Ohman, eds., *Rock Recall: Annotated Readings in American Popular Music from the Emergence of Rock and Roll to the Demise of the Woodstock Nation*, 295. Needham Heights, Massachusetts: Ginn Press, 1993.

Michael Lang Answers Questions about Woodstock '99. http://members.aol.com/Mary1 NYS/Lang2.html. Accessed October 23, 2003.

Miller, Paul. "A Weekend in Paradise." *The Village Voice* 39/35 (August 30, 1994): 28. This article contains the author's recollections of being a disc jockey (DJ) at the Woodstock '94 festival.

Milward, John. "Field of Dreams." *Rolling Stone* n688 (August 11, 1994): 36+. Milward contrasts the original Woodstock Music and Art Fair's emphasis on peace, love, and understanding with the emphasis on profit making of Woodstock '94.

Milward, John. "Joy in Mudville." *Rolling Stone* n691 (September 22, 1994): 61+. This article is a detailed recap of the Woodstock '94 festival.

Milward, John. "We Are Golden." *Rolling Stone* n694 (November 3, 1994): 37. The author reports on the optimism of Woodstock '94 organizers that the festival will turn a profit.

Morrison, Joan, and Robert K. Morrison. *From Camelot to Kent State: The Sixties Experience in the Words of Those Who Lived It.* New York: Times Books, 1987. Updated ed. New York: Oxford University Press, 2001.

Morrow, Lance. "Essay: Lance Morrow on the Latest Woodstock." *Time* (August 9, 1999): 82.

Mundy, Chris. "Green Daze." *Rolling Stone* n700 (January 26, 1995): 40+. This feature article on the band Green Day deals in part with their appearance at Woodstock '94.

Music Festival Home Page, The. http://www.geocities.com/~music-festival/. Accessed May 13, 2003.

"Music: The Rekindling of Woodstock." *Time* 144/8 (August 22, 1999): 78.

My Generation. VHS-format videocassette. Gary Busey, narrator; Obie Benz, writer, producer director; Andrew Solt, Quincy Jones, Bob Metrowitz, and David Salzman, executive producers; Jeffrey Peisch, series producer. Chicago: Time-Life Video and Television, 1995. Warner Home Video 13865.

Nanry, Charles, ed. *American Music: From Storyville to Woodstock.* New Brunswick, New Jersey: Transaction Books, 1972. This book attempts to place Woodstock within the context of historical American popular culture.

Navasky, Victor S., and Irving Kristol. "The 1960's." *New York Times Magazine* 145/50397 (April 14, 1996): 113+. This article includes reprints of articles concerning the Woodstock Music and Art Fair that were published in the 1960s.

Nazzaro, G. Review of *Woodstock: 25th Anniversary Director's Cut. Cineforum* 34/11 (November 1994).

Nelson, Tribby. *Woodstock, 1969.* Youngstown, Ohio: Youngstown State University, 1994. This is a thirteen-page transcript of a taped interview conducted by Christopher L. Helm as part of the Department of History's Oral History Program.

Newman, Andy. "Local Hopes for a Concert Windfall Are Dashed." *New York Times* July 25, 1999: 26. According to this article, concertgoers' lack of cash and the location of many of the shops in Rome, New York, caused area businesses to experience significantly less positive financial impact from Woodstock 1999 than had originally been anticipated.

Newman, Andy. "Police Investigating Reported Rapes at Woodstock." *New York Times* July 29, 1999: B5. This article concerns the gang rapes that were reported at the Woodstock 1999 festival.

Newman, Melinda. "Martin Is Artist of the Year . . ." *Billboard* 111–12/52–1 (December 25, 1999–January 1, 2000): 18+. Newman speculates that the problems that occurred at Woodstock 1999 will not mean the end of large, multiday rock festivals but will result in better crowd control in the future.

Newman, Melinda. "Mavericks, Radney Foster Say Hello to Pop Radio—Why Another Woodstock?" *Billboard* 110/35 (August 29, 1998): 18+. Author Newman wonders why promoters are planning a thirtieth-anniversary Woodstock festival, given the cultural significance of the original festival, the problems of the Woodstock '94 festival, and the fact that neither made money.

Newman, Melinda. "Rhino Commemorates Alice Cooper's *Life and Crimes* . . ." *Billboard* 111/15 (April 10, 1999): 12. The author includes a list of confirmed participants in the July 23–25 Woodstock 1999.

Newman, Melinda. "Woodstock '94: Mixed Aftermath." *Billboard* 107/33 (August 19, 1995): 1+.

"New York SPJ Chapter Sends Objections to Gov. Pataki." *News Photographer* 54/8 (August 1999): 22. This article is a reproduction of a letter from James Plante, president of the New York City Chapter of the Society of Professional Journalists, to New York state governor George Pataki protesting the New York State Police's unauthorized publication of copyrighted news photographs on the Internet to attempt to identify perpetrators of the Woodstock 1999 riots.

Nieves, Evelyn. "Can't Beat Woodstock? Then Join It." *New York Times* August 21, 1996: B1+. This article deals with owners of the former Yasgur farm, Jeryl Abramson and Roy Howard, and their decision to allow pilgrims to the site of the original Woodstock festival to set up camp on their land.

Nieves, Evelyn. "Still Haunted by the Spirit of Woodstock." *New York Times* August 10, 1997: 29. This article deals with plans for Woodstock '97, which was to be held at the site of the 1969 Woodstock Music and Art Fair.

"1994 Unplugged: The 94 Biggest Stories of '94." *Us* n204 (January 1995): 56. The twenty-fifth-anniversary Woodstock festival is included among the most significant events of 1994.

Niogret, H. Review of *Jimi Hendrix at Woodstock*. *Positif* n391 (September 1993).

Noack, David. "Covering Woodstock." *Editor and Publisher* 127/37 (September 10, 1994): 16+. This article details the "military-style planning" that enabled the three daily newspapers of New York's mid-Hudson Valley to cover the Woodstock '94 festival.

"Noise." *Spin* 15/11 (November 1999): 61+. This article contains information on the rapes that took place at Woodstock 1999.

Norman, Ken. "Tapes and Discs." *Video Magazine* 18/8 (November 1994): 71+. This article includes a review of *Woodstock: 25th Anniversary CD-ROM*.

Norman, Ken, and Brenda Butterworth. "Peace, Love and Multimedia." *Video Magazine* 18/8 (November 1994): 12. This article includes a report on the exhibits of interactive technology on display at the Woodstock '94 festival.

"Nostalgie de la boue." *New Criterion* 13/1 (September 1994): 2+. Among the interesting items noted in this article about Woodstock '94 is that "emergency medical workers compared the scene to 'a war zone' as doctors treated a new patient every twenty seconds" on Saturday of the festival.

"Notes." *Publishers Weekly* 241/32 (August 15, 1994): 34. This overview of upcoming CD-ROMs includes an announcement of the release of *Woodstock: Three Days of Peace and Music*.

"Notes and Comment: Woodstock Festival." *New Yorker* 45 (August 30, 1969): 17–21.

"Now Playing." *Rolling Stone* n688 (August 11, 1994): 63. This article contains a very positive review of the video release of the director's cut of the Michael Wadleigh film *Woodstock: Three Days of Peace and Music*.

"Of D-Day and Woodstock." *Alberta Report* 21/41 (September 26, 1994): 19.

"Offline: Cries and Whispers on the Internet." *Wilson Library Bulletin* 69/2 (October

1994): 16. This article includes mention of views of the Woodstock '94 festival that are being expressed on-line.

"On the Gravy Train." *The Economist* 317/7679 (November 3, 1990): 25. Although this brief article focuses on the political campaign Hugh Romney (Wavy Gravy) was waging at the time, his work at the 1969 Woodstock festival as part of the Hog Farm commune is mentioned.

Onkey, Lauren. "Voodoo Child: Jimi Hendrix and the Politics of Race in the Sixties." In Braunstein, Peter, and Michael William Doyle, eds., *Imagine Nation: The American Counterculture of the 1960s and '70s*, 189–214. New York: Routledge, 2002.

O'Rourke, John J., and John J. Murphy Jr. "Woodstock '94: Fire Planning for Large Public Events." *Fire Engineering* 148/1 (1995): 74+.

"Outliers." *Modern Healthcare* 24/32 (August 8, 1994): 164. This article includes a report on the plans for providing medical services at the Woodstock '94 festival.

Palmer, Robert. "Woodstock: Just Say No." *The Boston Phoenix* 23/30 (July 29, 1994): 6.

Panichas, George A. "The Woodstock and Ourselves." *Modern Age* 37/3 (Spring 1995): 194+. This article examines the increasing lack of emotional and behavioral restraints in society as reflected in Woodstock '94.

Pareles, Jon. "At the Woodstock Site, Measuring the Distance between Then and Now." *New York Times* August 17, 1998: E5. The author compares the music and the audience of the 1969 Woodstock festival with those of the 1998 A Day in the Garden festival, held at the same location.

Pareles, Jon. "This Woodstock Won't Inhale." *New York Times* August 7, 1994: B1. This article compares the music and audience of the 1969 Woodstock festival and that of Woodstock '94.

Pareles, Jon. "Woodstock: Old-Time New-Age Karma." *New York Times* October 25, 1996: C1. Pareles presents a look at the New Age features of 1990s Woodstock, New York, traditional values in the town, and the 1969 Woodstock Music and Art Fair.

Pareles, Jon. "Woodstock: Time to Face the Music." *New York Times* August 12, 1994: C1. This is a report on the opening day of Woodstock '94.

Pareles, Jon. "Woodstock's Children." *New York Times* August 28, 1994: B1. This is a follow-up on the Woodstock '94 festival.

Paul, Fredric. "Top 10 Entertainment." *PC World* 12/12 (December 1994): 145. This article includes a review of the *Woodstock: 25th Anniversary CD-ROM*.

Pielke, Robert G. *You Say You Want a Revolution: Rock Music in American Culture*. Chicago: Nelson-Hall, 1986.

Pike, Deborah. "You Said It." *Mademoiselle* 100/12 (December 1994). This article deals in part with the Woodstock '94 festival.

"Police Post Internet Photos of Woodstock Rioters." *New York Times* August 4, 1999: B2. A report on the New York State Police's use of copyrighted photographs to try to identify Woodstock 1999 rioters.

"PolyGram: Woodstock's Beautiful PPV Music." *MediaWeek* 4/33 (August 22, 1994): 4. This is a brief report on the success of pay-per-view live television broadcast of Woodstock '94.

Powers, Ann. "A Surge of Sexism on the Music Scene." *New York Times* August 2, 1999: E1. This article includes analysis of the rapes and other sexual mistreatment of women at Woodstock 1999.

Powers, Jim. "The Incredible String Band." *All Music Guide*. http://allmusic.com. Accessed December 22, 2003. Contains a biography and critical commentary on the group.

Prato, Greg. "King's X." *All Music Guide*. http://allmusic.com. Accessed April 14, 2004. Contains a biography and critical commentary on the group.

Pratt, Ray. *Rhythm and Resistance: Political Uses of American Popular Music*, 2nd ed. Washington, D.C.: Smithsonian Institution Press, 1994.

Quaif, G. "Woodstock, The Music." *Sight and Sound* 4/10 (October 1994). This is a response to Sinker's review of the video issue of the director's cut of the film *Woodstock: Three Days of Peace and Music*.

"Quick Clips." *PC Magazine* 13/17 (October 11, 1994): 473. This article includes a review of the *Woodstock 25th Anniversary CD-ROM*.

Reeves, Richard. "Mike Lang (Groovy Kid from Brooklyn) Plus John Roberts (Unlimited Capital) Equals Woodstock." *New York Times Magazine* (September 7, 1969): 34–35. A feature on the organizers of the Woodstock Music and Art Fair.

Reilly, Edward, Maggie McManus, and William Chadwick. *The Monkees: A Manufactured Image*. Ann Arbor, Michigan: Pierian Press, 1987. Contains information on Jimi Hendrix's ill-fated tour opening for The Monkees.

Ressner, J. "Woodstock Anniversary Plans Taking Shape." *Rolling Stone* n551 (May 4, 1989): 20. A report on plans for a Woodstock twentieth anniversary festival.

"Revenue Generation Clashes with the Peace Generation." *New York Times* September 30, 1992: B1. This is an article about the growing controversies surrounding the planning of a twenty-fifth-anniversary celebration of the Woodstock Music and Art Fair.

Review of *Woodstock Nation* by Abbie Hoffman. *New Republic* 161/22 (November 29, 1969): 38+.

"Reviews." *Video Magazine* 17/8 (November 1994): 68. This article contains a review of the *Woodstock* CD-ROM.

Revkin, Andrew C. "A More Sedate Woodstock Tries to Lure Yuppies, Not Hippies." *New York Times* August 14, 1998: B1. This article profiles the 1998 A Day in the Garden festival, organized by the then-current owner of the old Yasgur farm, cable television pioneer Alan Gerry.

Revkin, Andrew C. "With Nod to the Dead, Woodstock Lives." *New York Times* August 13, 1995: 35. This is a report on the twenty-sixth-anniversary celebration of Woodstock in Bethel, New York. The headline title alludes to the tribute to deceased Grateful Dead guitarist Jerry Garcia that took place at the event.

Richardson, Ken. "The Year in Headlines." *Stereo Review* 63/1 (January 1998): 91. This article includes a report on Alan Gerry's purchase of the site of the Woodstock Music and Art Fair and his plans to construct a music-related theme park at the location.

Richardson, Lynda. "Woodstock at 25: Adults Take Over." *New York Times* September 30, 1992: B5.

Roberts, K. Reply to "Mike Lang . . . Plus John Roberts . . . Equals Woodstock" by Richard Reeves. *New York Times Magazine* (October 5, 1969): 54. See Reeves, Richard.

"Rock Festival Fans Depart in Peace." *Denver Post* August 18, 1969: 1. Reprinted in Budds, Michael J., and Marian M. Ohman, eds., *Rock Recall: Annotated Readings in American Popular Music from the Emergence of Rock and Roll to the Demise of the Woodstock Nation*, 292. Needham Heights, Massachusetts: Ginn Press, 1993.

"Rock Festival's Instant City: Woodstock Festival." *Senior Scholastic* 95 (September 22, 1969): 26+.

"The Rocky Road to Fame, If Not Fortune: Woodstock Music and Art Fair." *Business Week* (August 30, 1969): 78–80.

Rodrick, Stephen. "Woodstock Postcard: Gone to Pot. Two Days of Mud and Pepsi." *The New Republic* 211/10 (September 5, 1994): 9.

Rogers, Adam. "Where Are They Now?" *Newsweek* 124/6 (August 8, 1994): 47. As the twenty-fifth anniversary of the Woodstock Music and Art Fair approaches, the author takes a look at what Woodstock performers are doing in 1994.

Rogers, Shelley L. Review of *Barefoot in Babylon: The Creation of the Woodstock Music Festival, 1969* by Robert Stephen Spitz. *Notes* 48/2 (December 1991): 531–33.

Rosenman, Joel, John Roberts, and Robert Pilpel. *Young Men with Unlimited Capital.* New York: Harcourt Brace Jovanovich, 1974.

Ross, Jay. "Earthlight Theatre Illumines out Times with Humor, Pathos." *Advocate* 4/16 (September 30, 1970): 14. This brief article discusses the formation of the Earthlight Theatre, their performance at Woodstock, and subsequent appearances at gay pride events.

Rothstein, Jeffrey. *The Apotheosis of Discontent: Representations of the Counterculture in 1960's Film and Television.* Thesis: Youngstown State University, 1999.

Rubin, Mike. "Summer of '69." *Spin* 10/6 (September 1994): 62. In light of the Woodstock '94 festival, the author takes a look back at events of autumn 1969, including Woodstock and the Manson murders.

Ruehl, Peter. "Sea to Shining Sea." *BRW* 21/29 (July 30, 1999): 106. This article, dealing with a variety of observations the author made after returning to the United States after living in Australia for ten years, mentions Woodstock 1999.

Ruhlmann, William. "Blues Traveler." *All Music Guide.* http://allmusic.com. Accessed April 12, 2004. Contains a biography and critical commentary of the band.

Ruhlmann, William. "Ten Years After." *All Music Guide.* http://allmusic.com. Accessed December 22, 2003. Contains a biography and critical commentary on the band.

Rusher, William A. "Mass Infantilism, Anyone?" *National Review* 21 (October 7, 1969): 1012. A highly negative report on the Woodstock Music and Art Fair.

Samudrala, Ram. *Woodstock 1994 Concert Review.* http://www.ram.org/music/woodstock/woodstock.html. Accessed March 7, 2004.

Samuels, David. "Rock Is Dead (Woodstock 1999)." *Harper's Magazine* (November 1999).

Sander, Ellen. "Monterey." In *Trips: Rock Life in the Sixties*, 91+. New York: Charles Scribner's Sons, 1973. Excerpted in Budds, Michael J., and Marian M. Ohman, eds., *Rock Recall: Annotated Readings in American Popular Music from the Emergence of Rock and Roll to the Demise of the Woodstock Nation*, 291. Needham Heights, Massachusetts: Ginn Press, 1993.

Sander, Ellen. "The Ultimate Pop Experience: Woodstock Music and Art Fair." *Saturday Review* 52 (September 27, 1969): 59+. A recap of the 1969 Woodstock festival.

Santoro, G. "Music." *Nation* 249/8 (September 11, 1989): 253+. This article contains a review of the compact disc reissues of *Woodstock* and *Woodstock II* recordings from the 1969 Woodstock Music and Art Fair.

Sardiello, Robert. "Secular Rituals in Popular Culture: A Case for Grateful Dead Concerts and Deadhead Identity." In Epstein, Jonathan S., ed., *Adolescents and Their Music: If It's Too Loud, You're Too Old*, 115–39. New York: Garland, 1994. An important study of The Grateful Dead's highly dedicated fan base.

Savage, Jon. "Rock Steady." *Artforum International* 34/4 (December 1995): 23+. Savage discusses the significance of the 1969 Woodstock Music and Art Fair in this article, which is dominated by discussion of mid-1990s rap and hip-hop music.

Schmid, Thomas, and Kees de Lange. "1969 Woodstock Performers Song List." *Woodstock '69*. http://www.woodstock69.com/Woodstock_songs.htm. Accessed June 29, 2003.

Schoemer, Karen. "Talking 'bout Our Generation." *Newsweek* 124/26–125/1 (December 26, 1994–January 2, 1995): 32+. This article deals with the sad state of Generation X and looks at examples of the lack of definition of the generation from the Woodstock '94 festival.

Schoemer, Karen. "Woodstock '94: Back to the Garden." *Newsweek* 124/6 (August 8, 1994): 44+. This article is a preview of Woodstock '94 that highlights some of the commercial aspects of the music festival.

Schoemer, Karen, and Patrick Rogers. "By the Time They Got to . . ." *Newsweek* 124/8 (August 22, 1994): 64+. A feature report on the Woodstock '94 festival.

Schowalter, Daniel F. "Remembering the Dangers of Rock and Roll: Toward a Historical Narrative of the Rock Festival." *Critical Studies in Mass Communication* 17/1 (2000): 86+.

Schwartz, J. "Woodstock '89: A Bad Trip." *Newsweek* 114/8 (August 21, 1989): 42. This is a report on the hopes expressed by promoters of the twentieth-anniversary concert, which contrasts with the modest ticket sales.

Scott, Janny. "On the Morning After, Memories and Debris of Woodstock '94." *New York Times* August 16, 1994: B1.

Scott, Janny. "Woodstock: Music Fades and Muddy Trek Begins." *New York Times* August 15, 1994: A1. A report on the mud and trash at Woodstock '94, as well as the long wait for shuttle buses, medical problems encountered by audience members, and so on.

Scott, Janny. "Woodstock '94: Peace, Dreams and Money." *New York Times* August 11, 1994: A1. The *New York Times* cover story on the Woodstock '94 festival.

Scott, Janny. "Woodstock Redux: New Sea of Young People." *New York Times* August 14, 1994: 1. The author contrasts the silence of Max Yasgur's farm with the weather-related problems the 200,000 attendees of Woodstock '94 are encountering.

Seavey, Todd. "On the Scene." *National Review* 46/17 (September 12, 1994): 21. This article deals with the author's difficulty finding any peace and harmony at the Woodstock '94 festival.

Seavey, Todd. "Once Is Enough." *National Review* 46/17 (September 12, 1994): 26+.

Seelow, David. "Listening to Youth: Woodstock, Music, America, and Kurt Cobain's Suicide." *Child and Youth Care Forum* 25/1 (1996): 49+.

Selvin, Joel. *Monterey Pop: June 16–18, 1967*. San Francisco: Chronicle Books, 1992.

Shaw, Arnold. *The Rock Revolution*. New York: Macmillan, 1971.

Sheffield, Rob. "Rage against the Latrines." *Rolling Stone* n820 (September 2, 1999): 52+.

"Shop Talk at Thirty." *Editor and Publisher* 127/40 (October 1, 1994): 48. This article deals with the wartime-like difficulties reporters faced in covering the Woodstock '94 festival.

Sia, Joseph J. *Woodstock 69, Summer Pop Festivals: A Photo Review*. New York: Scholastic Book Services, 1970.

Sideman, Andrew. "I Was There: Woodstock Music and Art Fair." *Seventeen* 29 (January 1970): 86+.

Sinclair, John, and Robert Levin. *Music and Politics*. New York: World, 1971.

Singleton, Carl, ed. *The Sixties in America*. Pasadena, California: Salem Press, 1999.

Sinker, Mark. Review of *Woodstock: Three Days of Peace and Music*, the director's cut. *Sight and Sound* 4/9 (September 1994): 55. See also Quaif.

Skelly, Richard. "Paul Rodgers." *All Music Guide*. http://allmusic.com. Accessed April 12, 2004.

Smith, Chas. *From Woodstock to the Moon: The Cultural Evolution of Rock Music*. Dubuque, Iowa: Kendall/Hunt, 2000.

Smith Kline & French Laboratories. Thorazine advertisement. Unknown date. Reproduced at http://www.biopsychiatry.com/chlorpromazine/thorazine.jpg. Accessed January 28, 2004.

Smucker, Tom. "The Politics of Rock: Movement vs. Groovement." In Eisen, Jonathan, ed., *Age of Rock*, vol. 2, 83–91. New York: Vintage Books, Random House, 1970.

Sobran, Joseph. "A Nation of Loners." *National Review* 41/16 (September 1, 1989): 28+. This article looks at the 1969 Woodstock festival as a place where loners and misfits could be accepted.

"Softwire." *Video Magazine* 21/5 (September 1997): 92+. This article includes a review of the video *Woodstock: The Director's Cut*.

Solomon, Jolie, and Robin Sparkman. "The Faithful Brace for Battle at Rock Music's Sacred Site." *Newsweek* 122/10 (September 6, 1993): 61. This is a report on the plans by the Multiple Sclerosis Society and its New York chapter head Robert Gersch to hold a Woodstock twenty-fifth-anniversary festival on the site of Max Yasgur's farm in Bethel, New York. By this time, objections were being raised to the plans, although the article suggests that Gersch's ongoing planning is proceeding.

Songs and Photos from Woodstock. New York: Warner Brothers, 1970. This book contains lyrics from some of the songs that were performed at the 1969 Woodstock Music and Art Fair and photographs from the festival.

Southworth, Ian. Personal e-mail to the author. December 19, 2003. Ian Southworth, a representative of Keef Hartley's current (spring 2004) record company (Kashmir Records), supplied the elusive partial set list for the Keef Hartley Band's performance at the 1969 Woodstock Music and Art Fair.

Spitz, Robert Stephen. *Barefoot in Babylon: The Creation of the Woodstock Music Festival, 1969*. New York: Viking Press, 1979. New York: W. W. Norton, 1989. An important study of the organization of the Woodstock Music and Art Fair.

"Splendor in the Morass." *People* 42/9 (August 29, 1994): 102+. This article presents a recap of the Woodstock '94 festival.

Stateman, Alison. "Bonfire of the Inanities." *Public Relations Tactics* 6/10 (October 1999): 1+. This article details the public relations problems encountered by the Woodstock 1999 festival due to what was seen as the overly commercial nature of the event, the riots, arson, and rapes that took place and the nature of the audience.

Steinberg, Jacques. "Love, Peace, Money, Lawsuits." *New York Times*, May 12, 1995: B1. This article reports on legal actions against Woodstock II promoters by vendors who were promised, but never received, donations from the festival's profits.

Steinberg, Jacques. "Woodstock, the Reprise, Under Way." *New York Times* August 13, 1994: 23.

Steiner, Andy. "The Last Days of Lilith." *Ms.* (June 1999): 60+. Steiner documents the way that the Lilith Fair music festivals, "feminist Woodstock for the 1990s," have changed the place and perception of women in popular music and American society. This citation is an example of how the 1969 Woodstock festival is still used as the bar by which other pop music festivals are judged.

Stevens, Jay. *Storming Heaven: LSD and the American Dream*. New York: Harper and Row, 1988.

Stevens, Kimberly. "Off the Shelf: Woodstock Memories." *New York Times* July 11, 1999: Section 14, p. 7. This article concerns Richie Havens' role at the 1969 Woodstock festival and the musician's new autobiography, *They Can't Hide Us Anymore*.

Stine, Peter, ed. *The Sixties*. Detroit: Wayne State University Press, 1995. Contains references to the 1969 Woodstock Music and Art Fair and to the hippie subculture.

Stothers, William G. "Rock and Roll in the Woodstock Mud." *Mainstream* 19/2 (October 1994): 10. This is a report on handicapped accessibility at the Woodstock '94 festival.

Strauss, Neil. "Eclectic Bill Shaping up for Next Woodstock." *New York Times* April 1, 1999: E1. A report on preparations for the ill-fated Woodstock 1999.

Strauss, Neil. "A Journey from Hippie to Hip-Hop." *New York Times* July 24, 1999: B5. This article includes a profile of musician James Brown and information about his appearance at Woodstock 1999.

Strauss, Neil. "Looking to a Woodstock '99." *New York Times* July 19, 1997: 16. This article reports on John Scher's announcement of plans for Woodstock 1999.

Strauss, Neil. "New Spirit of Woodstock: Music, TV, More TV, and Trashing." *New York Times* July 26, 1999: B8. A report on various negative aspects of Woodstock 1999.

Strauss, Neil. "On Night Music Died, Many to Blame for Mayhem." *New York Times* July 27, 1999: B5. A report on the riots and rapes that marred Woodstock 1999.

Strauss, Neil. "The Pop Life." *New York Times* October 6, 1994: C16. This article includes discussion of the Woodstock '94 live album from A&M Records.

Strauss, Neil. "The Pop Life." *New York Times* August 5, 1999: E3. This article includes discussion of the riots that marked July 25, 1999, the closing day of the Woodstock 1999 festival.

Strauss, Neil. " '69 or '99, A Rock Festival Is a Combustible Mix." *New York Times* August 8, 1999: C1. Strauss compares the 1969 Woodstock Music and Art Fair with Woodstock 1999. He suggests that the documentary movie of the 1969 festival helped to perpetuate the myth of Woodstock as a spontaneous gathering that came out of the hippie spirit, while downplaying the original commercial intent of the festival.

Strauss, Neil. "A Woodstock Where Teeny Is Everything." *New York Times* July 6, 1999: E1. This article concerns the former Yasgur farm in Bethel, New York, and new owner Alan Gerry's plans for A Day in the Garden festival to mark the thirtieth anniversary of Woodstock.

Stuessy, Joe. *Rock and Roll: Its History and Stylistic Development*. Englewood Cliffs, New Jersey: Prentice-Hall, 1990.

Szatmary, David P. Review of *"Woodstock": An Inside Look at the Movie That Shook up the World*, edited by Dale Bell. *Library Journal* 124/13 (August 1, 1999): 96.

Szatmary, David P. *A Time to Rock: A Social History of Rock 'N' Roll*. New York: Schirmer Books, 1996.

"Taking 'Stock." Entertainment Weekly n237–38 (August 26, 1994): 10. This article contains a brief report on the Woodstock '94 festival.

"Talent and Touring." *Amusement Business* 106/18 (May 2, 1994): 6. This article deals in part with arrangements for the Woodstock '94 festival.

"Talent and Touring." *Amusement Business* 106/29 (July 18, 1994): 8. This article deals in part with plans to add extra concerts to the Woodstock '94 festival and problems that are being encountered by the organizers of the twenty-fifth-anniversary concert on the site of the original Woodstock Music and Art Fair.

"Talent and Touring." *Amusement Business* 106/31 (August 1, 1994): 8. This article contains information on the settlement of the dispute over Woodstock festival trademark ownership.

"Talent and Touring." *Amusement Business* 106/34 (August 22, 1994): 6. This article deals in part with the difficulties the magazine's reporter had covering the Woodstock '94 festival.

Talty, S. "Invisible Woman." *American Film* 16/9 (September-October 1991): 42+. This is a feature article about film editor Thelma Schoonmaker, who worked on the *Woodstock: Three Days of Peace and Music* film.

"Tapes and Discs." *Video Magazine* 16/1 (April 1992): 47. This article contains a review of the laser disc *Woodstock: The Lost Performances.*

Tate, Greg. *Midnight Lightning: Jimi Hendrix and the Black Experience.* Chicago: Lawrence Hill Books, 2003.

Terwillicker, Max. "Woodstock '94: '1-2-3-4, We Don't Want a Tech-Compression War.' " *InfoWorld* 16/34 (August 22, 1994): 102. This brief article suggests that Woodstock '94 was a major event for the baby boom generation.

Thompson, Hunter S. *Hell's Angels: A Strange and Terrible Saga.* New York: Random House, 1967. Thompson's book contains insights into the Hell's Angels that help to explain the disaster at the Altamont concert.

"Three Companies File Suit to Protect Woodstock Name." *DNR* 24/154 (August 11, 1994): 11. A report on Woodstock Ventures, PolyGram Diversified Ventures, and Fine Host Corporation's lawsuit to prevent the unauthorized selling of Woodstock '94 merchandise.

"Three Days of Music, Mud and Myth: A Woodstock 1994 Survivor's Diary." *Billboard* 106/35 (August 27, 1994): 17+.

Tilsner, Julie, and Keith H. Hammonds. "The Woodstock Generation—Of Revenues." *Business Week* n3387 (August 29, 1994): 40. This is a brief report on the revenues generated by Woodstock '94.

The Top 10 Differences between Woodstock 69 and Woodstock 99. http://members.aol. com/Mary1NYS/Top10.html. Accessed October 23, 2003.

Tracy, Philip. "Birth of a Culture: Woodstock Music and Art Fair's Aquarian Exposition." *Commonweal* 90 (September 5, 1969): 532–33.

Traum, Artie. "Richie Havens." *Sing Out!* 18 (September–October 1968): 3+. A profile of Havens before Woodstock brought him into the national spotlight.

Turk, John R. *Woodstock Concert of 1969.* Youngstown, Ohio: Youngstown State University, 1989. This is a twenty-two-page transcript of a taped interview conducted by Molly McNamara as part of the Department of History's Oral History Program.

Turkalo, David M. Review of *Woodstock: The Oral History* by Joel Makower. *Library Journal* 114/11 (June 15, 1989): 60.

Turkalo, David M. Review of *Woodstock: The Summer of Our Lives* by Jack Curry. *Library Journal* 114/5 (March 15, 1989): 72.

"Ugly Side of Woodstock, The." *U.S. News and World Report* 127/6 (August 9, 1999): 28.

"The Underground Industrial Complex: After Woodstock." *Christian Century* 86 (October 1, 1969): 1237.

"Underperforming at Woodstock '94." *Broadcasting and Cable* 124/34 (August 22, 1994): 20. According to this report, the pay-per-view television rates were lower than anticipated for the Woodstock '94 festival. Compared with other concerts, however, the rates were good.

Unger, Irwin, and Debi Unger, eds. *The Times Were a Changin': The Sixties Reader*. New York: Three Rivers, 1998.

Unterberger, Richie. *Eight Miles High: Folk-Rock's Flight from Haight-Ashbury to Woodstock*. San Francisco: Backbeat Books, 2003.

Unterberger, Richie. "Sweetwater." *All Music Guide*. http://allmusic.com. Accessed December 22, 2003. Contains a biography and critical commentary on the group.

"Up Front." *People Weekly* (August 23, 1999): 58+. On the thirtieth anniversary of the Woodstock festival, this article profiles six prominent members of the 1960s counterculture. This bibliographical entry is an example of the type of iconic status Woodstock has achieved.

"Updates." *Mother Jones* 19/6 (November-December 1994): 18. In the progressive magazine's update on what was learned at the Woodstock '94 festival, it is noted that many of the women who stopped by the magazine's booth "seemed truly interested in saving the planet," while the men tended to ask, "So where are the 'shrooms'?"

VanBoven, Sarah, and Christopher John Farley. "Three Days of Peace, Music and *Hee Haw*." *Time* 144/7 (August 15, 1994): 12. The premise behind this article is that although approximately 400,000 American young people attended the Woodstock Music and Art Fair August 15–17, 1969, that left millions at home. The article lists the top-grossing movies, highest-rated television shows, and other news and best-sellers of the times.

Vansuch, Alexandra. *Woodstock, 1969*. Youngstown, Ohio: Youngstown State University, 1995. This is a fourteen-page transcript of a taped interview conducted by Christopher L. Helm as part of the Department of History's Oral History Program.

Verna, Paul. "A&M Team Gets Woodstock on Tape." *Billboard* 106/35 (August 27, 1994): 114+. This is a detailed report on the audio recording of the Woodstock '94 festival.

Verna, Paul. "Richie Havens Seeking Woodstock Royalties." *Billboard* 106/30 (July 23, 1994): 12+. This is a report on Havens' lawsuit against Time Warner and three of its subsidiaries for nonpayment of royalties and improper use of the singer's image in its audio and video recordings of the 1969 Woodstock festival.

Verna, Paul. "*Woodstock '94* Gets A&M Push." *Billboard* 106/41 (October 8, 1994): 1+. A feature on the marketing strategy A&M records will be employing with its live recording from the Woodstock '94 festival.

Verna, Paul. "*Woodstock '94* Set Emphasizes Modern Rockers." *Billboard* 106/42 (October 15, 1994): 14+. This is a short feature on the *Woodstock '94* live album.

Verna, Paul, and Marilyn A. Gillen. "Vital Reissues." *Billboard* 106/35 (August 27, 1994): 102. This article contains a review of the twenty-fifth-anniversary reissue of the audio recording *Woodstock: Three Days of Peace and Music*.

"Video Watch." *U.S. News and World Report* 117/8 (August 22, 1994): 73. Includes a brief review of the video release of the director's cut of the film *Woodstock: Three Days of Peace and Music*.

Von Hoffman, Nicholas. *We Are the People Our Parents Warned Us Against*. Chicago: Quadrangle Books, 1968. The author explains the late 1960s counterculture from a participant's perspective.

Waddell, Ray. "Volunteering Information." *Amusement Business* 111/34 (August 23, 1999): 3. This article deals with the riots that marred the final day of Woodstock 1999.

Wadler, Joyce. "Drug Counselor to New Woodstock Crowd." *New York Times* July 21,

1999: B2. This article profiles Paul Michael Ramirez, director of psychiatric services for the Woodstock 1999 festival.

Walker, David. "Pdnews." *Photo District News* 19/10 (October 1999): 14+. This report contains information on the controversy created when the New York State Police published copyrighted photographs of rioters at the Woodstock 1999 festival on the Internet without permission, in an attempt to identify the perpetrators.

Walls, Jeannette, and David Feld. "Ah-One and Ah-Two: Woodstock and Welk." *New York* 26/34 (August 30, 1993): 22. This article is a report on the ongoing battles between Woodstock Ventures, organizers of the Woodstock '94 festival, and the National Multiple Sclerosis Society, organizers of the competing A Day in the Garden festival.

Ward, Ed. "The Monterey Pop Festival." *Britannica.com.* http://www.Britannica.com/psychedelic/testonly/monterey.html. Accessed December 23, 2003.

Watts, Richard. *Woodstock, NY.* Youngstown, Ohio: Youngstown State University, 1989. This is a twenty-two-page transcript of a taped interview conducted by Molly McNamara as part of the Department of History's Oral History Program.

"We Are Olden . . ." *New York Times Magazine* 143/49788 (August 14, 1994): 12. This is a tongue-in-cheek advice article on how to celebrate the twenty-fifth anniversary of Woodstock for those who will not be attending Woodstock '94. The similarly tongue-in-cheek title is a deliberate misquote from Joni Mitchell's song "Woodstock."

Wechsler, Pat, and Roger D. Friedman. "Prime Sixties Mud Goes up for Sale." *New York* 28/23 (June 5, 1995): 12. This article deals with June Gelish's plans to sell the site of the original Woodstock festival. Concert promoter Sid Bernstein is assisting Gelish in her efforts.

Weimer, Daniel. *Woodstock, 1969.* Youngstown, Ohio: Youngstown State University, 1995. This is a thirteen-page transcript of a taped interview conducted by Christopher L. Helm as part of the Department of History's Oral History Program.

Wein, George, with Nate Chinen. *Myself among Others.* Cambridge, Massachusetts: Da Capo Press, 2003.

Weiner, Rex, and Deanne Stillman. *Woodstock Census: The Nationwide Survey of the Sixties Generation.* New York: Viking, 1979.

Weinstein, Norman. "Relive Woodstock with New Hendrix Release." *Christian Science Monitor* 91/161 (July 16, 1999): 17. This article is a review of the recently released compact disc *Jimi Hendrix: Live at Woodstock.*

Weisbard, Eric. "The Year in Music." *Spin* 10/9 (December 1994): 62. This article contains a report on the Woodstock '94 festival of 1994, including issues revolving around the corporate sponsorship of the festival.

Weisel, Al. "Ravestock." *Rolling Stone* n691 (September 22, 1994): 61.

Weiser, Glenn. "Woodstock '69 Remembered." *Woodstock History.com.* http:www.advol.net/wood5.htm. Accessed May 27, 2003.

Wenner, Jann. "British Groups 'Smash' at Monterey." *Melody Maker* 42 (June 24, 1967): 8–9. Reprinted in Budds, Michael J., and Marian M. Ohman, eds., *Rock Recall: Annotated Readings in American Popular Music from the Emergence of Rock and Roll to the Demise of the Woodstock Nation,* 290. Needham Heights, Massachusetts: Ginn Press, 1993.

Whitburn, Joel. *Joel Whitburn's Top Pop Singles, 1955–1996.* Menomonee Falls, Wisconsin: Record Research, 1997.

Whitmer, Peter O., with Bruce Van Wyngarden. *Aquarius Revisited: Seven Who Created the Sixties Counterculture and Changed America*. New York: Macmillan, 1987.

"Who Will Control the Legacy of the Woodstock Nation?" *New York Times* August 18, 1990: 1.

"Whole New Minority Group: Woodstock Music and Art Fair." *Newsweek* 74 (September 1, 1969): 20–22A. This article concerns the battles between Max Yasgur and Bethel, New York, area developers over the commemorative celebrations at the site of the 1969 Woodstock festival.

Wiener, J. Review of *Woodstock: The Summer of Our Lives* by Jack Curry. *New York Times Book Review* 138/4777 (May 21, 1989): 19.

Willis, Ellen. "Rock, etc. Woodstock Music and Art Fair." *New Yorker* 45 (September 6, 1969): 121–24.

Wilson, Brian, with Todd Gold. *Wouldn't It Be Nice*. New York: HarperCollins, 1991.

Wolfe, Tom. *The Electric Kool-Aid Acid Test*. New York: Farrar, Straus, and Giroux: 1968. Also published New York: Bantam Books, 1969.

"Woodstock." *News Photographer* 49/9 (September 1994): 4.

"Woodstock Generation Revisited, The." *Broadcasting and Cable* 124/31 (August 1, 1994): 38. This article reports on the plans to broadcast ten hours of live and taped concert highlights of the Woodstock '94 festival on Media America, Inc.'s over 200 affiliate stations.

"Woodstock: Making Hay from Memories." *Newsweek* 122/10 (September 6, 1993): 61.

Woodstock Master Tapes for Sale. http://www.digibuilders.com/jobs/woodstock/index.html. Accessed August 4, 2003.

The Woodstock Music Festival. New York: Time, 1969.

Woodstock Nation Foundation. *For Perpetual Free Assembly*. http://www.woodstock nation.org/history.htm. Accessed May 27, 2003. This Web site contains the rather convoluted post-Woodstock history of the property on which the original 1969 festival was held.

Woodstock 1969. Video. 60 minutes. Westlake Video.

"*Woodstock '94*." *New York Times* December 23, 1994: B15. This is a review of the video release of concert footage from Woodstock '94.

"Woodstock '94: By the Time They Got To." *Newsweek* 124/8 (August 22, 1994): 64.

"Woodstock '94: High-Tech Reunion." *Broadcasting and Cable* 124/30 (July 25, 1994): 31. This article contrasts the 1969 Woodstock Music and Art Fair and the Woodstock '94 festival in the area of technology, with a focus on the on-demand broadcast of the 1994 event and the various interactive technologies that will be displayed at the festival.

Woodstock '94: The Book. New York: Polygram Diversified Entertainment, 1994. This book contains photographs from the Woodstock '94 festival by Albert Watson, a foreword by Amy Wu, and essays by John Milward and Christopher John Farley, as well as contributions by various musicians who performed at the festival.

Woodstock '94: 3 More Days of Peace and Music. New York: Woodstock Ventures and Polygram Diversified Ventures, 1994.

Woodstock '94: 2 More Days of Peace and Music. New York: Welsh, 1994. This is the official concert booklet for the Woodstock twenty-fifth-anniversary festival.

"Woodstock '94 Site Is Clean and Green." *New York Times* October 29, 1994: 26. A report on the cleanup of the Woodstock '94 festival site in Saugerties, New York.

"Woodstock '94's Mine 'Field.'" *Billboard* 106/30 (July 23, 1994): 78. This is a brief report on the interactive technology "village" planned for Woodstock '94.

"Woodstock, 1999 (With Apologies to Bob Dylan)." *The Economist* 352/8130 (July 31, 1999): 25.

"Woodstock '99: Mega MSW Management." *Waste Age* 31/4 (2000): 284+. This article deals with difficulties waste management personnel had with removing garbage from the site of the Woodstock 1999 concerts due to looting and fires that concertgoers set.

Woodstock 1999 Truth Network Web Ring, The. http://www.geocities.com/TheTropics/Bay/9641/wring.html. Accessed October 23, 2003. This Web site claims that it is "devoted to getting out the message that there was both good and bad at Woodstock 1999." It seeks to counter the negative image of the thirtieth-anniversary festival that was featured by the mainstream popular media in the United States.

"Woodstock Notion." *Business Week* n3621 (March 22, 1999): 66. This article deals with Alan Gerry's plans to build a music-related theme park on the site of the 1969 Woodstock festival and the controversy Gerry's plans were generating.

"Woodstock Redux." *Brandweek* 35/34 (September 5, 1994): 32. This article deals with commercial aspects of the Woodstock '94 festival.

"The Woodstock Regeneration." *Mediaweek* 4/28 (July 11, 1994): 18. This article concerns Joel Rosenman's plans for interactive video and pay-per-view television of the Woodstock '94 festival.

"Woodstock Revisited." *The Economist* 332/7871 (July 9, 1994): 31.

"Woodstock Revisited: What Pharmacists Dealt with There." *Drug Topics* 138/17 (September 5, 1994): 19.

"The Woodstock Spirit Is Alive and Well among the Rainbow People." *Time* 138/2 (July 15, 1991): 74–75.

"Woodstock Then, Woodflop Now." *U.S. News and World Report* 117/7 (August 15, 1994): 17. This article is a report on the failure of a Woodstock twenty-fifth-anniversary reunion concert on the site of the original 1969 event, due to poor ticket sales. The lack of prefestival sales for Woodstock '94 is also noted.

Woodstock: Three Days of Peace and Music. Two VHS-format videocassettes. Michael Wadleigh, director; Bob Maurice, producer. Burbank, California: Warner Home Video 13549, 1994. Also reissued as *Woodstock: Three Days of Peace and Music, The Director's Cut.* Burbank, California: Warner Home Video, 1997. This is a rerelease of the video of the original 1970 film and contains thirty extra minutes of concert footage.

"*Woodstock: 25th Anniversary CD-ROM.*" *CD-ROM World* 9/10 (November 1994): 82. This article reviews the new CD-ROM product.

Woodstock: 25th Anniversary CD-ROM. Computer optical disc and user's guide. Burbank, California: Time Warner Interactive, 1994.

"Woodstock 2019." *The Economist* 332/7877 (August 20, 1994): 68. A humorous projection of what a Woodstock reunion festival might look like in the year 2019.

"Woodstock II: Regeneration Gap." *World* 9/15 (August 27, 1994): 16. Dealing with the Woodstock '94 festival in generally negative terms, this article describes the sense of rage and contempt that members of "Generation X" brought to the Woodstock II festival.

"Woodstock Watch: For Peace and for Profit." *Newsweek* 123/24 (June 13, 1994): 49. A report on the commercial and philosophical basis for Woodstock '94.

"Woodstock Weekend." *Christianity Today* 13 (September 26, 1969): 37–38.

"Worst of Tube." *People* 42/26 (December 26, 1994): 16.

"Year in Pictures, The." *Life* 18/1 (January 1995): 54+. Contains photographs from the Woodstock '94 festival.

"The Year That Was." *Entertainment Weekly* n255–56 (December 30, 1994): 56. The twenty-fifth anniversary Woodstock festival is included among the most notable events of 1994.

Zeman, Ned. "First, Kill all the Boomers." *Newsweek* 121/8 (February 22, 1993): 71. This article contains a critique on the Woodstock festival.

Zielbauer, Paul. "Fans Rampage in Last Hours of Music Show." *New York Times* July 26, 1999: B1. This article concerns the riots that marred the final day of the Woodstock 1999 festival.

Zielbauer, Paul. "In Woodstock's Wake, Debates Erupt over Security." *New York Times* July 31, 1999: B5.

Zielbauer, Paul. "Inquiry Pressed into Reported Rapes at Woodstock." *New York Times* July 30, 1999: B1.

Zielbauer, Paul. "Oneida County Seeks Fines from Woodstock '99 Organizers." *New York Times* July 10, 1999: B4.

Zielbauer, Paul. "The Way to Woodstock? Look for the B-52." *New York Times* July 12, 1999: B1. The author points out the irony that the route to the site of Woodstock 1999, Griffiss Air Force Base, is marked with a B-52 bomber, the very type of airplane used in the Vietnam conflict, the source of so much protest by the generation of young people who attended the original Woodstock festival.

Zielbauer, Paul. "Woodstock Arrives and Mood Is Mellow." *New York Times* July 22, 1999: B5. In hindsight, the relative smoothness of preparations for Woodstock 1999, as described in this article, proved to be the calm before the storm. See also Zielbauer's subsequent articles in the *New York Times*.

Zielbauer, Paul. "Woodstock Festival Faces a Bad Hangover." *New York Times* July 27, 1999: B1. This article focuses on the riots and other violent incidents that marred the last day of the Woodstock 1999 festival.

Zielbauer, Paul. "Woodstock '99 Has Heat, Laconic Fans and One Death." *New York Times* July 25, 1999: 26.

Zielbauer, Paul. "Woodstock '99 Kicks off, but without the Stardust." *New York Times* July 24, 1999: A1.

Zito, J. S. "Music Medicine." *Medical Laboratory Observer* 32/2 (2000): 40–45. This article deals with medical care provided at the Woodstock 1999 festival.

Index

About the Author

JAMES PERONE is the author of eleven books, including *Music of the Counter-culture Era*, *Songs of the Vietnam Conflict*, *Paul Simon: A Bio-Bibliography*, and *Louis Moreau Gottschalk: A Bio-Bibliography*. He is associate professor of Music at Mount Union College, where he teaches Music in America, Vernacular Music and the Vietnam Conflict, Music Theory, and Clarinet.